SHALLOW THOUGHT
DEEP MIND

SHALLOW THOUGHT
DEEP MIND

*What you need to succeed, thrive
and make the world better*

Dr Wayne Somerville

CREEK'S BEND
Toonumbar, Australia

2019

Creek's Bend
Toonumbar, Kyogle, NSW, 2474, Australia

First published by Dr Wayne Robert Somerville 2017. Revised May 2018, June 2019.

Copyright © Dr Wayne Somerville 2017, 2018, 2019

All rights reserved. Without limiting the rights under copyright reserved above, no part of this publication may be reproduced, stored in or introduced into a retrieval system, or transmitted, in any form or by any means (electronic, mechanical, photocopying, recording or otherwise) without the prior written permission of the publishers of this book.

Every care has been taken to trace and acknowledge copyright. Please let the author know of any accidental infringement and it will be addressed.

Shallow Thought, Deep Mind is educational material designed to inform and entertain. The information in this book is made available on the understanding that the author is not providing any form of specific legal, medical or psychological advice relevant to any individual reader's circumstances. In all cases, readers should consult appropriate professionals for legal, medical or psychological advice and treatment. The author shall have neither liability nor responsibility to any person or entity with respect to any loss or damage caused or alleged to be caused directly or indirectly by the information contained in this book.

If you do not wish to be bound by the above, you may return this book to the publisher for a full refund. If you have questions about this disclaimer, please contact the author.

Typeset in Adobe Garamond 12/15 by the publishers
Layout and design by Performingdesign

National Library of Australia
Cataloguing-in-Publication data

Creator: Somerville, Wayne, author.

Title: Shallow thought, deep mind : What you need to succeed, thrive and make the world better / Wayne Somerville.

ISBN: 9780648062820 (paperback)
ISBN: 9780648062806 (e-book: epub)
ISBN: 9780648062813 (e-book: mobi)
ISBN: 9780648062844 (hardcover)

Subjects: Philosophy of mind
           Human information processing
           Thought and thinking
           Self-actualisation (Psychology)

For everyone who wants to make their life
and the world better.

Contents

Illustrations	xiii
Acknowledgements	xiv
Preface	xv

Introduction   1

    The One Thought Solution   2
    What's in This Book   2
    Thought Experiments   4
    Checking With Your Intuition   4
    Stories and Studies   6
    References   6

Part 1: Tackling Big Challenges

1   Nature's Basic Problem-Solving Strategy   9

    What is the One Thought Solution?   10
    Wisdom   12
    Parts of a Whole   15
    Our Animal Friends   17
    Being Human   22
    Symptoms as Solutions   24
    Fear and Learning   25
    Protective Phobias   27
    The Ultimate One Thought Solution   30
    Evolution through Learning   32
    Horse Sense in an Age of Nonsense   34
    We'll Determine Our Future   36

2 War Trauma and a New Psychology — 39

    A Country Divided 41
    A Fractured Psychology 43
    Freud and Psychoanalysis 43
    The Rise of Rat Psychology 45
    The Computer Revolution 47
    The Mind–Body Problem Solved? 48
    Systems Theory 51
    The New Hypnosis 51
    Healing with the Deep Mind 55
    Meeting Professor "X" 58
    Brief Treatment for Phobias 59
    The Curse of Memory 61
    Big Pharma and the Mind 64
    Exposure Therapy Exposed 68
    Moving Your Eyes to Change Memories 72
    Evidence-based Treatment 73
    Giving Memories a New Ending 77
    Taking Control 80
    Cognitive Control Training 85
    Natural Trauma Resolution and PTSD 86
    An Information Processing Model 87
    How Trauma Therapy Works 88

3 Native Forest Dieback — 93

    Logging's Legacy 94
    The Hunters' Story 95
    Family Therapy for Forests 96
    Ill-suited Labels 101
    Birds Nest in Lantana 103
    Glyphosate Should be Banned 103

4   Unconventional Gas: The One Thought Solution goes to the dark side   107

    Down the Rabbit Hole   108
    The Physical Reality   109
    A Fractured Earth Responds   112
    The Human Dimension   114
    One Thought Solutions as Risk Management   117
        Risk, What Risk?   118
        Relax, We've Been Doing This for Years   119
        I Know Nothing   119
        Attack and Demean   120
        Befriending Rocks and Gases   122
        Regulation to the Rescue   123
        Double Standards for Proof   125
        You Can't Prove It   127
        Misrepresenting Information   129
        Ignoring Evidence   133
    Economics of Gas Mining   136
    An Activist's Journey   139
        Reluctant Health Professionals   141
    A Community Protects Itself   143
        Protectors, not Protesters   144
        Practical People Power   145
        Democracy's Pointy End   146

Part 2: Using the Deep Mind

5   The Key Mental Processes   155
    The Problem-Solving Mind   155
    Awareness   158
    Behind the Scene   159

6 **Perception: Where mind meets the world**   161
7 **Memory and Imagination: Visions of past and future**   171
    Media Hypnotists   173
    When Talking Harms and Silence Heals   175
    Lure of the Unfinished   177
    Mastering Memory and Imagination   178
        Working with Imagery   178
        Set and Setting   178
        Using Training Memories   179
    Sensory Qualities and Perspective   181
        Distance   181
        A Matter of Size   182
        Colour versus Black and White   184
        Changing Viewpoint   185
        Don't Shout, This is My Memory   187
        The Power of Elmer, Goofy and Donald   188
    Adding New Elements   189
        A Circus Monkey   189
        Extra Characters   190
        'All's well that ends well'   191
    Adjusting Imagery for Best Effect   192
    Multistage Imagery Techniques   194
        Your Inner Coach   194
        Supporting Your Younger Self   196
        Envision the Future   198
    Guided Imagery   201
8 **Beliefs to Limit or Liberate**   203
    Optimism and Pessimism   203
    Self-esteem and Efficacy   205

Learning New Things   206
Look to the Big Picture   207
Truth and Lies   208
Attitudes to Time   209
The Predictably Unpredictable   210
Trance of the Terminal   211
The Challenge of Suffering and Evil   213

9 Language: The wonders that words work   215
Names and Labels   218
Putting Words Together   221
Word Spells   222
   Words in Therapy   224
   Using Truth to Deceive   226
The Analogy/Metaphor Strategy   227
Reverse Psychology Words   228
Words to Set Goals   231
Words that Bind   233
Troublesome Words   234
   What Ifs   234
   Failure Words   235
   Pressure Words   236
Warm-up Words   238
   The Alphabet Technique   238
   Think the Unthinkable   239
Deconstructing Complex Information   239
Getting Your Words Out   241
   New Media and email   242
   Using Silence   243

10 Emotions: Reason's judge — 245

- Fear and Anxiety 247
  - Using Anxiety as a Tracer 247
  - Letting Go of Unnecessary Emotion 248
  - Remember to Breathe 249
- Anger 251
- Finding Courage 252
- The Voice of Conscience 255
- Balancing 259

11 Intuition, Sleep and Dreams — 261

- Is the Unconscious Ally or Foe? 261
- Tides and Waves of Consciousness 263
- The Day Shift 265
  - Ernest Rossi's Problem-Solving Procedure 268
  - The Natural Everyday Trance 269
- The Night Shift 271
  - Sleeping Well 272
  - Sleep Apnoea 272
  - Make Good Use of Your Time 273
  - First and Second Sleeps 274
  - Use Your Bed Wisely 275
- Creative Sleep and Dreams 276
  - The Magic Theatre of Hypnagogia 277
  - Night Dreams 280

12 What It Will Take — 285

- The Three Case Studies 286
- Big Challenges Ahead 288

REFERENCES — 291

INDEX — 299

Illustrations

The One Thought Solution   10
Beyond the One Thought Solution   15
Yin-Yang Symbol   17
Susan with Happy and Honey   20
Snake Phobia   28
Our Apple-munching Jill   33
Hypervigilance   63
Exposure for Fear of Heights, Spiders, Snakes and Storms   69
Creek's Bend and the Toonumbar Valley   93
Lantana Understorey Choking Forest   95
A Systems Model of Forest Dieback   99
Coal Seam Gas Field in Queensland's Darling Downs   109
Final Dawn at the Bentley Blockade   150
Awareness and the Key Mental Processes   157
The Arrow of Time   161
Many Lines Illusion   162
Logs on Road Illusion   163
Mueller-Lyer Illusion   163
Adelson's Shadow Illusion   164
Wayne, Katie and Rainbow   167
Duck Illusion   168
Young Woman Illusion   168
Sad Imagery, Happy Imagery   180
To the Future   200
Which Do You Choose?   204
Negative Thinking   228
Bad Habits   232
Measuring Unnecessary Anxiety   248
Cranky Cow   251
At One with the Universe   269
Bovine Insomnia   273
Bucolic Sleep   275
Sweet Dreams   282

Acknowledgements

I owe a lifetime of gratitude to Susan: my wife, muse and editor-*extraordinaire*. Without Susan there would be no book, no stories to tell, and likely no 'Dr Wayne'.

I want to thank my mother, Elaine Somerville, for her love and support throughout my life.

Special thanks to Dr Sarah Antill for her indispensable editing. Sarah's insight and sense of humour made the work a joy.

Special thanks also to Greg Somerville and Paula Martin for the book's cover and layout.

Thanks to my friends Allan Andreasen, Simon Chance and Ian Glover for their comments on early versions of the book.

Thank you to my fellow activists Richard Deem and Brendan Shoebridge for their help with the book, and much else.

I would like to thank John Hunter, Stephanie Horton, John Nagel, Jim Morrison, Bob Jarman and Tara Patel for their contributions to the bush regeneration work on Creek's Bend.

This book is graced by cartoons of cows drawn by my now adult, youngest daughter, Kieran. Most were created when she was 14 years old. I hope you enjoy them.

I acknowledge the Githabul traditional owners of the country where we live and this book was written. We need the wisdom of their elders, past and present, to live gracefully on this precious land.

I also acknowledge my ancestors who left Africa long ago, wandered the planet, and by coming to the Great South Land, made my life possible.

Preface

We've been the problem. It's time to become the solution.

No God, no space alien, no other creature is going to take responsibility and make things right. It's up to us to realise the futures we desire.

This book is for everyone who takes on life's challenges and dreams of a brighter tomorrow. The ideas apply to all the opportunities and problems, from the everyday to the profound, that we meet in our personal, social, spiritual, professional and political lives.

Now in my mid-60s, I have a grandfather's stake in the future. I'd like to give you a head start so you don't have to reinvent all the wheels I had to chisel out and roll around.

These stories from my life as a clinical psychologist, horseman, bush regenerator and environmental activist are about experiences that changed the way I think and do things. They might also help you discover who you really are, what you could be, and how you can make the world better.

This book is based on reason, science and philosophy. I believe that the wisdom of our deep mind can transform lives and the world.

But please be warned. There's no quick fix on offer here, no secret to make wishes manifest, no '6-steps' formula. Learning what you need to know takes time and effort. But once you've got it, you'll never lose it.

Dr Wayne Somerville
Creek's Bend
Toonumbar, NSW, Australia
2017

Introduction

It's always been a challenge to live, work and raise a family, and the task is getting harder. We can no longer take our well-being for granted, or rely on others to give us the lives we want. Not for the first time in history, we have to look inward to secure sufficiency. And on top of the usual demands, we confront threats the likes of which we've never seen before.

The media soundtrack to modern life buzzes with talk of war and tales of catastrophe and suffering. Ever spreading human activity degrades our planet's air, water and soil, and puts at risk civilisation that millennia of clement weather made possible. Climate destabilisation drives mass extinctions of plants and animals, as all-time records of heat and cold and drought and flood are reset with each passing year.

And as problems proliferate, reason retreats. Science is under attack. In this so-called 'post-truth' age, emotion and personal beliefs, rather than objective facts, shape public opinion.

But this is also a time of great promise and possibility. Science is breaking through longstanding barriers. Renewable energy technologies are transforming the way we power our lives and move about. In medicine, treating cancers with a pill is no science fiction, human genomes are sequenced routinely, and there's talk of genuine elixirs of life. The information revolution rolls on as social movements push back against divisive politics and harmful developments. And knowledge, once restricted to a few, is now available to everyone.

The One Thought Solution

The human mind can be the source of both our prospects and our problems. Our mental abilities make it possible for us to meet challenges in new, creative ways. But the way we think is also crucially involved in generating the perils we face. If we are to make the world better, we have to change the way we use our minds. Our personal and collective futures depend on how we think and act.

Some claim that for the sake of our species and the planet, humans have to transcend an innate self-serving irrationality and evolve more rational and compassionate ways of thinking.

I believe there's nothing essentially wrong with our minds. Rather, a near-universal, natural, but inherently limited 'One Thought Solution' dominates the way we think. Honed by evolution, this 'train of thought with one carriage' works, or works well enough, to give us the impression that we can see off challenges quickly and solve most personal, political and scientific issues with minimal effort. But this strategy from ancient times causes grief when it's applied inappropriately in our complex modern world.

This book shows you how to go beyond shallow thought to unlock the power of your deep mind and tackle life's challenges.

What's in This Book

- Part 1: Tackling Big Challenges

We begin by examining the One Thought Solution: what it is, how it can create trouble, and what it takes to find solutions to big problems.

Chapter 1, Nature's Basic Problem-Solving Strategy, gives an evolutionary perspective on the role that the One Thought Solution plays in the survival of our kind and other creatures across eons of time.

Chapter 2, War Trauma and a New Psychology, tells a story, 45 years in the making, about the aftermath of the Vietnam War and the search for gentler psychological therapies for trauma survivors.

Chapter 3, Native Forest Dieback, describes the 20-year journey that led my wife Susan and me to a cure for a dieback disease which is devastating eucalypt forests along Australia's eastern seaboard.

Chapter 4, Unconventional Gas, gives my perspective on the problem of gas field industrialisation and the history-making Gasfield Free campaign in the Northern Rivers of New South Wales.

These stories from my life are examples of the kinds of smaller problems that make up the big challenges that confront humanity. The search for humane treatments for trauma is but one aspect of the overarching task of dealing with interpersonal violence and war. Dieback in Australia's eucalypts is just one example of the troubles that afflict forests around the globe. And the campaign against invasive gas fields is one instance of the worldwide struggle to promote reason over propaganda and reconcile the interests of people and the environment with those of the fossil fuel and mining industries.

This book is not so much about the problems that came my way, but rather, what these tell about how you can successfully take on challenges in your life.

- Part 2: Using the Deep Mind

The second part of the book explores the knowledge and skills you need to harness the deep mind.

Chapter 5 introduces the 'Key Mental Processes' that make us who we are and determine how we think and act.

Chapter 6, Perception, zeros in on where our bodies end and the external world begins, and examines how our minds generate the reality we inhabit.

Chapter 7, Memory and Imagination, investigates the way we create visions of past and future.

Chapter 8, Beliefs to Limit or Liberate, surveys ideas that assist or block our potential for positive change.

Chapter 9, Language, delves into the profound effects that words have.

Chapter 10, Emotions, discusses the positive and negative feelings that affect the way we respond to challenges.

Chapter 11, Intuition, Sleep and Dreams, takes us into the mysterious realm of the unconscious and sleeping mind.

Chapter 12 takes stock, looks to the future, and asks, 'What's it going to take?'

Thought Experiments

Albert Einstein imagined that the streetcar he was riding accelerated to the speed of light as he looked back at a clock tower. He realised that the hands of the clock would appear stationary: time would be frozen. Einstein then did the maths and gave the world his special theory of relativity.

In this book, you'll be invited to work with thought experiments, though none as mind-bending as Einstein's. I'll ask you to think about, or to say, or to imagine something, and to rate your feelings on a '-10' to '+10' scale that we'll call the 'Emot-o-Meter'. These exercises in active mindfulness make it possible for you to imagine situations, take perspectives, and see implications that you could not otherwise realise. The experiments are ruled off in the text.

There are no right or wrong answers: no correct way to respond to the thought experiments. You are unique and can take from these experiences what's relevant to you. Requested images might come clearly, vaguely, or not at all, and it really doesn't matter. All you have to do is make believe that you can imagine, see, hear or do the things that we talk about.

Checking With Your Intuition

Your 'gut feeling' whether something is right or not comes from a part of the mind that psychologists call the 'intuition', or the 'deep', 'subconscious' or 'unconscious' mind.

INTRODUCTION

The thought experiments in this book invoke real feelings – there's not much difference between real and imagined sadness and happiness. So, before each exercise, I want you to check with your intuition that, deep down, it feels all right for you to do this work at this time.

That's not as strange as it might sound. Have you ever felt that something was not quite right and it took a while to work out what was wrong? Your intuition let you know that something was amiss before you consciously knew what it was.

When you check with your intuition, encourage any negative feelings to come through. Heed and respect the deep mind: it is rational, cooperative and protective, and knows more about you than you do.

Your deep mind does not communicate by talking, so we need to set up nonverbal signals. If this was a face-to-face consultation, I would ask your intuition to indicate 'yes' and 'no' with finger or head movements. Known as 'ideomotor signals', these slight, automatic movements tend to naturally accompany our thoughts of 'yes' and 'no'.

Because I'm working with you via the written word, we'll conduct the training differently. You will control the running of the thought experiments, and interpret your own responses using a method known as 'ideosensory signalling'.

The first step is to identify the sensations that you can use as signals. We'll do that now. Make yourself comfortable, and ask your intuition for a feeling you can interpret as a 'yes' signal. Take all the time you need. When you discern a clear 'yes' feeling, ask your intuition for a 'no' signal. Repeat the process of asking for 'yes' and 'no' signals until you can readily distinguish the two.

If the signals are not clear, compare the feeling you get when you say things that are definitely true or untrue. You might contrast what it feels like when you say 'I am a man' and 'I am a woman', or 'I am a giraffe' and 'I am a human'.

If the signals are still unclear, take a break and think about whether your deep mind might not want to communicate in this way. Perhaps some part of you is reluctant, or you might need more information or more time. Perhaps your intuition is protecting you. Whatever the reason, respect and heed your deep mind.

If you would like personalised help to get started on your work with the deep mind, you might see a registered psychologist with expertise in 'Ericksonian hypnotherapy' or 'neuro-linguistic programming'. Organisations such as the Australian Psychological Society and the American Psychological Society can direct you to an appropriately qualified practitioner.

In any case, you can get what you need by just reading the book without doing any of the thought experiments.

Stories and Studies

This is a work of nonfiction. As far as I know, everything in this book is true and based on real events and research. Dialogue with clients was reconstructed from clinical notes or, where indicated, taken verbatim from recorded conversations or client's letters and responses to questionnaires. Quotations from politicians and executives are from emails and letters sent to the author, speeches in the NSW Government's Hansard, or media reports.

To protect identity and privacy, I have changed some names. These are indicated by double quotation marks around the initial presentation of the name. When known, animals are referred to by their real names.

References

At the end of the book, for each chapter, you will find the references indicated by the superscript numbers in the text.

Let's get started.

Part 1

Tackling Big Challenges

Chapter 1

Nature's Basic Problem Solving Strategy

No problem can withstand the assault of sustained thinking.
Voltaire (1694–1778)

SOMETIMES THE OBVIOUS HIDES a deeper truth. Many who witness the grand folly of history despair that human thought is inherently shallow, self-serving and illogical; they see our actions as impulsive, unpredictable and dangerous. But they do not understand the true nature of the ubiquitous One Thought Solution.

This ancient response to life's challenges can function as a gift or a curse. The One Thought Solution is not inherently dysfunctional or pathological. Rather, it's an efficient, protective, problem-solving strategy that has been tempered by the struggle for survival and proven effective across millennia. Our minds developed in a world that has changed. Like a plant that becomes a weed if it grows out of place, the One Thought Solution stymies personal development and problem-solving when it's applied to challenges that demand a more sophisticated response.

In this chapter we explore the One Thought Solution from an evolutionary perspective. I argue that our genetics and history liberate rather than limit us. Even the most biologically rigid One Thought Solutions yield readily to training and deeper thought. If we decide to do so, we can learn to go beyond simple thinking to realise our potential and solve the most pressing problems.

What is the One Thought Solution?

The One Thought Solution can come into play anytime we face a challenge. When we use this train of thought that seems to have just one carriage, we are only consciously aware of a simple image or phrase. This induces an accompanying emotion which automatically directs us to ideas and actions that we think are solutions. We then use sound-bite slogans to communicate our thoughts. Characteristically, the thought or image that comes to mind is true, or true enough. The associated emotions give us the impression that we've done the job and dealt with the challenge, so we move on.

Shallow Thought
Quick & Easy
Simple Problems
Atomistic

The One Thought Solution

Conscious awareness is like a radar that constantly scans, looking out for trouble and things of interest, and this takes effort. Attending to unpleasant or dangerous things is especially taxing. Hence the One Thought Solution – it's easier to form a single thought than it is to think something through. This ancient way of dealing with challenges conserves energy; it helps us make decisions quickly.

Like much human thinking and behaviour, One Thought Solutions run on automatic, as habits controlled by unconscious mental processes. Habits are essential. Life would grind to a halt if each morning we had to think about what we're going to have for breakfast or how to brush our teeth.

For everyday decisions of no real consequence, the One Thought Solution works well enough. It usually doesn't matter if we don't think things through, or if we end up with a less than ideal outcome. For instance, there's little risk in choosing the colour for a new car with the thought 'I like blue' and with no consideration of such factors as the cost, availability, visibility in poor light, heat absorption in sunlight, ease of keeping clean, or cost of repair of different tints.

For choices concerning jobs, relationships, education and other personally important matters, One Thought Solutions can work, but are unlikely to produce optimal results. For example, the truthful thought 'I can't stand this job', with its associated image of being stuck in a rut for years to come, can make us desperate to quit. In such cases, a One Thought Solution might work, but the chances of a good outcome improve if we add more carriages to our train of thought, explore other possibilities, and ask, 'What makes the job so distasteful?', 'Could I improve things?', 'What are the consequences of leaving?' Even if after asking such questions we do not quit the job, we will be less likely to regret our decision to stay.

At the high end of the scale, with challenges that could affect the future of humanity and life on Earth, One Thought Solutions have no legitimate role to play in making policy. Decisions to promote coal and gas mining and to oppose renewable energy can never be justified by a simple, but true, statement that people need jobs. Such complex challenges demand a proper consideration of costs, benefits and risks to communities and the environment.

One Thought Solutions appear simple, but appearances are deceiving – and I do apologise for stretching the metaphor to near breaking point – because what we are dealing with here is a kind of 'ghost train'. When we use this strategy, our train of thought does have a number of carriages, but these are concealed, hidden from us and from others. When this pattern of thinking is running, we are oblivious to the unstated assumptions, beliefs, implications, images, motives, emotions, memories and other mental processes that connect our simple thought to our decisions and actions.

Even when we use One Thought Solutions to disastrous effect, it does not mean that there's anything wrong with our mental equipment or with the strategy itself. Rather, the error lies in our choosing to apply a technique that is not suited to challenges that have no simple solution. The strategy is neither inherently positive nor negative. Our preference for this style of thinking is just human.

For good and for bad, skilled persuaders make use of our fondness for shallow thought by presenting their ideas as One Thought Solutions. Simple statements and images can have a legitimate role in communicating complex ideas if, when made explicit and thought through, the hitherto hidden train of thought takes us to deeper truths and insights. By contrast, when we examine the concealed carriages of a One Thought Solution designed to mislead and manipulate, we find only untruths, distortions and groundless assumptions.

One Thought Solutions block us from using our deep minds. The strategy restricts our attention, prevents us from appreciating the complexity of problems, and has nothing to do with true wisdom.

Wisdom

The One Thought Solution fits well with the now common idea that too much thinking is bad for you. The globally dominant, extroverted American culture discourages deeper thought and sees it as weakness. Nowadays, the public tends to rate politicians who espouse simplistic notions, regardless of how daft they are, as decisive and independent (e.g., 'She speaks her mind'), rather than as the impulsive, shallow thinkers they are.

Simple thinking is easy and quick, and many believe that quick and easy is good while slow and difficult is bad. Politicians demand decisive action and an end to regulations that impede development, so mining projects are fast-tracked with no accounting of risks to the economy, health or the environment. Fast is good, faster is better, and a fast-food drive-in drive-out never-leave-your-bulldozer processing of mining applications would be best. Few question such commitment to rapid, thoughtless action, and what it says about how we understand wisdom.

I have a maths problem for you.

A man paid $1.10 for a bat and ball. The bat cost $1.00 more than the ball. How much did the ball cost?

The question comes from the work of Nobel Prize-winning economists Daniel Kahneman and Amos Tversky.

Back to the question. If you answered that the ball cost 10 cents, you're in good company, but wrong.

Check your reasoning. If the ball costs 10 cents and the bat costs $1.00 more than the ball, then the bat will cost $1.10 and the two together would cost $1.20, not $1.10.

Well done if you got it right that the ball costs 5 cents. But did the 10 cents figure come to mind first, before you did the wise thing of taking the time to think things through, and went beyond the obvious to the truth?

Professor Jacqueline Goodnow (1924–2014), an expert in child development, told us undergraduates in the 1970s about children she tested at a Hong Kong school. Prof Goodnow could not understand why students with a Western background scored higher on tests of intelligence than kids with a traditional Chinese heritage. One day she asked a student from a Chinese background why he gave an incorrect answer and the boy replied, in effect, 'Because that's what a wise person would say'. Taken aback, the professor asked, 'How would a foolish person answer?' and the student gave the officially sanctioned response. Psychologists reckoned they knew the smart answer, but this child considered it inferior.

Intelligence is the ability to successfully adapt to one's environment. But in practice, intelligence gets defined as 'what intelligence tests measure'. IQ, the 'intelligence quotient', is calculated from scores on a battery of tests of cognitive abilities involving vocabulary, general knowledge, attention span, arithmetic, comprehension, abstract thought, pattern recognition, auditory and visual memory, planning, practical reasoning, and visual and motor skills. Many tests have a time limit. You get no score if it takes you more than 60 seconds to rearrange a mixed-up set of six cards so they tell a story, as in a cartoon.

Can you guess where this is headed?

Ask a question in a typical Australian or American classroom and hands shoot up, attached to students busting to show off their knowledge. You might not even finish your question before kids anticipate what you're about to say. They get the game. They're in training for a world ruled by the extrovert. Rapid-fire responses work in a society where glib, quick answers trump a considered response. The strong act, even if they have no idea what they're doing. Only the weak take time to think.

As Professor Goodnow's Chinese student explained, ask a wise person, 'In what way are a dog and a lion alike?' and of course they know they're both animals. This is the answer that scores top points, but how trivial is that? A wise person does not rush to state the obvious; rather, they take time to think. They look to inject something human and interesting into an otherwise mundane situation. But our cultural assumptions about wisdom – what it is, how it's gained and how we should use it – impacts on much more than the answers children give in tests.

Distorted notions of wisdom and a reliance on shallow thinking lock us out of the deep mind, away from the abilities we need to successfully take on the great challenges of our time. As Albert Einstein put it, 'No problem can be solved from the same level of consciousness that created it'. Shallow thinking led to many of the problems that bedevil us. Answers will only be found when we go beyond One Thought Solutions.

True wisdom is built on knowledge and technique. We need to know how our minds work, understand the world we live in, appreciate the complexity of a challenge, and then be able to think and act effectively. This takes time, consideration and persistence.

Deep Mind
Considered & Wise
Big Problems
Holistic

Beyond the One Thought Solution

Parts of a Whole

Simple thinking obscures the fact that we are part of a great system that goes beyond the individual. The One Thought Solution is by nature 'atomistic' rather than 'holistic'. That is to say, this form of thinking cannot cope with complex problems because it focuses only on simple cause and effect relationships between things. It ignores the bigger picture – the blooming, buzzing confusion of the real world with its nuanced interactions. One Thought Solutions only deal with pieces of a challenge, never the whole thing. Such thinking fractures the world into isolated parts and alienates its user from the unity out of which all things arise.

In a debate, Member of Parliament Dr Peter Phelps said, 'What is the environment? It is an ill-defined, amorphous, quasi-religious mass with no intrinsic dollar value but is instead invested with a completely spurious, bogus emotional value'.[1] (© State of New South Wales through the Parliament of New South Wales)

What sense can we make of a world in which there are things, but no environment: a world with content, but no context; figures, but no ground? How could you understand a politician's words without appreciating their political, social and economic context? Can you understand the behaviour of any person without taking into account the systems in which they live: be it a family, a political party, a community, a country or a culture?

Psychological therapy can go wrong if you don't take account of the context that gives a problem or a possibility its meaning. Forget that people live in families, and it doesn't matter what you do to help an obese woman lose weight. If her doing so makes her husband jealous, your intervention will likely come to naught. And how could you make sense of a nine-year-old boy's aggressive behaviour at school if you do not know that he's trying to protect his wheelchair-bound younger sister from bullies?

To benefit from a challenge and to solve big problems, we need to look beyond the obvious to the greater stage on which we play out our lives. In a letter to a grieving father, Albert Einstein wrote that human beings are 'a part of the whole' known as the 'Universe', and our feeling of being separate from the rest is a 'kind of optical delusion' of our consciousness.[2] A cascade of challenges is coming our way, and a holistic, not atomistic, perspective is essential.

When we focus only on the causal connections between isolated things, we perceive delusion, not reality. All things relate to each other as parts of multi-layered systems. For instance, communities of bacteria, insects, fungi, shrubs, trees, birds, reptiles, mammals and much more, interact to make a living forest. And the forest is a part of systems that make up a water catchment, a mountain range, a country and the planet.

If I could look outside my window through a time-lapse camera that condenses years into seconds and decades into minutes, I would see our animals being born, eating grass, living, dying and dissolving back into the paddock. The animal and the environment that sustains it appear different, but are really interdependent, interacting components of a system known as 'life'.

We are of this Earth. We come from dust, and we will return to dust. There's not one atom in our bodies that has not inhabited other forms and will not be recycled endlessly in the future. We are like whirlwinds, eddies that come out of the ground of being, form for a while, and then dissolve back into the environment.

NATURE'S BASIC PROBLEM SOLVING STRATEGY 17

Yin-Yang Symbol

The Buddhist Yin-Yang symbol depicts the insight that the great dichotomies such as 'on and off' and 'life and death' go together, as aspects of an underlying unity. You can't have one without the other. There is no life without death and no light without the dark.

As the *Bible* tells it, our problems began when the first of our kind, Adam and Eve, ate fruit from the forbidden 'tree of the knowledge of good and evil'. Thus began our expulsion from paradise and our sense of separateness from all things. But our fellow creatures weren't tempted by the serpent. They do not suffer our sense of being different from the rest of life. And they have much to tell us about how they and their ancestors have gone about tackling life's challenges.

Our Animal Friends

The ancient evolutionary struggle to survive defines and explains much about how animals look, think and act. You can see it in their bodies, the way their minds work, and in the behaviours that protect them.

Susan and I live at the end of a road, surrounded by animals. Some are friends; all are teachers. As I write, a mob of 20 or so wallabies graze outside the window. A mother with joey (baby wallaby) in pouch nibbles at the grass, lifts her head every 10 seconds or so, looks around with ears scanning back and forth, then goes back to grazing.

It is spring and our red-necked wallabies (*Macropus rufogriseus*) are especially rambunctious. Yesterday, a couple of boxing young males, heads bent way back to protect their eyes, managed to career into our front gate and knock it off its hinges. Standing all of 90 cm from furry foot to radar ears, the wallabies know that under our house is a safe haven from passing dingos (*Canis lupus dingo*). The thumping and growling under our feet last night suggested that hiding under the house might not work so well for female 'jills' trying to avoid amorous male 'jacks'.

Our wallabies have never become tame. We tried to tempt them with 'macropod' (literally, 'big foot') pellets – yes, you can buy such feed – but the pasture is good and they were never interested. The big jacks are gamest, but all the wallabies bound away in a flash if we walk too close for their comfort. Unlike our sheep and cattle, when the wallabies' ancient flight response kicks in, they bounce away helter-skelter in every direction. Even a mother and her joey go their separate ways, giving would-be predators something to think about and a choice to make.

A wallaby's brain is not big like ours; there's not a lot of forehead above that snout and below those ears. But constant hypervigilance and an explosively quick escape plan complement a body with powerful legs, haunches and tail. Wallabies are built for speed. To see a wallaby or kangaroo skip up a boulder-strewn cliff is a treat: a graceful show of skill honed in tough country and dangerous times.

Unlike us, wallabies are not celebrated for their reasoning. Their response to threat is a typical One Thought Solution stripped back to basics. At the first hint of anything that looks, smells or sounds different, they fly away, and they don't look back until they feel safe. But modern horses (*Equus ferus caballus*) have evolved to be perhaps Nature's foremost exponents of the flight response.

As a young man, I worked draught and light harness horses in singles and pairs, pulling logs and slides, sulkies, carts and wagons. In Old English, 'Wayne' means 'wagon maker', but that doesn't account for the pleasure that knowing horses gives me. There is much of interest in the way the horse evolved to cope with challenges as it changed from the 35 cm (14 in) tall *Eohippus*, some 60 million years ago, into the modern horse, about a million years ago.

In its natural state, the horse is the quintessential apex prey animal: a big, fast, powerful scaredy-cat that, with no fitness training at all, can cover 100 kilometres in a day, at pace, while carrying a load. Thanks to its ancestors who lived on open grass plains in the company of big cats and other fearsome hunters, the horse is supremely prepared to get away from predators.

Our human eyes are close together, looking forward, with overlapping visual fields that give us stereoscopic vision. This was an essential ability for our tree-dwelling primate ancestors whose lives depended on being able to judge distances to branches. But the horse's eyes are on the sides of its head, giving it about a 350° range of monocular vision, with only about 65° of binocular vision where its visual fields overlap at the front. The horse's ancestors lived on grassy plains and didn't need to judge distances to branches. Rather, for them, it was important to see all around, and especially behind, from where an attack was most likely to come.

Horses have two-colour, dichromatic vision. They naturally see the blue, yellow and green colours of the spectrum, but cannot distinguish red and are not sensitive to intermediate hues. Grass is grass, some green, some brown, and ancestral horses didn't need to finely discriminate colour gradients. Humans can normally see four basic colours of red, green, blue and yellow, and finely distinguish intermediate hues. For our primate ancestors, and indeed for us today, our omnivorous fascination with exotic foods and our taste for just about any type of game, fungi, fruit, flesh or vegetable, makes our ability to finely distinguish colour potentially lifesaving.

You might have heard the joke, 'A horse walks into a bar and the barman asks the horse …' But do you know the answer? Why does the horse have a long face?

The horse's long head allows it to graze while its eyes are far enough off the ground to watch for predators. As the horse's long head evolved, its jaw developed gaps, known as 'bars', on the gums between the front nipping teeth and the chewing molars further back. This made it possible to put a bit in a horse's mouth – otherwise, it would scrape on teeth – and inadvertently facilitated the human–horse partnership which powered civilisation up until fossil fuel technology took over. That's why the horse's long face has been so important in human history.

When their water trough was near our verandah, we witnessed an ancient drama re-enacted when our three horses, Happy, Honey and Geena came to drink. Happy and Honey are 17+ hand Standardbred harness horses: a breed celebrated for their strength and heads that look better in winkers. Geena is a retired Thoroughbred mare that our eldest daughter used to gallop everywhere.

Susan with Happy and Honey

The routine was always the same. The gelding Happy is top horse, so he had the onerous job of approaching the water trough first. His faltering, weaving approach, never straight, never smooth, began some 30 metres away, as Happy, ears scanning overtime, checked, and checked again, and again, for the lions, tigers and bears that might be lying in wait near the waterhole. Behind, the younger mare Honey and old Geena relaxed and waited patiently. It would be cruel to make a noise just as Happy touched lips to water, but if a bird flew by or the wind blew at that crucial moment, with a snort, a rear and a thunder of hooves Happy was gone.

Horses have a prodigious memory. If you teach something to a young horse, months later you can take up the lesson pretty much where you left off. And they seem to never forget things that frighten them. I never figured out what spooked my long-gone Arab gelding Ra to turn a relaxed canter into a sideways bolt whenever we rode down a certain bush track.

You need patience when you ask a young horse to do anything new. It takes a lot to reassure these powerful, trembling creatures that it's safe to cross a creek or to go through a gate for the first time. The horse's One Thought Solution is straightforward. If there's any sense of risk, they snort, bolt and don't go that way again, at least not without a lot of checking first.

Horses evolved One Thought Solutions that protect them in the natural world, but which limit them in a more complex, human-engineered environment where water sources and tracks are safe and they might have to live without a herd.

Sleeping is not easy for horses. It's something they really can't do alone. Mostly they nap while standing. Horses can't lie down for long because their internal organs put pressure on their lungs. But beyond such physical limitations, a horse can't relax enough to sleep unless someone stands guard for them. Our horses take it in turns, with one horse on alert, while the other two rest.

A horse forced to live by itself can become sleep-deprived and develop mental and behavioural problems. I've heard of a tired horse that stood guard over its only companion, a cow, while the cow chewed its cud, only to be disappointed when its bovine buddy didn't reciprocate and stand guard so it could rest.

For every species, the history of their ancestors' solutions to Nature's great challenge is etched in the form and function of their minds and bodies. And we are also animals of this world.

Being Human

Life on Earth originated from a single genesis spark about 3.5 billion years ago. Consequently, we humans (*Homo sapiens*) share a genetic history with every other form of life on the planet. We are biologically related to all bacteria, viruses, plants, fungi and animals that exist or have ever existed. If we could time travel down our genetic line, we'd see our modern human form morphing through ancestors that we share with other species. No life form exists that does not have this common genetic inheritance. If an unrelated creature is ever found, the event will be as momentous as finding life on another planet.

Human weaknesses are often highlighted. But we and every other creature here today have an unbroken line of ancestors that connects us back to the beginning of life. We follow a very long line of survivors indeed. And every generation of our predecessors not only reproduced but successfully protected their offspring so they could reproduce.

We know that our ancestors were resilient and persistent. How could they have been otherwise? They survived billions of years, endless ages of ice, planet-busting asteroid strikes, volcanoes, climate chaos, wars, pestilence, and much more. It follows that human nature is profoundly adaptable, strong and functional. We can find realistic hope for our future in the stories of how we and other creatures made the journey from deep time to now.

Much that defines us and our civilisations – our pro-social traits of cooperation, empathy and love, as well as antisocial stereotyping, prejudice and inter-group aggression – make sense as evolved responses to the challenges of life and ever-present danger. These abilities and strategies improved our species' prospects for survival and breeding.

We descended from African ancestors, but we're quite different from other extant primates. Instead of long arms for climbing trees, our pelvis, upright stance and long legs mark us as an ape suited to walking and running. We're good breeders. We have no obvious oestrus heat and can have sex anytime, any day, in any season, and in lots of positions. Our brains and long vocal chords allow us to use complex language. We are able to read and write because our visual system can discern the fine angles and shapes in letters that are similar to those between twigs and branches. Prominent frontal lobes and large brains signal that we're specialists in cunning, planning and higher forms of thinking.

Our extraordinary ability to cooperate with strangers is on show as we effortlessly synchronise vehicles in great daily migrations that, for spectacle, rival the flow of herds of wildebeests on the Serengeti. And it's no problem for 100,000 humans to travel from afar to pack together in a sports stadium and share the pleasure of a ritualistic replay of ancient tribal warfare.

Where would our love of sport be without arms and shoulder joints superbly adapted for throwing? We are the only primate who pays to watch balls, pucks, disks or shafts, being hit, thrown or kicked, back and forth from player to player, under, through, over, or into, all kinds of holes and goals. The flight of projectiles must be dear to our hearts. Due to this distinctively human characteristic, our ancestors not only survived but now our type dominates the planet.

Humans are expert at recognising faces and interpreting subtle expressions. So good, in fact, that we can see a man in the moon and Jesus in a piece of toast. This ability helps us to instantly distinguish in-groups and out-groups, which we do on the basis of minimal cues. A simple act of wearing a shared colour at a football game engenders instant bonhomie and a sense of fellowship that's not extended to those wearing the other team's colours. In the past, when meeting someone from another tribe could be fatal, prejudice based on stereotypes enabled our ancestors to tell friend from foe. At different times in history, this protective One Thought Solution was well adapted to its task.

Evolutionary theory and clinical psychology point to an insight. Some attributes and behaviours that appear to be problems today are actually solutions that worked in the past. The old solution only becomes problematic when it's used inappropriately to deal with a new challenge. It follows that we can solve some problems by bringing an old solution up to date and modifying it to suit the task at hand.

Symptoms as Solutions

People seek help from a clinical psychologist because they feel defeated by emotions, memories or impulses that they can't understand, let alone control. Healing in therapy begins with new knowledge and progresses with the learning of skills.

"Tim" arrived with a common request. 'Please hypnotise me. I've tried to quit smoking many times, but I just can't do it. I guess I'm weak ... lousy willpower ... please put me under and take smoking away.'

So it begins with many who seek hypnotherapy to give up tobacco. They arrive feeling inadequate, hoping that they will not have to use their willpower which has let them down so often in the past. They want their problem solved while they're blissfully unaware in a hypnotic trance. There is magic in hypnosis – indeed there's much about the human mind that's magical – but the key to becoming a non-smoker lies within, not in a hypnotist's spell.

My smoking clients do not realise that they already have all they need to become non-smokers again. My task is not to induce hypnosis; they're already entranced by their problem. Rather, my job is to break the spell that gives tobacco its power over them.

'Tell me about when you took up smoking. Why did you begin?' I ask Tim.

'It was so long ago. I was 19, everyone smoked in those days. It made me feel cool and grown up. I always looked forward to "smoko" (the morning break) at work. I suppose smoking relaxed me, gave me something to do with my hands in crowded places. No one knew it was dangerous back then. No one thought it was bad for you.'

I continue, 'If tobacco had turned out to be a miracle herb, and we now knew that smokers are healthier and have stronger hearts and lungs than non-smokers, would you be here?'

Tim is silent, not sure what to say. He hasn't been asked that question before. Confusion and uncertainty prepare Tim for change.

'If I could speak to that part of your mind that controls smoking and ask it why you took up the habit, the answer would be along the lines that everyone was doing it, it made you feel good, and it helped you to relax. Is there anything wrong with any of that?'

'No … no, I guess not. But smoking's such a hassle. I hate having to hide when I need a smoke. People look down on you. I don't like coughing every morning. I don't want to get emphysema and lung cancer. I want to be healthy.'

'So, smoking made good sense when you took it up. There was nothing wrong with the habit back then. Some doctors even prescribed it. But now you know more about the dangers and you want to change the old habit, bring it up to date so that it works better for you now?'

'Yeah … I guess that's it.'

For Tim, change is well underway with the question, 'Is the part of your mind that controls the old smoking habit ready to work out new ways to achieve the good things that smoking does for you?'

Fear and Learning

If humans did not fear harm and humiliation and could readily forget stressful experiences, clinical psychologists would be out of work. Fear and anxiety signal that a threat is present. Evolution designed these natural, protective emotions to warn us of danger. A client's presenting symptoms are often solutions that made sense when they confronted a challenge at an earlier time in their lives. But trouble can arise when the old response becomes an out-of-date habit that runs automatically in new situations.

If you feel terrified about the prospect of giving a speech or performing in public, suspect that somewhere in your past, you were embarrassed.

You'll never hear me sing in public, and you can thank "Miss Dowdy", my primary school teacher, for that. I was about nine years old, standing halfway back, on the right-hand side of the room facing forward, as Miss Dowdy conducted the class singing.

'Stop! Someone is out of tune. That half of the class, stop singing now' was how it began.

Then, 'The front three rows stop singing'.

Miss Dowdy zeroed in on me. Now face-to-face, I stared into her glasses. 'You sing Wayne.'

I tried, but not for long, before Miss Dowdy cut me off and announced to all, 'You're tone deaf, don't sing again'. I was led from the class and given a job to do in a storage room.

Miss Dowdy solved her problem, restored harmony and launched my lifelong habit of lip syncing 'Happy Birthday' and 'Advance Australia Fair'.

I can maybe accept that Miss D was right. The world could be better off for my not singing. Nonetheless, as the adult I am now, the diagnosis of tone-deafness and the demand for silence seem a tad harsh.

Mine is no victim's tale: just a common experience really. My One Thought Solution powered by the memory of Miss Dowdy and the desire to avoid embarrassment has not shut me up completely. I can sing (sort of) when in the shower or driving alone in my car. I was not treated cruelly – not like my 62-year-old friend "Anne" who will never enjoy playing the piano because she can't forget the nuns hitting her over the knuckles with a ruler every time she struck a wrong note during practice. Nor do I suffer hurtful emotional echoes like 93-year-old "Mary" who still bristles when she tells how teachers punished her for making writing mistakes after they forced her to give up her natural left-handedness as a child.

Throughout life, and especially during childhood, we build up networks of autobiographical memories (recollections of life events) related by emotional themes: Carl Jung called them 'memory complexes'. These linked memories underpin what we know about ourselves, other people, and the world around us. Such experiences and our responses to them affect the way we grow up and who we become.

The lessons we take from life are encoded in sequences of One Thought Solutions that help us manage similar situations when we confront them again. Childhood recollections of success, of being loved and encouraged, engender thoughts along the lines, 'This is all right, I can do this'. More stressful lessons, like that imparted by Miss Dowdy, also become personal history and inform our sense of who we are. Such memories generate useful thoughts like, 'Be quiet, you can't sing'. Whatever limitation this imposed, I don't feel cheated out of a career as a singer, and this One Thought Solution protected me from embarrassing myself by singing in public again. But, of course, this came with some loss of potential from my life.

Our adult personalities reflect strings of One Thought Solutions that determine whether we passively avoid or actively engage with life: whether we are confident or timid, shy or outgoing. These lessons tell us about the trustworthiness of other people, and whether the world is safe and friendly or dangerous and unpredictable.

But for more serious, potentially life-threatening challenges, Nature gives us special strategies – the automated, biologically driven, genetically determined One Thought Solutions known as 'phobia' and 'posttraumatic stress disorder'.

Protective Phobias

Phobias, the intense fear and avoidance that some people experience when exposed to potentially dangerous or threatening situations or things, are so common that they are considered near normal.

Most phobia sufferers manage anxiety by structuring their lives to avoid the thing they fear. People who do not like meeting people look for jobs in back rooms. Someone with a fear of heights avoids working on rooftops. Few with phobias seek treatment.

'Specific phobias' relate to dangers in the natural world, and are classified into types depending on the nature of the threat. 'Situational' types (e.g., tunnels, bridges, flying, enclosed places, driving) are most common, followed by 'natural environment' phobias (e.g., storms, heights, deep water), 'blood-injection-injury' type, and 'animal' type (e.g., snakes, dogs, spiders, birds). 'Social phobia' is intense anxiety about what others might be saying or thinking about us. 'Agoraphobia' is not fear of open spaces, but rather anxiety about having a panic attack in public.

As you might expect, people with specific phobia One Thought Solutions tend to tune in to the natural world around them. They check weather forecasts, know where every dog lives in their neighbourhood, and react instantly to curvy sticks on the ground as if they've seen a snake.

Snake Phobia

As I write this, it is late summer and it seems that every time I walk through long grass on our property I nearly step on a red-bellied black snake (*Pseudechis porphyriacus*) or carpet python (*Morelia spilota*). I do not have a snake phobia, but I'm used to jumping backwards giving my snake squeal before I realise why.

Folk who have a social phobia are exceptionally sensitive to real and imagined nuances in people's facial expressions. For agoraphobia sufferers, signs of impending panic are important, so they go through life paying close attention to their bodily feelings.

Phobias are 'biologically prepared'.[3] Evolution genetically wired our nervous systems to develop a phobia if certain dangerous things threaten us at particular stages of life, usually when we're young.

In the 1980s, psychologists demonstrated that evolution prepared monkeys to fear certain things, but not others.[4] Like humans, monkeys learn to fear something if they see another of their kind acting afraid of it. When researchers showed laboratory-raised rhesus monkeys a video of another monkey reacting fearfully to a snake, the monkeys quickly developed a fear of snakes even though this was the first time they had ever seen one. The observing monkeys also developed a fear response when a toy crocodile was substituted for the snake in the video. But other monkeys never learned a fear response when they watched an edited video of a monkey reacting in fear to a flower or a stuffed toy rabbit. Why would that be? Primates are biologically prepared to fear dangers that they might meet in the natural world.

In humans, phobic fear usually develops after something frightens them as a child. At my phobia treatment program in Sydney during the late 1980s, I studied a brief, low-stress technique which relieved clients' phobias by working with the memory of the first time they encountered their fear.

"Joan", a 40-year-old businesswoman, sought help for a phobia that overwhelmed her when she walked across the ramp onto the Manly Ferry, which she had to do every day to get to work. Joan felt ashamed because other commuters had seen her quivering like a frightened child.

In therapy, Joan recalled an incident that occurred when she was six years old. Her brother had held her head under the bath water, and she believed she was drowning. Joan's phobia was relieved after she reviewed, from an adult's perspective, what had happened to her as a child all those years ago. She was then able to let go of the old, out-of-date fear that had protected her for so long.

For Joan, when the sight of deep water triggered her phobia One Thought Solution, she was aware only of intense fear, a desperate need to escape, incoherent thoughts about personal weakness, and little else. Joan would never have spontaneously thought about the long-forgotten memory of her brother holding her underwater.

Psychiatry classifies phobia as a 'mental disorder': a psychological syndrome that creates clinically significant distress or disability. But these fear reactions are natural and healthy One Thought Solutions, similar to the fight-or-flight response to threat. Phobias protect us from danger. If you're afraid of heights, there's less chance that you will die by falling; a phobia of deep water diminishes the risk of drowning and shark attack; a fear of storms reduces the likelihood that you'll be outside where lightning could strike.

It makes sense that phobias begin with just one fright. In our ancestors' world, children who did not learn to avoid deep water after nearly drowning, or who went back to explore holes along the creek even though their mother warned them about brown snakes, were less likely to pass on their genes.

But evolution has given us a survival strategy even stronger than phobia – you could call it the pinnacle of phobias – Nature's top-drawer One Thought Solution known as 'posttraumatic stress disorder' or 'PTSD'.

The Ultimate One Thought Solution

"Jim", his weary wife "Claire" by his side, stiffened as his gaze shifted up and to the side. Jim's facial expression signalled the onset of a natural trance in which he attended only to his memory.

'Where are you Jim? What can you see? What's going on?' I asked.

'Firefight. Rubber plantation. Smell machine gun ... mud. Shredded leaves on my arms.'

Every day for more than 30 years, Jim had time travelled back to this firefight in the Vietnam War. Jim was strong and young then, but the burden of years and too much fear had worn him down.

Back in the Vietnam jungle, as was usual, on his first day out on patrol, Jim was forward scout. This most dangerous position was rightly his because he had the least to lose. The men behind Jim were nearer to their '365 days and one wakey' countdown to going home. They'd earned their safer positions on patrol.

When his tour of duty ended, Jim was lifted out of the jungle, flown home, and smuggled into Sydney in the dead of night to avoid anti-war protesters. But Jim hadn't really come home. He never left his mates. Now, in my office, Jim was with them, heart, body and mind, fighting a battle that had no end.

'Come back Jim. Look at me. You're here, in my office. You're safe now.'

Jim hated coming to see me at first, and that was usual. He would never have come except that his respected ex-military medico ordered him to do so. Like many survivors of violence, Jim felt ashamed when his doctor told him that he had PTSD. He figured that this meant he was crazy.

'In restaurants,' Claire said, 'Jim has to sit facing the door with his back to the wall'. She hesitated, 'And it takes him forever to park in town, he keeps driving around and around'.

Jim knew it sounded strange, but he had to keep driving until he found a parking spot that looked safe from ambush and crossfire.

Jim's therapy began with a thought experiment. I asked him to 'Think about what it would have been like in Vietnam to have none of the symptoms of PTSD. Imagine that you were a relaxed, easy-going fellow who trusted other people, never felt paranoid, slept soundly at night, never became angry, was incapable of violence and didn't drink alcohol. How would you have gone in the war?'

Jim thought, and said, 'I'd be dead'.

Memories of trauma underpin the PTSD One Thought Solution. These intrusive recollections, and the terror and compelling urge to escape they bring with them, are just about all that a sufferer is aware of when this survival strategy kicks in. And their nightmares are never far away, ever ready to bite when something triggers the past into life.

As distressing as post-trauma symptoms are for the sufferer, these reactions are not a sign of mental illness or personal weakness. In fact, in the scientific literature, posttraumatic stress disorder has been described as a third form of human learning alongside 'classical conditioning', made famous by Ivan Pavlov's experiments with bells and salivating dogs, and 'operant conditioning', associated with B. F. Skinner's lever-pressing rats.[5]

PTSD is a One Thought Solution that was forged in our ancestors' encounters with extreme danger. It is specifically designed for coping with life-threatening situations. It prepares us to quickly learn and never forget life's most important lessons.

Evolution through Learning

Evolution has endowed humans with genetic potentials that are flexible and nuanced. Our ancestors had to adapt not just to the demands of one era – they had to successfully manage every new, unpredictable situation they confronted through the ages.

Species inherit more than physical and mental traits. Intergenerational change is also driven by learning and the passing on of 'memes': those useful ideas, values and behaviours shared across generations. For instance, there's little about our modern world that does not reflect the ongoing impact of the 'agricultural revolution' and memes discovered some 12,000 years ago when our ancestors learned to breed plants and gave up hunting and gathering for more settled agrarian lifestyles.

The cultural transmission of new knowledge about food has also transformed the lifestyles of animals. A community of Japanese macaque monkeys took up the practice of washing potatoes in salty water after a pioneering individual discovered that this made spuds taste better.[6] Passed down from parent to offspring, this meme changed the diet and behaviour of a macaque colony across generations. And urban macaques in Cambodia solved their dental problem of sore gums due to eating junk food when they learned to floss their teeth with hair pulled from the heads of tourists.[7]

A tropical apple tree used to grow in our yard. The bitter fruit never ripened and fell to the ground where, some years ago, a creative redneck wallaby jill acquired the taste and worked out how to eat apples.

Our Apple-munching Jill

A wallaby uses its front paws for grooming, scratching fleas and grappling with other wallabies, but not for much else. When grazing, a wallaby's front legs lightly touch the ground as they lean forward to eat. Our apple-munching jill learned to hold the fruit steady with her paws while she nibbled. And next season, she taught her joey how to eat apples. Unfortunately, we cut down the tree before we found out whether the apple-eating joey would pass on the skill to its offspring.

Other wallabies and mammals such as possums eat apples, so this behaviour, while unusual for us to see, is not a big stretch for a wallaby's genetically endowed abilities. We will never know if apple eating could have become a cultural tradition, like potato washing in the Japanese macaque colony, passed down through generations to enrich the diet of Toonumbar's wallabies.

Horse Sense in an Age of Nonsense

What are we to make of the fact that in the 19th century, when horsepower really was the power of horses, the term 'horse sense' meant the ability to make sensible decisions?

How does my earlier description of horses as scaredy-cat prey animals fit with the opinions of prior generations who saw dependability and doing the right thing as commendable characteristics in the horses they worked with day to day?

Horses appeared in Cro-Magnon cave art 15,000 to 20,000 years ago. But humans used them only as food until some 5,000 to 6,000 years ago when nomads around the Black and Caspian Seas figured out how to train the horse.

It is incredible what horses and humans — two creatures with an exquisite sensitivity to social cues and an innate capacity for learning — can achieve together.

Look at it from the horse's point of view. Why would you let someone climb on your back? For an untrained horse, having a large, carnivorous predator such as a human climb onto its back, behind its neck, would be its worst vision come true: a terrifying trigger for every fight/flight/buck/bolt One Thought Solution it's capable of. And yet, with patient instruction, horses not only accept us riding on their backs, but can enter into a relationship of such skill, subtlety and joy that horse and rider seem to function as one.

What does it take to transform a horse with its native propensity for flight into the celebrated partner who has dependably worked with humans throughout history: ploughing fields, hauling loads, and carrying us through the chaos of war? How does the horse learn to override its genetically determined One Thought Solution flight response? What enables them to achieve their remarkable potential?

No horse left to itself will become skilled at riding, driving, dressage, jumping, polo or any of the other performances they are capable of. A young horse can learn from other educated horses – I used to tether a green horse beside an experienced worker – but most important new lessons come from humans.

I attained a farmer's skill as a horseman. I taught them a thing, maybe two; they taught me more. My Arab gelding Ra was skittish by nature, but readily learned to ignore my stockwhip cracking about his head as we mustered cattle. And it didn't take Ra long to learn to stand still as my young daughters jumped on, one in front and one behind me, to ride around our farm.

Initial training for a horse involves a series of strategically timed lessons early in its life. But it takes many more years of work before a horse is fully educated. In the horse world, 'bombproof' is the gold standard: a horse that's so experienced and disciplined it behaves impeccably and safely in all situations, regardless of distractions.

In a sense, a bombproof horse has completed the '10,000 hours' of practice that it's said humans need to achieve expertise. These are the horses that demonstrate horse sense as our grandparents understood the term: the milk cart Clydesdale who walked to the next house while the milkman ran bottles to front doors; the Australian Waler who charged into battle amidst gunfire and explosions; and the farm carthorse who plodded on safely while the driver dozed, asleep at the reins.

Evolution endowed the horse with physical attributes and One Thought Solutions that have stood its kind in good stead through millions of years in a challenging, dangerous world. Beyond that, evolution made it possible for horses to enter into relationships with humans. Evolution equipped horses with traits that enable them to learn complex, subtle skills that go way beyond anything you would suspect from observing horses in their natural state.

The horse serves as proof that new knowledge gained through learning can profoundly change even rigid, genetically determined patterns of thought and behaviour. And clinical experience shows that with new understanding and skills, people can free themselves from the One Thought Solutions of phobia and posttraumatic stress disorder.

We'll Determine Our Future

Evolution shaped the One Thought Solution, but that does not mean that it will be impossible, or even very difficult, for us humans to learn how to respond effectively to the complex challenges we face today. Indeed, our species' long history of creative problem-solving gives hope that we can go beyond our current over-reliance on shallow thought.

In this chapter, we have gone from wisdom to war via some physical and mental traits that define what it means to be a wallaby, a horse or a human. We have seen how specialised forms of the One Thought Solution evolved to protect us from threat, and how we use this basic strategy to respond to life's challenges.

We could choose to go through life applying One Thought Solutions to almost every problem, but to do so would be to live like an untrained horse. In such a life we would show off our natural proclivities but, as impressive as these are, we're capable of so much more.

We know what it takes to train a horse to a bombproof standard. Why would we doubt that *Homo sapiens* cannot also learn more sophisticated ways of thinking and behaving?

When a challenge comes our way, we have choices to make. If we decide that we don't care and there's nothing we need to do, One Thought Solutions will suffice. 'It's none of my business.' 'It's too hard.' 'There's nothing I can do.' If we decide that we do care and want to succeed, we have to leave the comfort of shallow thought for the more demanding, but vastly more rewarding, realm of the deep mind. From here on, whatever we decide, there will be consequences for us and for the challenge we take on.

If we do one thing, we can't do other things. The best choice might be a considered decision not to pursue a potentially valuable opportunity. Sometimes, running from a dangerous problem is the only viable option; if there's no other way to protect your family, you might have to move them to safety regardless of the losses this entails.

But when we decide to take on a challenge, we meet the conundrum expressed by Gandalf in J.R.R. Tolkien's *Lord of the Rings*: we can't determine the times we live in, but it's up to us what we do with the time that's given us. So begins a search to find out what we need to know about the problem, ourselves and what it will take to succeed. Easier paths are more travelled, but the way to the deep mind leads to greater satisfaction.

In the following chapters, we'll look at three challenges from my life. I confronted pressing needs to help my traumatised clients, cure forest dieback on our property, and do what I could to protect my country and community from gas field industrialisation. These problems differed in kind but shared common features.

In each case, trouble arose when natural systems – the human mind, native forests and the physical environment – were disrupted. The problems could be solved when the pathogenic factors (things causing or capable of causing disease) were identified and dealt with so that healing processes could restore balance to the system.

Shallow thinking with One Thought Solutions helped create and sustain the three challenges. Success was built on effort, new learning and the work of the deep mind.

Chapter 2

War Trauma and a New Psychology

> Great is the guilt of an unnecessary war.
> John Adams (1735–1826)

THE NAME HAS CHANGED: it was 'shell shock' in the Great War, 'combat neurosis' in World War II, and posttraumatic stress disorder after Vietnam, but the suffering was similar for veterans returning from Gallipoli, Kokoda, Long Tan, Iraq, Afghanistan and all theatres of martial violence. For me, the challenge of how best to help victims of trauma began in the 1970s.

It was a time for revolution when seismic shifts fractured Australian society, politics and the science of psychology. Coming of age in the 1960s and 70s was exciting, at times frightening. Nothing focuses the mind of a young man like the prospect of violent death and a legally enforced duty to kill other people.

From the mid-1960s, males turning 20 were entered in the 'birthday ballot' or 'lottery of death' as it was known. If the marble bearing your birth date fell, the prize was two years in the Australian Army, three more years on active reserve, and the prospect of the experience of a lifetime – a one year tour of duty fighting in the jungles of Vietnam. I was lucky. My shot at being press-ganged was deferred until I finished university, and Gough Whitlam ended conscription before I was called up.

From 1962 to 1973, almost 60,000 Australian military personnel served in the Vietnam War: 521 were killed, over 3,000 were wounded and, in accord with the usual one to four deaths to serious injury ratio, about 2,000 returned home with permanently broken bodies. Upward of 3.3 million Vietnamese and 58,220 soldiers from the United States died in the war.

You can't quantify the mental harm from fighting in Vietnam. The toll mounts still as physical, genetic and emotional damage passes down through sons and daughters to the grandsons and granddaughters of our war veterans and their families. For many, the emotional wounds never heal.

Vietnam was the first televised war. Who can forget the images of 'napalm girl' running from her bombed out village (in 2015 Phan Thi Kim Phúc finally received treatment for lifelong pain from her napalm scars[1]), or the headshot street execution of a Viet Cong? For the first time, mental rehearsal and other psychological techniques lifted the kill rate of infantrymen and countered the natural human reluctance to kill others.

The American military-industrial complex tested technologies of destruction. Agent Orange herbicides defoliated vast tracts of forest, leaving a toxic legacy for the ages. Aerial bombardment of defenseless towns and villages was not new, but the One Thought Solution offered as justification was: 'We had to destroy the village in order to save it'. Vietnam is not a big country – it takes six minutes for a commercial flight to cross the narrowest section near Da Nang – but the US dropped more bombs there than were deployed in the entire European theatre of World War II.

For the first and hopefully only time, Australian soldiers returning from war were denied the respect they deserved. By the late 1960s, anti-war Moratorium marches in Australia eclipsed the scale of World War I's anti-conscription rallies.

The Vietnam War was popular at first, well sold with a One Thought Solution known as the 'domino theory'. Fear was the motivating emotion. The pitch was that if we didn't defeat the Communists in their backyard, they would stream down from China through Southeast Asia and we would have to fight them here. For Australians, memories 20 years fresh of Kokoda and the Japanese bombing of Darwin lent credibility to the story.

The hidden carriages in the domino theory One Thought Solution concealed a false assumption. Australia was not under threat of invasion. The Viet Cong and North Vietnamese were fighting to reunify their country and expel foreign powers. They were not looking to invade other countries. Citizens in western nations gradually learned the truth, and later in the 1960s, a great protest movement arose. The government fined or gaoled draft resisters, conscientious objectors and protesters. Families and communities split into pro and anti-war camps.

Tragically, on their return home, many servicemen and women were treated with contempt. To avoid protesters, they were often delivered back to an uncaring country in the dark of night. There was no heroes' return or welcome home march for our Vietnam veterans: a healing honour accorded returning soldiers since the first ANZACS. Thankfully, in October of 1987, our veterans held their own welcome home march.

A Country Divided

My 85-year-old mother still becomes teary when she remembers the arguments between anti-war me and my pro-war father. I was against the war but opposed protests that targeted returning service personnel.

'We have to stop the Communists, and military service is good for young men' were my father's One Thought Solutions to the problem of having three teenage sons. Years later, Dad told me that he never understood what I was on about. He said that he left school at 15 years of age and had believed the government's line that the war was necessary to protect Australia. I'm grateful we resolved our differences before my father died.

Until my teens, my parents and their five children – I was the eldest – lived with my Pop and Nanna. Pop fought in the trenches of France during World War I. For Australia and many other nations, the Great War remains the most deadly and dangerous conflict in history. From a population of fewer than five million, 416,809 Australian men enlisted, with over 60,000 killed and 156,000 wounded, gassed or taken prisoner. My grandfather was hospitalised and returned to the front on three separate occasions after being shot in the shoulder, blown up by an artillery shell, and poisoned with mustard gas. As a kid I went with Pop to Anzac Day marches. They were never good times.

I could not understand why Vietnam War protesters spat on and threw paint at the 'diggers' but mostly left the politicians alone. Those responsible for sending Australian troops to war seemed unburdened by guilt as they enjoyed healthy, successful lives. It was left to the Vietnam Veterans and their families to pay the bill.

Australian society never fully recovered from the Vietnam War. Old ways broke down and a chasm opened up between generations. Sons no longer looked to their fathers and older men for guidance or wanted to follow in their footsteps. Reducing complex problems to One Thought Solutions flourished.

For the young, the old became the enemy. 'Hope I die before I get old,' sang The Who, though they might have changed their minds by now. Mass killings perpetrated as righteous war tarnished the conservative values of mainstream society. The young welcomed almost any 'radical' or 'alternative' idea that promised change. Few questioned whether the changes were for the better.

Things are clearer looking back. During the '60s, university students joined Stalinist and Maoist groups thinking they were supporting good over evil. In 1972, when I was hitching around the United States, anti-war university students told me that Richard Nixon was their peace candidate. They knew nothing of the secret bombing of Laos and Cambodia. Nixon, on a Peace in Vietnam ticket, went on to secure his second term as president by a landslide. But Nixon couldn't lock a Watergate, and you know how that went.

The Vietnam War generation has never properly thought through One Thought Solutions about the generation gap, conservatism and radicalism, and the nature of patriotism which helped them make sense of the mayhem they lived through.

A Fractured Psychology

For some, the early 1970s meant hell in Vietnam. For fortunate others, it was a great time to be a university student. I was the first in my family privileged to go to university, where I studied psychology and philosophy. Social revolution was transforming fashion, sex, drugs, rock-and-roll and just about everything that interests the young. In the world of science, a divided psychology was coming to some profound insights into the human mind.

Psychology was not a unified science. It still isn't. With no accepted general theory, no paradigm or common method to pull it together, psychology was a grab bag of intellectually isolated, competing schools of thought: 'psychoanalysis', 'behaviourism', 'Gestalt', 'transpersonal' – the list was long. There was no cross-fertilisation of ideas. Practitioners did not talk to others outside their preferred tradition, nor did they read their journals. In truth, many psychologists had little in common.

There were pretenders for the title of a scientific psychology, but no real contender.

Freud and Psychoanalysis

Back then, Sigmund Freud's psychoanalytic theory dominated European psychology and influenced art and thinking about the human condition. The technology of a time inspires the metaphors that scientists use to explain how the human mind and brain work. In Freud's day, it was steam power and electricity.

In Freud's model, 'libido' powered the human mind. Poorly translated as 'sexual energy', libido is more properly understood as a 'life force'. Emotional problems develop when the flow of libido is blocked – 'cathected' is the term – stuck somewhere in the mind's structure.

As you would expect in a steam-driven system, when things get blocked, you need to unblock them. So to resolve psychological difficulties, you promote 'catharsis': a purging of the emotional tension. You free up the flow of libidinal energy, reduce the pressure, let off some steam, as it were. In electric terms, you overcome the resistance and get the current flowing. To this day, when it comes to treating trauma, steam-driven metaphors dominate clinical psychology's thinking and practice.

The Europeans liked it, but American psychologists dismissed Freud's psychoanalytic theory out of hand. They said it was unscientific and untestable, more literature than science. 'How do you measure a libido?' and 'What's sex got to do with it?' they asked.

American psychologists didn't buy Freud's theory that five-year-old boys develop a male sex-role identity because they fantasise having it off with their mothers – the well-known 'Oedipus complex'. Freud's idea was that young boys, realising that their fathers might get in the way of their incestuous plan, and fearing that their fathers would castrate them as punishment (the 'castration complex'), solved the problem by 'identifying with the aggressor' and becoming like their father. I guess they hoped that mother would find that appealing.

Outside of Europe, Freud's theory about how young girls take on a female sex role, the 'Electra complex', with its notion of 'penis envy', was no more popular.

From our contemporary perspective, Freud's ideas about sex seem odd, even bizarre. But we need to understand them in the context of the early 20th-century Viennese society in which the young Jewish doctor Sigmund Freud worked.

Early in his career, Freud treated women who suffered 'hysteria', which today would be diagnosed as a trauma-related condition such as posttraumatic stress disorder, 'dissociative disorder' or 'conversion disorder'. When Freud hypnotised patients and took them back to childhood memories, they often described horrific sexual abuse.

Freud's investigation of children's bodies in morgues confirmed his initial opinion that his clients were recalling genuine assaults.

Then, for reasons too complex to describe here, Freud changed his mind and came up with 'psychoanalytic theory'[2]. He recast his patients' recollections of sexual abuse, not as genuine memories, but as fantasies which arise from unconscious sexual drives. This shifted responsibility for the apparent incest and sexual assault from the likely perpetrators to mental processes within the client. From then on, many psychiatrists took women's memories of sexual abuse to be fantasy, rather than fact.

In the United States, mid-20th-century academic psychology took a different tack.

The Rise of Rat Psychology

Impressed by the power and influence of physicists during and after World War II – science contributed nuclear bombs, radar, jet engines and lots of other neat things – the Americans reasoned that if psychologists mimicked the hard sciences and did things as the physicists did, they too would become successful and powerful. The psychologists got it wrong on a number of counts.

Since Einstein, Rutherford and Maxwell, physicists had dealt with curious entities such as atoms, force fields and space-time, and they were comfortable working with things that no one could see. Ideas that seemed counterintuitive or even impossible did not trouble physicists, provided that their theories accounted for the data and were testable.

Now, a century on from Einstein, theories of relativity and quantum dynamics seem as impossible as ever: no one truly understands them. But these ideas have survived all tests and are indispensable for modern technologies such as solid-state memory storage, light emitting diodes and the global positioning system.

Physicists knew that something can be real even if you cannot see it or directly measure it. But when the American 'behaviourist' psychologists looked at physics, all they saw were the technicians' white coats and the dazzling instruments and machines they got to use. So, with a brilliant One Thought Solution, psychology decided to lose its mind.

Behaviourists solved the problem of how to study mental processes by decreeing that they don't exist. They banished subjective experience from science and would tolerate no talk of the mind. Henceforth, no respectable scientific psychologist dared dabble with anything that sounded mental. Psychology was to concern itself only with what could be seen and measured: the 'stimulus', what the organism experienced; and the 'response', the way it responded. Behaviourists relegated everything that went on inside the mind – imagination, memory, desires, dreams – to a 'black box' that was not to be opened. And so 'rat psychology', also known as 'behavioural psychology' or 'learning theory', was born.

The American psychologists knew that humans are complicated, contrary creatures, so they donned white coats and spent decades and millions of dollars studying rats running through mazes and pigeons pecking targets. Their One Thought Solution was that because they were looking for a universal theory of learning, it made sense to study creatures less complex than humans.

This fanciful agenda should have collapsed sooner than it did. Philosophers in the early 20th century knew that behaviourism was untenable. Just because you can't see something doesn't mean that it doesn't exist or it's not worth studying.

What do you think would have happened if, instead of asking a pigeon to peck a target and a rat to pull a lever, researchers had swapped the tasks and asked the pigeon to pull the lever and the rat to peck the target? The answer is: not a lot. Neither the pigeon nor the rat would have done much at all.

It's natural for a rat to explore with its paws, and for a bird to look for food with its beak. The psychologists' research depended on their unwitting decision to look only at behaviours that came naturally to these animals. If the behaviourists' train of thought had a few more carriages, they might have realised that evolution shapes every creature's form and function, and what was going on in the brains and minds of laboratory animals was centrally important for a truly scientific psychology.

Behaviourism's demise was assured when the US Air Force asked psychologists about optical illusions that were inducing false sightings in their radar operators: a potentially catastrophic problem during the Cold War nuclear standoff between the USA and the USSR.[3] The psychologists had nothing to say about the problem because they had deliberately avoided thinking about such things. If the Air Force had asked them about rats or pigeons, they might have been able to help.

No forced marriage of behaviourism and psychoanalysis was imaginable. They shared no common interest, spoke different languages, and seemed to inhabit alternative universes. They did not agree on what a scientific psychology would look like or what it should study, so there was no chance of any theoretical synthesis. It seemed that psychology would never enjoy the kind of unifying theory that powered physics, chemistry, biology and other sciences.

But then a brand new technology arrived to transform psychology and the world.

The Computer Revolution

The digital computer was a new, powerful machine to inspire metaphors and fresh ideas about human nature. The computer not only gave psychology its mind back, it offered the prospect of a unified scientific theory.

In the mid-1970s, there was no personal computer: it was still a decade away. But the integrated transistor chip had been invented and, with it, the 'information age' and the 'cognitive revolution' were on the way. Psychologists could now create metaphors for the mind that went beyond systems inspired by steam and electricity.

Freud's notion of a hierarchically arranged mental system was compatible with the way that computer components and software operations are organised. But the steam-driven model of emotions was difficult to integrate. Freud's theories couldn't offer a satisfying account of how the human bio-computer worked.

The behaviourist method that only took account of stimuli and responses had no chance of describing what a computer did. For this, you have to understand mysterious entities known as programs.

The computer was a device of undoubted power – a mechanical brain to drive new military, industrial and civilian machines – and at the heart of its operation was the program. In those days, programs were physically represented on punch cards or tape, but these are not the program itself. Programs are not physical. They have nothing to do with atoms, molecules, wires or microchips.

If you had superhero X-ray and microscopic vision and could see through the casing of your laptop or tablet, down into every circuit, even to the atomic and quantum levels, you still couldn't describe how your computer works by referring only to its physical components. You have to take account of the way the machine's programs process information.

A program exists, but it is an ethereal thing: a flow of symbols, a set of instructions for manipulating information. In computer programming code, you'll find logical operations such as 'if this, then that', but you will never find the chemical makeup of a metal or plastic component of the machine.

The arrival of the computer even offered a solution to a problem that had perplexed philosophers for ages.

The Mind–Body Problem Solved?

For millennia, philosophers have tried to understand how consciousness and the mind arise from the physical operations of the brain and nervous system.

The mind and the body are clearly not the same thing, but they are intimately linked. Drinking alcohol can make us feel happier and gamer than we ought to be, so a physical substance can affect our feelings and actions. Thinking about something sad can make us cry, so words, an image, or a memory can induce our bodies to shed tears.

The mystery deepens in the fields of pharmacology and neuropsychology. Ingesting 100 millionths of a gram of LSD-25, a barest mote of chemical, profoundly alters a person's sense of identity and reality, and a small dose of a benzodiazepine such as Valium blocks anxiety and induces sleep. A client I assessed performed normally on intelligence tests not long after doctors removed a tumour the size of an egg from her brain. I have also treated a man whose life was ruined because he could not plan or think ahead after he fell from his push-bike and sustained a tiny scar on the underside of his brain's frontal lobes.

Head injuries can leave patients with startlingly specific deficits, but otherwise intact, normal functioning: a dairy farmer who forgot only the names of his cows; a woman whose vision was normal, except that movement appeared as a series of snapshots; people who lose only the verbal ability to understand pronouns, or conjunctions, or names of places; and clients who draw clocks with the numbers 1 to 12 on only half of the clock face.

Brain injuries reveal surprising distinctions between perception and recognition, and between conscious and unconscious mental processes. A brain-injured patient with 'blindsight' cannot see, but they can catch a ball thrown in their direction. At the conscious level they see nothing, but at an unconscious level, they're aware of what's around them. Try as you might, you cannot convince some brain-injured patients that their arm, which they can clearly see, is actually theirs. In a potentially tragic condition known as 'Capgras delusion', the sufferer sees that someone looks like a family member, but because they don't have the feeling of recognising the person, they can come to believe that their relative is an impostor.

The bio-computer metaphor offered a new way to think about the relationship between mind and brain. We now had a machine made up of connected, interacting physical components controlled by a microchip brain, and programs with an eerie resemblance to mind that ran the show. As with cases of human brain injury, damage to a computer's visual processors would likely affect its visual system; damage to a soundcard, the auditory and speech systems; a fault in the memory chip would likely affect memory, and so on. It was now clear why a minor brain injury could cause profound disability, while a major injury might have little impact. We could understand how a minuscule physical fault or software error might crash a computer, while some components could be removed altogether with no obvious effect.

But most importantly, the relationship between a computer's software and its hardware seemed similar to the way the human mind relates to the human body. In computers, instructions to move, store, retrieve and coordinate information in and between subcomponents produce the observed performance. In humans, thoughts, images, beliefs and other mental processes, initiate and control our body's behavioural and emotional reactions.

Here's a thought experiment.

Imagine that you're lying on a table with the top of your skull removed so that, with mirrors, you can see your brain. Monitors tell you about every physical process in your brain. You can see the electroencephalogram trace of electrical activity, and have access to all information about nerves, hormones, proteins, genes, etc.

Now ask yourself, where is love? Where's your sensation of the colour red? Where will you find your ambitions?

How could you use this wealth of information about the brain to make the simplest prediction, such as whether you will choose tea or coffee later on?

Don't be concerned if you couldn't find love in the brain. Nobody can. But if you do, please let me know.

The mind cannot be explained in terms of the brain because they operate at different levels of reality. They require different types of explanations and call for different kinds of theories. Knowing how the nerves in your arm work will never help you understand why you reach for a pen instead of a pencil.

But perhaps the computer's greatest gift to psychology is 'systems theory'.

Systems Theory

Computer-inspired systems theory was a potent new way to think about reality and the way that organisms and environments interact. The perspective is holistic. The focus is on 'organised wholes' and 'active systems', rather than one-at-a-time causal connections between isolated, elementary parts.

You could spend lifetimes studying how computer components interact and be none the wiser about how a computer works. To understand that, you have to look at what's going on in the computer's 'brain' and 'mind'. And these are complex, interacting, physical and nonphysical systems.

The computer re-awoke psychology to the insight that what goes on in our minds affects the way we interpret and react to the world around us. From the mid-1960s, cognitive psychologists opened the black box and went about creating models of attention, perception, imagery, memory and all kinds of other mental processes.

By the mid-1970s, the Vietnam War was over, there was hope for a truly scientific psychology, and I left the city for the bush.

The New Hypnosis

For the next decade or so my life revolved around farm and horses, raising a family and working as a small-town psychologist in private practice. For clinicians it was an exciting time: a golden age of innovation in psychotherapy and what was known as the 'new hypnosis'.

The therapy of Milton Erickson (1901–1980), an Arizona-based psychiatrist, inspired clinical practitioners to transform psychotherapy.

I could see parallels between Milton Erickson's ideas and the gentler ways of working with horses which began in the 1960s with Tom Roberts, and continues today with Pat Parelli, the 'natural horse training' movement, and others.

Like in old cowboy movies, you can break an untrained horse by throwing gear on its back and bucking it out. This is risky and stressful for both horse and trainer, but you might end up with a rideable, if not entirely reliable, horse. I followed Tom Roberts, who treated horse training as a process of communication, not subjugation. The attitude was gentle, persistent and respectful. The trainer worked to keep the animal calm and assumed that the horse was essentially cooperative, but naturally concerned for its safety and prone to fright and flight. Ideally, you ended up with a horse that had never bucked, never kicked, and had never been frightened or harmed by a human.

It's up to the trainer to use skilful means to help the horse reach its potential. If things aren't going well, if communication between horse and human is coarse and dull, or breaks down entirely, the responsibility is in the hands of the human. A well-handled driving horse is attentive to information conveyed through reins and voice. If this information is 'noisy' due to the driver giving inconsistent signals, the horse cannot understand what's expected of it, so its behaviour appears erratic. If the voice commands and pressures transmitted through the reins consistently relay the driver's intention, the horse's responses become increasingly subtle, until they seem to synchronise with the driver's thoughts. Then the magic begins.

As with my horses, when working as a psychologist I looked to help clients solve their problems gently and quickly, and for that, Milton Erickson's ideas were priceless.

From experiences of growing up on a farm, a lifetime coping with chronic pain and confinement to a wheelchair, and work with difficult psychiatric cases, Milton Erickson created a practical wisdom that was at odds with traditional ways of doing therapy.

Erickson recognised early that unconscious mental processes are important. When an attack of poliomyelitis in 1919, just after he graduated from high school, left Erickson almost totally paralysed for months, he lay at home and observed his family communicating with each other on intuitive levels outside of conscious awareness.[4]

Erickson was an early 'systems theorist'. He likened therapy to starting a snowball rolling down a hill: a small, strategic change in one part of a person's life could set off a self-generating healing process.

From Erickson's work, a new spirit of creative problem-solving fostered a raft of innovative therapies including neuro-linguistic programming, 'solution focused therapy', 'systemic family therapy', Ericksonian hypnotherapy, and more. Now, some 40 years later, I am as impressed as ever when clients use these methods to resolve problems that mainstream psychology still considers difficult to treat. The good begun by Erickson goes on.

Some therapists are entranced by what they think is their power to heal. Erickson's antidote to this idea was to tell a story about a lost horse that turned up outside his family's house when he was a boy.[5] Erickson climbed onto the horse's back, gave it a giddy-up with his heels – there were no reins – and the horse walked home. As Erickson explained, the therapist stimulates the client with ideas, but does not know how the client's deep mind will use this information or how it will resolve the problem.[6]

Unlike Erickson, neither Freudian nor cognitive psychology inspired therapists trust the deep mind. They blame it for the problems that people bring to therapy. For Freud, the unconscious mind, which he dubbed the 'id', was a dangerous, untrustworthy region of the psyche ruled by base aggressive and sexual instincts. Freud trusted the 'ego', with its reason and connection to external reality. He believed that emotional problems could only be solved when unconscious conflicts were understood at a conscious level. Freud described his goal in therapy as, 'Where id is, there shall ego be'.

Cognitive therapy practitioners also distrust the unconscious mind. They identify dysfunctional 'automatic thoughts' which, like all One Thought Solutions, occur rapidly with little conscious awareness. For instance, if someone interprets the look on another person's face as being critical, the automatic thought 'They don't like me' can trigger a feeling of rejection. Like Freud, cognitive therapists work to bring problematic unconscious thoughts to a conscious level, and they encourage clients to rationally discuss, challenge and think through their beliefs.

Milton Erickson took a radically different approach. He downgraded the role of the conscious mind and portrayed it as mainly concerned with generating cover stories and rationalisations to give us the illusion that we're in control of what we think, do and feel. Erickson believed that conscious awareness can get in the way when we're taking on challenges and solving problems. So he sometimes deliberately distracted a client and gave their conscious mind things to do, while the real therapy went on at deeper levels.

Erickson believed that Nature designed the unconscious mind to be a rational, health-minded system that's capable of making sophisticated decisions to help and protect us. It follows that therapists should respect and not criticise clients who are reluctant to take directions. Erickson offered an analogy for working with such resistance. If you want to change the course of a river and you try to block it, the water will go over and around you. But if you accept the power of the river and divert it in a new direction, the force of the water will cut a new channel.

Erickson respected the unconscious mind. The goal of Erickson's hypnotherapy is to liberate the deep mind's creativity so that clients bring their own memories, knowledge and abilities to bear on their problems. For clients, psychotherapy becomes a process of learning about who they are, what they're capable of, and how they can improve their lives.

Erickson thought of hypnosis as a natural state akin to a daydream or letting your mind wander. For him, hypnotic inductions were more invitation than instruction. Erickson might say, 'You can enter trance in your own way and in your own time'. How could you object to that? The style is respectful and undemanding, and you're in control.

By contrast, in traditional hypnotherapy, the client is given direct suggestions, much like being ordered what to do: 'As you look at the watch, your eyes will get heavier and heavier'. The hypnotist wants to give the impression that they're in control. If you stare at a spinning watch, or anything that's difficult to look at, for long enough, your eyelids will get heavy, and you will want to close your eyes. It's called blinking and it happens all the time. If you buy the idea that the hypnotist somehow ordered your eyelids to feel heavy, you're on your way to ever more interesting suggestions.

Not everyone reacts well to being directed, so traditional hypnotists believe that only some people can be hypnotised. In fact, everyone can use hypnosis provided they're invited, not ordered, to respond.

Healing with the Deep Mind

Trauma can leave people bedevilled by horrific memories that won't leave them alone: any mention of the past triggers suffering. Milton Erickson's work raised the intriguing possibility that severely traumatised clients could be helped gently if their deep mind solved problems while they were consciously unaware of what was going on. Working with "Sylvia", I learned that such a thing is indeed possible.

32-year-old Sylvia felt depressed and was thinking of taking her life. Over a half-dozen consultations, we addressed the thoughts that seemed to trigger her despair. I intuitively steered away from exploring Sylvia's dreams because they suggested to me that she might have been sexually molested as a child. Sylvia gave no indication that she was aware of any such thing. She hadn't told me about any abuse, and I didn't want to breach what could be a protective amnesia. Sylvia's depression did not lift until I talked with her deep mind.

We communicate not just with what we say, but with how we say it, and what we do while we say it. 'Body language', the tone and inflection of voice, posture, and facial and hand gestures, can reinforce or contradict what we say. How convinced would you be if I told you 'I feel great' in a slow, monotone voice with my eyes downcast? Would you trust someone who agreed with you while their head was moving slightly side to side as if to indicate 'no'? Body language can tell us how a person is feeling and thinking, even when their words indicate something different.

When we agree with an idea, we tend to nod our heads slightly. When we disagree, our heads move side to side. Skillful operators use these slight, automatic movements to guide their efforts at influencing others. A politician might delay a vote at a meeting until she sees most heads nodding agreement with her favoured proposition. A fortune-teller will pursue a line of patter that produces subtle head nodding. A salesperson will shift from pitching to closing a sale when he sees his target's head moving up and down.

During hypnotherapy, these ideomotor behaviours make it possible for a client to communicate with a therapist without speaking. I set up Sylvia's ideomotor signals so I could talk with her deep mind.

With Sylvia comfortably in trance and her conscious mind distracted with tasks, I began the conversation. 'Is the unconscious mind willing to talk with me?' A tremulous movement of Sylvia's right-hand index finger and a slight nod of her head signalled 'yes'.

I then explored the history of Sylvia's problems.

'Is there anything in the past that's still creating uncomfortable feelings or tensions?' 'Yes,' Sylvia signalled.

'Did these events occur after the age of five years?' 'No.'

'Did they occur at five years of age?' 'No.'

'Did they occur at four years of age?' 'Yes.'

'Did they involve feelings of sadness, hurt, anger or guilt?' 'Yes.'

'Would it be alright to discuss these experiences with me?' 'No.'

'Would it be alright for Sylvia to know about what happened back then?' 'No, no,' the signal kept repeating.

'Would it be alright for the unconscious mind to work with this memory while Sylvia is unaware of what happened in the past?' 'Yes' was signalled, and from there I followed a procedure for reformulating memories at an unconscious level.

Sylvia's ideomotor signals guided me as we located and worked with her problem memories. At an unconscious level, Sylvia learned what she needed to know from these experiences, and then used her adult resources to let go of the old tensions. The session ended with me suggesting that Sylvia recall a good memory to bring with her as she drifted back to my office.

I didn't know what happened to Sylvia when she was four years old, and neither did she. Sylvia seemed relaxed, and there was no sign that she was aware of the work we had done. At subsequent meetings, Sylvia said that she felt better, and therapy ended when it was clear that her depression had lifted. I invited Sylvia to contact me again should she ever feel the need. Unfortunately, years later, Sylvia again needed help.

When she came back, Sylvia said that her severe depression hadn't returned, but something else was troubling her. She had volunteered for a demonstration in a counselling training course. When the lecturer asked Sylvia to concentrate on a feeling of tension in her body, there in front of the class, Sylvia relived a memory of being sexually assaulted when she was a child.

It might sound innocuous, but the lecturer's request was the initial step in a hypnotic technique known as the 'affect bridge', in which a feeling links to a memory. I don't use the method because it tends to produce uncontrolled, highly emotional reliving of trauma memories.

By the late 1980s, I was drawn back to university. I wanted to learn more about the intriguing things I was seeing in my clinical practice. And I knew what I wanted to do as research for a Master of Clinical Psychology degree.

Meeting Professor "X"

Clinicians deal mostly with the bad stuff in people's lives. Since the pioneering days of Pierre Janet, Sigmund Freud and Carl Jung, psychologists have worked with the memories that underpin symptoms. My plan was to use ideomotor signalling to study the good memories, the instances of success, support and love that build positive traits such as confidence, self-esteem and resilience.

Looking back, my project would have been an example of 'positive psychology', the study of the strengths that enable individuals and communities to thrive. But positive psychology did not come into being until 1998, some 10 years later.

I was looking forward to studying with Prof X, the author of a book on hypnosis. When we met I pitched my positive memories project and waited.

'No one has studied that. You can't do that. This is what you'll do instead.'

Trying to hide my disappointment, I asked Prof X what he had in mind.

'It's a study of traumatic amnesia. I want you to hypnotise subjects, ask them to open their eyes, and show them medical pathologist's photos of the faces of deceased motor vehicle accident victims. We'll have numbers and letters in the corners of the photos, and you can study how they remember or forget this information.'

I don't know how long it took me to speak. It could have been a case of the traumatic amnesia the professor was keen to study. Some two years before that meeting, I had to do something that no big brother should ever have to do. I had to identify my youngest sister's body at the morgue. I had met my sister earlier that day and she was later killed when her car rolled. The doctor kept asking, 'Is this your sister?' All I could say was, 'I think so, I think so'.

Pulling myself back to the present, I said in effect, 'Professor, I couldn't do that. You're not going to warn the subjects. They'll have no idea what we are going to do to them, so there's no informed consent. What you propose would violate every guideline for ethical research on human subjects'.

Professor X had that covered with a One Thought Solution to the ethical issue I raised. 'That's no problem. A paper published in a European journal used this research design, so I'll have no trouble getting it through the ethics committee.'

I mumbled something like, 'We'll talk later' and left.

A few days later, a professor whom I had worked for during my undergraduate days explained, 'X (as he was known to his friends) gets his research approved because he's on the ethics committee'.

I found a new supervisor and set up a program to study a therapy for relieving phobias.

Brief Treatment for Phobias

In my 1992 study, subjects with specific phobias were randomly assigned either to a group that received treatment straight away or to a 'control group' which was given treatment later on.[7] Therapy involved two or three sessions in which I used hypnotherapy to locate and resolve phobia-related memories. Depending on their signals, subjects either worked with their memories unconsciously, as Sylvia had done, or at a conscious level by reviewing what had happened from an adult perspective, and then comforting their 'younger self' in the memory.

The phobia therapy resulted in rapid, significant easing of many clients' fears. By two weeks after treatment, half of the subjects had lost their phobias, and they maintained these gains at follow-ups over the next five months. One case was especially interesting.

56-year-old "David" was intensely afraid of heights and medical procedures. He was depressed and could not face much-needed heart bypass and back surgery.

David was Jewish and his parents emigrated to Holland when he was born. David had an early memory of his mother describing her goitre operation performed without anaesthetic. In another memory from seven years of age, David recalled his sister telling him and his brother not to return home because German soldiers were there waiting for them. David's sister and parents were killed in Auschwitz, his brother was given sanctuary, and David hid for four years in the attic of a farmhouse. When Nazis abducted neighbours and shot the house owner, David was shunted from location to location until the liberation.

In the immediate postwar years, David suffered an intense fear of dying, but this eased over time. At 20 years of age, he enjoyed the flight to Australia in a small plane. The first time David felt a fear of heights was when, six years later, a workmate removed the ladder while he was working on a building frame. For the next 30 years, until his treatment, David's phobic fear of heights never let up.

David was tense and depressed the first time we met. His ideomotor signals were inconsistent and difficult to establish, suggesting a deep reluctance to undertake therapy. Nonetheless, David worked through two memories in the session. Afterwards, he said it was difficult for him to relax. He was particularly unsettled when I referred to his unconscious mind as an 'ally' – he thought of it as his enemy. David said that he had no visual images at all during the session, and each time I asked him to review a memory, he had 'dropped into a void'.

At his second session, David could not relax, but his ideomotor signals were strong and clear. He signalled that a memory was not suitable for conscious review, but he was willing to unconsciously work on the material. Each time I asked David's deep mind to locate a memory, he appeared to fall asleep and started to snore, but the signalling remained clear, so I continued. David later said that he had enjoyed the session, and he had experienced a powerful feeling of satisfaction when I asked him to support his 'younger self' in the memory.

At our next meeting, David asked if it was possible that the therapy was already working. During the week, on a regular delivery job, he had to pass by a large window on the 12th floor of a building: a task he usually managed by looking away and squeezing up against the opposite wall. But this time, David startled himself by standing and quietly looking at the view before he realised what he was doing.

Two weeks after treatment, David wrote, 'Looking down from the 11th-floor stairs air shaft, I felt a mild to moderate fear. I certainly would not anymore avoid that situation'. At four weeks post-therapy, David rated his fear of heights as 'mild', and his fear of surgical operations as 'mild to moderate'. He wrote, 'At a lookout, where there was a great fall, I felt very little fear and certainly would not avoid this situation'.

When I last contacted David six months after therapy, he rated his fear from both phobias as 'mild' and his avoidance as 'rare'. He wrote, 'Looking down from a great height I noticed the absence of panic feelings. There was just a little fear but no panic, not even deep down. Previously, when I could control my fear I could still feel the panic deep down, ready to take over. Last time when I looked down, I was a little surprised at the total lack of panic feeling'.

With some useful research, a degree completed, and a better understanding of the divide between academic and clinical psychology, I returned home to the country.

The Curse of Memory

Over the next quarter-century working as a clinical psychologist in private practice, I had the privilege and challenge of treating about 2,000 clients, many of whom were traumatised Vietnam veterans and their families; victims of violence; train drivers; or members of the police, military, firefighting and ambulance services.

As the Vietnam War raged, I thought that fighting in a war and killing people was not good for you. I had no proof, no peer-reviewed research and no scientific evidence – just a gut feeling. Now I know. Killing people and being present when others are killed are experiences to avoid.

William Shakespeare understood the role that memories play in the emotional aftermath of trauma. In Act 5, Scene 3, of *Macbeth*, his bloody tale of political intrigue, Shakespeare suggested that the key to healing lies in the individual, and not in the 'sweet oblivious antidote' of drugs.

> MACBETH. How does your patient, doctor?

> THE DOCTOR. (Referring to Lady Macbeth): Not so sick, my lord, as she is troubled with thick coming fancies, that keep her from her rest.

> MACBETH. Cure her of that. Canst thou not minister to a mind diseased, pluck from the memory a rooted sorrow, raze out the written troubles of the brain and with some sweet oblivious antidote cleanse the stuff'd bosom of that perilous stuff which weighs upon the heart?

> THE DOCTOR. Therein the patient must minister to himself.

Scientific understanding of trauma advanced rapidly after the Vietnam War as veterans presented with similar symptoms at clinics across the United States and Australia. And in 1980, posttraumatic stress disorder first appeared in the psychiatric bible, the *Diagnostic and Statistical Manual of Mental Disorders* of the American Psychiatric Association, or DSM as it is known.

Disturbing recollections that won't go away curse sufferers of posttraumatic stress disorder. Many restrict their lives, hide, and try to avoid the triggers that bring back memories. Some distract themselves with work or numb their senses and emotions with drugs, alcohol and medications. But all remain on high alert, primed to jump at any sign of trouble. And even if they manage to keep their demons at bay in the daylight, nightmares come in the dark.

War Trauma and a New Psychology

Hypervigilance

I faced a big challenge. I was seeing more and more traumatised clients, and their suffering was severe and debilitating. I wanted to do what I could to help within the limits imposed by working in an outpatient setting. The path from hell to health is not without risk. Clients have to negotiate with their demons, work through problems and unpack sometimes tortuous personal histories. Treating trauma survivors in a hospital is one thing, but working in private practice with no immediate medical backup is an altogether different task.

I could have just counselled clients, but I knew that wouldn't put a stop to their nightmares and flashbacks. To really help, I needed to calm their inflamed memories.

Most of my clients took prescribed antianxiety, antidepressive and sometimes antipsychotic medications. I assumed that this was useful. Lady Macbeth's doctor had no 'sweet oblivious antidote' for traumatic memories, but pharmacology had come a long way since Shakespeare's day. Medical science seemed to have a substance for every symptom, so why not a pill for posttraumatic stress disorder?

Big Pharma and the Mind

In psychology, a One Thought Solution known as 'reductionism' reduces mental states to bodily processes. The thinking goes: when people become anxious or depressed their brain chemistry changes, so taking a substance that counters those physiological effects should relieve their emotional distress. Take the right pill and *voilà*, the problem is fixed.

Reductionism diminishes the role of mental processes and emphasises the physical functioning of the brain. This One Thought Solution has profound implications not just for psychology, but for all humanity.

If we believe that consciousness and emotions like love, anger, hope and despair are best understood as the chemical and electrical activity of the brain, do we need psychology at all? Why struggle with life's challenges if a pill can cure suffering?

The invention of the computer should have put paid to the reductionist One Thought Solution, but it hasn't. The belief persists – even amongst health professionals – that our mental lives are not as real or as important as the physical processes that go with them.

The postgraduate clinical psychology students at a seminar I conducted in 2004 were young, intelligent and motivated to pursue a career helping others. I was their clinical supervisor, and after we reviewed their work with clients at the university's clinic, I posed a question and they gave an answer I wasn't expecting.

I asked, 'If the revolution in brain science gives us technologies to measure every biological, electrical and chemical process that goes on in the brain, will there be a place for psychology? Will we need psychologists at all?' They thought a bit, and to a person answered, 'No'.

I was surprised. If postgraduate psychology students truly believed the One Thought Solution that reduces psychology to physiology, why were they investing time and money in a career that, by their own estimation, was likely to disappear, and soon?

Did they really believe that history would relegate clinical psychology to a footnote in science, alongside phrenology, astrology and alchemy?

There were gaps in their education. The students knew little about the philosophies of mind or science, but the problem went deeper than that and was more sinister.

A 2014 Scientific American article declared this the 'new century of the brain'.[8] Neuroscientists are developing maps that show specific areas of the brain becoming active when people do things in their minds. And the discovery of such associations comes with the promise that research could lead to new drug treatments for mental problems.

In this thought experiment, we compare the emotional and bodily effects of taking two different attitudes to the same event.

First, assume that you know me as a friendly fellow, given to playing and joking around. Imagine that I'm standing in front of you, holding up a ball in my hand. Picture me raising my arm as if I'm about to throw the ball to you. You know that I am being friendly, and I just want to play catch with you.

Notice the feelings that come with that scene. How does your body react to the scenario? What emotions does it generate?

Rate the feeling on an Emot-o-Meter where '-10' is 'very unpleasant' and '+10' is 'very pleasant'. Record your rating.

After you've done that, let those images and feelings gently fade away.

Now imagine an identical setup with me standing in front of you and raising my hand which holds a ball. But this time, assume that you don't know me. Imagine that you see the situation as threatening, as if I might throw the ball hard at you, meaning to hit and hurt you.

Notice how your body reacts. What feelings come when you imagine this scenario?

Now rate the feeling on our Emot-o-Meter. Record your rating.

When you're ready, allow those images and feelings to fade away.

I'm guessing that in the first part of the thought experiment, where you interpreted my holding the ball up as friendly and playful, you felt more relaxed, your blood pressure might have dropped, maybe you smiled, and it would have been easy for you to think of other times when you enjoyed playing catch.

In the second part, where you see my actions as aggressive, you're unlikely to have felt relaxed and your blood pressure might have gone up. Instead of smiling, perhaps you clenched your jaw, and it would've been easy for you to remember other times when people were aggressive. Maybe you felt a touch of the ancient fight-or-flight response.

Your reactions differed depending on whether you thought I was being friendly or aggressive. What does this tell us about how we should treat emotional distress?

There's no doubt that our bodies react when we think we are under threat and feel anxious. Does that mean that in such situations we should rely on a drug to counter our body's physiological response? Or would it be better to learn how our interpretation of the situation determines our feelings, and how we might think differently about similar situations in the future?

For my postgrad students, their reductionist One Thought Solution gave them a ready answer: prescribe drugs. For them, medications were the way to go because they relieve the bodily symptoms of stress and lower blood pressure and hormone levels.

It's simpler to take a pill than it is to learn how to manage stressful reactions. But Nature gave us the emotions of anxiety and anger for good reasons.

Anxiety signals that danger is present, and anger prepares us to run or resist. Using medication to counter anxiety is like putting masking tape over a warning light that flashes on your car's dashboard and doing nothing more to address the problem indicated by the signal. The tape solves the immediate problem of seeing a flashing light, but if you investigate no further you'll never know what the signal was trying to tell you, at least not until your engine breaks down.

Taking a sedative to soothe anger is akin to lowering your guard before you know what kind of threat is coming your way and what you need to do to protect yourself. A sedative might solve the immediate problem of feeling angry, but it could weaken you when you need to fight.

Swallowing a pill is easy and quick, but learning to manage your mind and emotions is a better investment. The new skills you acquire will be yours to keep; you don't forget how to ride a bicycle. The choice is between learning a skill that takes effort in the short run but works forever, and the option of taking pills which can come with side effects and ongoing costs.

The pharmaceutical industry has given us medications for physical illnesses that have blighted humanity. And there are times when antianxiety and antidepressive medications are valuable tools. When severe anxiety or depression makes it very difficult to think or act effectively, medications can provide relief and free the mind to work on the underlying issues. Once the problem has been properly thought through and resolved, the medications can often be discontinued.

But Big Pharma is trying to convince us that many difficult human experiences are pathological, and that drugs are the preferred treatment for emotional suffering. Increasingly, doctors prescribe amphetamines for children's behavioural problems, redefine grief as illness, and bolster sales of antidepressants and sedatives. Big Pharma touts benzodiazepines and antidepressants as good for just about everything that troubles us.

How many will resist the advertising promise, 'Do you feel shy or anxious? Have trouble sleeping? End your problems with our scientifically proven, extra-strength Solve All'.

How difficult will it be for loving parents to forego the opportunity to 'Give your child the new improved Look at Me formulation? Shy children never do well. Make your child a winner. Wallflowers blossom with these mind vitamins'.

Big Pharma wants doctors and consumers to believe that taking a drug is the best way to smooth out life's emotional bumps. The slogan 'better living through chemistry' has never been more vigorously promoted. But regardless of the pharmaceutical razzle-dazzle, my heavily medicated clients still endured plenty of nightmares and flashbacks.

There is no magic pill for treating trauma. For genuine solutions, we have to go beyond medications and return to the realm of the mind.

Exposure Therapy Exposed

When I looked to academia and my professional society for guidance on how to help traumatised clients, clinical psychology seemed stuck in the past. It was as if the computer and cognitive revolutions had never happened. Therapies had not progressed much since the 1890s when Freud was treating hysteria.

In the 1950s, the behaviourists developed phobia treatments that exposed clients either 'in vivo' (in reality) or in imagination to their feared situation until the anxiety subsided. You might have heard of people with phobias being asked to touch snakes: that was in vivo exposure. If they imagined that they were touching snakes, it was 'imaginal' exposure. Psychologists applied these therapies to posttraumatic stress disorder soon after the diagnosis appeared in 1980.

Recommended treatments for adults with posttraumatic stress disorder required clients to undergo lengthy exposure to traumatic memories, or a process known as 'eye movement desensitisation and reprocessing', or EMDR. Neither therapy was suitable for my severely traumatised clients.

Exposure for Fear of Heights, Spiders, Snakes and Storms

The One Thought Solution that underpins exposure-based therapies goes back to Freud's observation that in treating hysteria, 'Recollection without affect almost invariably produces no result. The psychical process which originally took place must be repeated as vividly as possible; it must be brought back to its *status nascendi* (state at birth) and then given verbal utterance'.[9]

The idea is that an extended reliving of the original horror, either in reality or in imagination, is necessary to relieve trauma-related stress. For behaviourists, anxiety is a learned fear response, not a warning signal that danger is about. For them, it follows that you need to unlearn the fear. As with most One Thought Solutions, there's some truth in the idea.

Pat a dog and give it food every time it approaches and it will come to you more often. Stop feeding the dog and growl at it and it will come to you less often. What would you do if you wanted to teach your pet rat to stop pushing a bar to get food? You'd stop feeding the rat. If you wanted to speed things up, you might even give it an electric shock each time it pushed the bar. Behaviourists call the process 'habituation', and define it as the tendency of a learned behaviour to give up if it's repeated often enough without being reinforced. This sounds scientific, but that doesn't mean that this is a good way to treat trauma survivors.

'Exposure therapy' tries to wear out a client's anxiety. The notion is that you solve the problem if you can get a trauma victim to relive their horror while you stop them from running away long enough for their fear and anxiety to diminish. Freud did a similar thing, but exposure therapy is more gruelling. For severely disturbed people, the recommended dozen or more 90-minute-long sessions of reliving horrific memories is a tough assignment. It's heavy going even for experienced therapists.

In a recorded conversation, "Carl", a Vietnam veteran, told me about an exposure therapy program conducted in the Northern Rivers in the early 1990s. Carl said that the treating psychiatrist told veterans 'I'll take you back and bring you out' and he would 'keep you overnight ... there's speakers in the walls and they play machine gun fire, helicopter sounds, guys yelling out, "I'm hit, I'm hit, help me ... incoming" and all that sort of hoo-ha'. Carl declined the offer and told his referring doctor, 'I'm not subjecting myself to all that. I've been trying to forget that sort of stuff'.

Traumatic memories and images are dangerous. It's not the original insult that causes long-term harm: you only endure that once. Rather, it's the oft-repeated reliving of disturbing memories over years that damages mind and body. And clients are not the only ones at risk. The harm can be contagious.

A clinician's challenge is to help each client, harm none, and stay well themselves. It's the nature of the work that creates an occupational hazard for clinical psychologists. How do you keep your heart open as you help hundreds of people? If a therapist takes into themselves a fraction of the suffering that goes with each client's story, then emotional burnout and vicarious traumatisation are not far away.

Therapies that use imagery are effective because the emotions we feel when we remember or imagine something are real emotions. Imagery engages similar neural networks to those involved during an actual event. Immerse yourself in a sad or frightening memory, and you will feel sad or frightened. The sadness and fear are real.

Briefly consider what it would be like to relive a traumatic memory over and over during a dozen or more lengthy sessions. I'd escape. I don't accept that reliving horror is good for you so long as you don't let up. Some come out better for the experience, but I'll bet it's not because the therapy habituated their fears.

Exposure therapy comes with caveats and risks. The scientific literature cautions that some clients do not benefit or drop out of treatment. Some are left worse off due to the 'iatrogenic effect': the harm induced by a clinician's words or treatment.

Exposure therapy is unsuitable for people who suffer from psychosis, substance abuse, cognitive deficits, serious personality pathology or poor physical health. The method is not recommended for trauma victims whose memories generate emotions of guilt, shame or anger, or when memories involve being a perpetrator. Nor should exposure be used with rape victims whose memories involve mental defeat or a feeling of alienation or permanent change. In short, best practice guidelines ruled out exposure therapy for just about every trauma survivor I met.

Nurses used to enforce a rigid four-hourly schedule for giving pain relief medication. But experiencing pain is now considered toxic in itself, so analgesics are given preemptively to keep pain to a minimum. We used to think that training a horse had to be stressful, but now we know that horses, like humans, learn new skills best when they're calm.

Times had changed, and I needed better methods than exposure therapy to help my traumatised clients.

Moving Your Eyes to Change Memories

In the 1980s, American psychologist Francine Shapiro invented eye movement desensitisation and reprocessing (EMDR) when she noticed that her disturbing thoughts eased when she moved her eyes back and forth. From this observation, Dr Shapiro created an influential treatment for posttraumatic stress disorder.

When you attend an EMDR session, the therapist asks you to describe a problematic memory and, as with our Emot-o-Meter, rate the unpleasant emotion that goes with the recollection. You then focus on an aspect of the memory, such as a visual image, a negative self-statement, or an emotion, while at the same time tracking the therapist's index finger as it moves rapidly back and forth in front of your eyes. After a while, you're asked to 'Blank it out and take a deep breath'. Then you recall the original memory and give another rating of the emotion. If your stress rating hasn't gone down, you get more of the same. When your ratings stay low, the therapist deems you cured.

It's not clear how EMDR works, and the procedure is just as effective without the eye movements. Its practitioners do lots of things that other therapists do. Clients discuss their problems with a sympathetic psychologist who encourages hope. They learn new ways of thinking about their symptoms. They bring memories repeatedly to mind and blank them out, and they make lots of ratings on scales.

The technique is well marketed and popular with psychologists, but it is not so well received by every client. For some, remembering the trauma is distressing and they drop out when they discover that they'll have to do this repeatedly: a review of eight EMDR studies reported an average dropout rate of about 11%.[10]

Some Vietnam veteran clients told me that they felt anxious as they moved their eyes back and forth. One said, 'You learn very quickly what you have to do to stop the bloody finger'. He worked out that the therapy would continue until he lowered his distress ratings.

"Gillian", a 28-year-old woman with severe posttraumatic stress disorder following a motor vehicle accident, saw me for a medico-legal assessment.

'Your psychiatrist said that you've been successfully treated with EMDR. But two years later, you're still troubled by memories of the accident. What can you tell me about that?' I asked her.

Gillian said, 'I hated it. The psychiatrist was very keen. Every time I saw her we had to do the finger thing again and again. I kept giving her low ratings so she'd stop'.

Gillian's lowered ratings did not mean that she was cured; they were just her means of escape.

Clinical psychology seemed stuck in the past, rigidly applying stressful therapies that were not suitable for severely traumatised people. There was little creative evolution of method or insight into what was really going on during treatment. Exposure and EMDR were fixed and likely to stay that way. Few practitioners saw this as an issue. And it seemed that the profession had taken on a faulty One Thought Solution to solve the problem of how it could identify genuinely effective therapies.

Evidence-based Treatment

What does it mean to say that a treatment works?

In an early 1970s lecture, psychiatrist "Dr Allen" described how he relieved a 10-year-old boy's severe symptoms of anxiety and 'obsessive-compulsive disorder' by performing a frontal lobotomy. He pushed a needle through the boy's skull behind the eyeball up into the frontal lobes of his brain and wriggled it back and forth. In those days, per head of population, brains were surgically adjusted in New South Wales as often as anywhere else in the world.

The lobotomy 'worked', in the sense that the boy lost his symptoms. At the time, many psychiatrists considered psychosurgery scientific and acceptable, and Dr Allen seemed pleased that he'd helped a distressed boy.

You could only believe that the lobotomy One Thought Solution was a good idea if you restricted your thinking to the simple relationship between symptom, treatment and outcome. The boy is anxious, you cut his brain, and now he's not anxious.

Add more carriages to your train of thought, and consider the treatment in the context of the boy's overall physical and mental well-being. A lobotomy damages the brain's frontal lobes, thereby affecting the ability to anticipate and imagine. Hence the reduction in anxiety – you can't worry about something you can't anticipate or imagine. But the doctor-induced brain injury was likely to have far-reaching impacts on the boy's life.

Even if you thought that the lobotomy worked, that didn't mean that there weren't better ways to solve the problem. It seems obvious now, but it wasn't back then.

When psychological therapies proliferated in the 1960s and 70s, practitioners wondered how they could scientifically evaluate treatments. Psychology again looked to another profession for the solution to its problem.

Medical science had protocols for testing new medications, so why not use these procedures to sort genuine from ineffective psychological treatments? As before, white coats and prestige were involved. And again, the situation was not as straightforward as it seemed.

The 'evidence-based approach' is now the cornerstone of modern psychotherapeutic practice and is used to determine what works and what doesn't. Psychologists everywhere believe this One Thought Solution. They sense that basing practice on evidence is a good thing. After all, what's the alternative? Hunch-based practice? That doesn't sound right.

In 1972, epidemiologist Archie Cochrane introduced the evidence-based approach when he argued that properly designed studies could evaluate new medications.[11] And the most reliable evidence comes from experiments known as 'randomised controlled trials'. The essential feature of such studies is the 'double-blind' comparison of a medication with a 'placebo' (a treatment that only works because a subject expects it to). In a double-blind experiment, neither the subject nor the experimenter knows if the pill being given is placebo or medication. The placebo has to be identical to the medication in all respects, except for the presence of the active drug. It even has to taste the same and produce the same physiological reactions when ingested. If and only if you satisfy these conditions, can you conclude that a medication is more effective than a placebo.

The problem is that you can't use these methods to evaluate psychological treatments. It's not possible to design a proper control condition that equates to a placebo. Comparing two pills that look and taste exactly alike – a necessary condition for testing a medication – has no counterpart in the field of psychology. How could you construct a control which resembles exposure therapy in every respect except for the active ingredient? What is the active ingredient?

Unlike a medication, psychological therapy is not a discrete, definable thing. Therapy brand names are codes for all that a client experiences during multiple sessions conducted over months or even years, as well as all that goes on in a client's mind during every day and night between consultations.

Psychology fudged a solution to the control group problem by decreeing that a treatment be accorded evidence-based status if subjects receiving the therapy did better than others who were waiting to be treated. But this meant that they had to abandon the requirement that the experiment is double-blind. It was obvious to everyone who got the treatment and who was waiting, and this knowledge profoundly affects the way people think and behave.

As with all big-ticket One Thought Solutions, the sting is in the implications that trail along unnoticed. Psychology is paying a price for the *faux* comfort of thinking that they could adopt this technique from medical science.

Well-marketed therapies such as 'emotional freedom technique' (EFT) now satisfy criteria as evidence-based treatments for phobias, anxiety, depression and trauma. These practitioners do the kinds of things that other therapists do, but they claim their method works because they tap acupressure points and balance the body's 'ch'i' energy. And clinical psychology seems to have nothing much to say about that.

Exposure therapy is much as it was 50 years ago, and little has changed in EMDR over more than a quarter of a century. These treatments cannot have been so perfect at birth that there's no room for improvement.

The evidence-based approach cannot tease out the strengths, limitations or usefulness of the myriad components that make up complex therapies. Nor can it evaluate claims about the therapeutic mechanisms responsible for an effect. There's an unrealised potential for controlled studies to improve psychological treatments. For example, a simple comparison of outcomes for two groups who receive identical emotional freedom therapy, but with one group tapping acupressure points and the other group tapping nearby skin, would inform debate about the role that ch'i energy plays. And a comparison of the effects of exposure therapy on groups that recall trauma memories from the 1st person and 3rd person perspectives would tell much about the role of habituation and the need for high levels of stress during therapy.

Beware of the One Thought Solution that renders clinical psychology incapable of distinguishing good science from bad. Like the Trojan's hollow horse, it could bring questionable cures and dubious ideas into the profession. If lobotomised children had lower anxiety scores than children waiting for brain surgery, would that make lobotomy an evidence-based treatment?

Like putting winkers on a horse, the evidence-based practice One Thought Solution restricts therapists' vision. The computer and cognitive revolutions profoundly changed scientific thinking about mental processes, but not when it comes to treating trauma.

Exposure therapy clearly manipulates memories, images and beliefs, but practitioners continue to invoke old behaviourist concepts and use stressful, lengthy treatments from the 1950s.

The situation is reminiscent of the history of the QWERTY keyboard. In 1873, engineers solved the problem of levers jamming on newly invented typewriters by deliberately arranging the letters on the keyboard to slow typists down. Today, this solution to a 19th-century problem reduces the speed and efficiency of every keyboard user on the planet, and will likely always do so.

As with the QWERTY keyboard, just because everyone uses a particular therapy, it doesn't mean that there aren't better ways to help trauma survivors.

Giving Memories a New Ending

Research and clinical experience told me that the memories underpinning phobias could be relieved quickly and gently. And to me, posttraumatic stress disorder looked like the supreme phobia. Back at work after my sojourn at university, I found that the methods I tested on phobias worked well with trauma. With the necessary groundwork in place, a client's traumatic memories could often be relieved in a single session.

But I did not understand why these methods would not work with all clients. Nor did I know why so many apparently different interventions could be effective in relieving PTSD. In therapy, as in life, unexpected challenges that you can't manage with old ways trigger new learning. It was when therapy failed that I had to think differently about the problem of traumatic stress and how it could be treated.

In 1990, I met "Rob", a 60-year-old veteran who had been a professional soldier in Malaysia, Korea and Vietnam. Rob was depressed, traumatised and taking a mix of medications. Rob's doctor referred him for 'sleep difficulties' but, as his wife "Cathy" explained, this diagnosis didn't do the problem justice. Over the years, Cathy had been bruised and battered when Rob punched and choked her while he slept.

Rob didn't want to talk about his war experiences. He'd cried when his doctor made him do that, and he wasn't going there again. But he did tell me about his recurring dream of an event in the Vietnam jungle. He was in command and had to leave a young wounded soldier behind, concealed until the patrol could come back for him. They returned to find that the enemy had tortured and killed the soldier. Rob coped with this while he remained in the army, but now the dream about the dead man kept coming back.

With characteristic discipline, Rob applied himself to the things we worked on – relaxation, pain control, sex therapy, medication withdrawal – but his recurring nightmare would not let up.

I'd read that nightmares could be relieved if sufferers, while awake, imagined different endings to their recurring dreams. I asked Rob to close his eyes, recall what happened to the young soldier, and give the memory a better ending. I could tell from Rob's ideomotor signals and the way his eyes moved under his eyelids that something was going on, and when he opened his eyes I found out what it was.

Rob said that he saw himself order another soldier to stay with the wounded man. As soon as he did that, the soldier multiplied, over and over, until there were dozens of identical soldiers standing there. Rob knew instantly that this was what he'd have to have done to save the wounded man's life. But that was impossible. He couldn't have left enough men to save him.

Guilt is a difficult emotion to shift. Anxiety signals danger, and when we take care of the threat we can let the anxiety go. But guilt tells us that we have done something wrong, committed a sin, or broken a law. How do you make that go away?

Rob's guilt had condemned him to a life sentence of regret. No counselling could convince him that he was not culpable for another man's violent death. The solution to this problem had to come from within. My request for a better ending suggested no specific content and I had no idea what a new ending might look like. It was Rob's deep mind that created the experience he needed, and it was a brilliant solution. His guilt lifted as he understood the broader reality he confronted all those years ago in the jungle.

Rob's nightmare didn't return. As Milton Erickson predicted, effective therapy for Rob came from what Rob did. But what was it about the simple suggestion that helped him come up with what he needed? The psychologists who wrote about new endings for nightmares thought that the positive effect might stem from a client's improved sense of mastery. It seemed like more than that to me. A few metaphors came to mind.

Some clinicians liken therapy to helping clients repair their life story so that the trauma no longer seems like an ending, but rather becomes just another chapter in the ongoing narrative of their lives.

To put it another way, a trauma survivor's life can get stuck in the past, as if they've been given a posthypnotic suggestion to endlessly replay an old horror. From this point of view, the therapist's job is to break the trance so clients can think about all the things that have happened in their lives, before and after the trauma.

In cinematic art, movie genres have distinct structures and rules. Traumatic memories follow the trajectory of a horror movie which ends the story at the worst possible time and place, with some terrible event like the death of the hero or the return of zombies. In drama and adventure genres, while it's sometimes acceptable for a hero to die at the climax of the movie, the more usual ending is for the hero to survive.

With the cinematic metaphor, the therapist's job is to give the memory – the mental movie – a new ending that changes the genre from horror to a drama or, even better, to a hero's story. Protagonists suffer great hardships in a drama, but suffering is not the central theme, and the movie ends with hope for the future.

For Rob, the request that he give his memory a better ending broke the trance. His deep mind was then able to script a new scene that transformed his horror movie into a drama. It was still a tough story, but now his redemption was possible.

Over years of helping traumatised clients, I came to expect rapid improvement. Along the way, none of my clients became emotionally overwhelmed during work with their memories (yes, I touched timber as I wrote that). I gave presentations at conferences and seminars. Then I met "Bill" who taught me more about what makes therapy work.

Taking Control

Bill, a 67-year-old veteran of the Korean War, arrived agitated, panicked and gasping from emphysema. Bill was dubious about entering my room. He stood in the doorway, told me he was only there because his doctor insisted, and said he'd be off if I mentioned the war. Bill reminded me of my deceased grandfather who was a World War I veteran. If I was to help Bill, I had to do something credible straight away, and that couldn't involve talking about the war.

There's a long history of psychologists changing the elements in distressing memories. In the 1800s, Pierre Janet hypnotically suggested that a mother substitute an image of flowers thrown into the air to change her memory of soldiers tossing up and bayoneting her child. Sitting with Bill, the idea came to me to adapt a procedure that Richard Bandler described in 1985.[12]

I asked Bill if anything had upset him lately. I was looking for some unimportant event, more an irritation than an insult. It took Bill a second to come up with something, and then he began his growling, wheezing account.

'Bloody young copper, I was at the club bar and he knocked my beer over with his elbow and didn't apologise. If I was younger, I'd have him.'

Bill was not inclined to forget or forgive. He wanted to fight the policeman.

'I think about the mongrel all the time. I can see his face, his stupid smirk. Every time I see a police car or go past the police station I want to punch him.'

Bill could see the policeman in his mind's eye as clearly as he could see me in the office. I asked, 'Would it be all right to use your imagination to muck around with the policeman who knocked your beer over?' Bill agreed.

'To make things easier, there's no need to talk. Just nod your head to answer "yes". Shake your head side to side to answer "no".' Bill nodded.

'Close your eyes and remember what happened at the club. Nod your head when you can feel what it was like.' Bill nodded straight away.

'Now rate the feeling from "0" to "10". "0" stands for "no anger" and "10" means "as angry as possible". Then tell me the number.' '10' said Bill. It was not the kind of memory I was after, but it'd have to do.

'Check with your gut feeling. Does it feel okay deep down for you to work with this memory today?' Bill nodded.

'At all times, you're in control. You can open your eyes when you want. I'm going to ask you to change the way you remember this incident. As you make each change, I want you to notice the feelings, and then I'll ask you to rate the level of distress like you just did. Is that all right?' Bill nodded.

'Imagine that you're drawing yourself out of the scene, pulling back so you're watching yourself and the policeman over there, at a distance. Nod your head when you've done this.' Bill nodded.

'Notice how that feels. Give me a rating, "0" to "10".' 'That's an "8",' said Bill.

In like fashion, I proceeded to guide Bill through a series of changes to the memory of what happened at the bar. Some transformations, such as making the scene duller, switching from colour to black and white, and giving the policeman a woman's voice, did not dent Bill's anger. But some changes had an effect.

Bill flinched and rated the feeling as '10' when I asked him to bring the policeman 'up close' so he was right in Bill's face. But when I had Bill push him away 'over there', his rating dropped to a '5'.

When I asked Bill to make the policeman bigger, so he was seven foot tall, towering over him, his anger shot straight back to '10'. When Bill shrunk the policeman down until he was only four foot tall, the emotion dropped to a '4'.

Bill smiled for the first time when I asked him to imagine a circus monkey standing on a box behind the policeman. 'You can see the monkey, the copper can't, and the monkey is imitating everything he's saying and doing,' I told him. Bill rated that as a '1'.

Continuing with humour, I had Bill give the policeman a cartoon voice. He chose Elmer Fudd, smiled again, and gave a '2' rating.

I asked Bill to use the changes we had worked with to adjust the memory of the policeman so it had the least possible emotional impact on him. When he'd done that, I asked Bill if it would be all right to remember the policeman 'so he has no power over you'. Bill nodded, and I had him open his eyes.

Bill and I had come a long way since he stood at my door a half hour earlier. We talked and I suggested that he might use what he had learned with any bad memories or nightmares that came his way. I warned him that he couldn't use humour for serious events, but I suggested he might look at things from a distance, from the perspective of the man he is now.

Bill did come back, and I am privileged to have known him as a friend. At our next meeting, Bill told me how he now smiled whenever he thought about the policeman or walked past the club or the police station. But Bill had changed more than the memory of the policeman.

During World War II, Bill served with Australian forces and participated in the demilitarisation of the Japanese Army and the Hiroshima Guard not long after the Americans dropped the atomic bombs. Bill subsequently served with the Australian Army in Korea, and during the severe winter of 1951, Bill's battalion lived in the open in trenches with the enemy nearby. Every day since then, Bill had relived in memory and nightmare what happened in Japan and Korea.

Bill's worst recollection was of an event that occurred after battle died down in Korea. In the frozen trenches, Bill had to deal with his dead mate's eviscerated body.

Bill was keen to tell me how each time he woke from his nightmare about Korea, he would put the scene over there, look at it from a distance, turn it into a black and white picture, adjust the volume down, and then talk to his 'younger self'. He reassured the younger Bill that he had survived. Bill went on with therapy and found much relief.

After Bill, I used versions of the imagery-changing procedure with other clients to near-universal good effect. With low-stress training memories, clients could practice different strategies for relieving their traumatic recollections. The method proved to be quick, safe and well-tolerated. For some, it was all they needed to relieve their posttraumatic stress disorder.

I now had a kitbag of techniques that I could draw on to treat most traumatised clients in my outpatient practice. Then a couple of cases provided more clues about what effective treatments for trauma might have in common.

"Barry", a 46-year-old Vietnam veteran, told me how he ended a nightmare that had plagued him for years. Barry was in his dentist's chair, inhaling nitrous oxide and listening to the pulsing air conditioner. As he looked into the bright light through closed eyelids, Barry began to relive combat. He was back in an intense firefight that continued into the night when a helicopter made a daring landing. Sitting in the dentist's chair, in his mind's eye, Barry saw the helicopter turn its spotlight on and drop through heavy fire, as boxes of ammunition were kicked out the doors. The helicopter touched down to pick up wounded men as Barry lay behind a narrow tree while shrapnel shredded the canopy above and he waited for the bullet that would surely kill him.

Barry opened his eyes and 'came half out of it'. Realising where he was, Barry told himself that he survived this battle and there was no way the dentist was going to let him die now. Reassured, Barry determined to 'go back in and see it out'. He did, and that was the end of his nightmare.

My problem was much less serious and the solution nowhere near as dramatic. In my mid-30s, an inner ear infection ruptured my eardrum, and a doctor prescribed ototoxic (toxic to the auditory nerve) antibiotic drops that left me with severe tinnitus, a continuous, high-pitched, hissing noise in my left ear. Another doctor told me that my nerve would not recover, the sound would worsen as I got older, and there was nothing I could do about it. Losing forever the sound of silence was sad enough, but finding out that the condition could be fatal – the doctor told me about a patient with tinnitus who shot himself – made it quite depressing. Then, I heard a psychologist interviewed on a radio program.

The psychologist said that tinnitus is a problem because sufferers think of the noise in their head as a threat. I certainly did. This sense of threat triggers the familiar fight-or-flight response and sets up a state of high alert and obsessive thinking about the sound. The psychologist's solution was, in essence, to tell his tinnitus clients, 'A noise in the head can't hurt you, it's just the music of the brain' or something like that. That information solved my problem. I'll always have tinnitus – it's clear and loud as I write this – but I usually don't notice it and it causes me no grief. It's not so much what happens to us, but the way we think about it, that creates suffering and determines what we do about it.

Clinical psychologists understand that many things together make for good outcomes in therapy. Trust, a sense of safety, explaining symptoms, learning to control imagery, engaging rather than avoiding problems, and gaining mastery, all play a role. But as the millennium ended, I wanted to know more about what makes trauma therapies work.

So again, and for the last time, I went back to university.

Cognitive Control Training

Studying for a Doctor of Psychology degree gave me the chance to read everything I could find in the scientific literature about memory, hypnosis and trauma. I also got to experimentally test the imagery-changing intervention that I first used with Bill: an approach that I call 'Cognitive Control Training'.[13] Best of all, I found a systems theory model from the 1980s which, with tweaking, could explain why posttraumatic stress disorder develops and what makes successful treatments work.

I recruited 26 subjects, most of whom suffered post-traumatic stress disorder, for a program that offered 'training to control distressing thoughts, memories and dreams'. The research found that two one-hour sessions of Cognitive Control Training resulted in significant reductions in symptoms. For a number of subjects, the treatment relieved their posttraumatic stress disorder. The 'effect size' statistic, a measure of the therapeutic power of the intervention, was 'large', and exceeded figures reported for lengthier, more stressful exposure and EMDR treatments.

No subject had difficulty with the Cognitive Control Training. For a few, it seemed that the initial one-hour introductory meeting was all they needed to solve their problem.

"Elizabeth", a 79-year-old subject, had long been troubled by memories of her deceased husband emotionally abusing her. When she arrived for her treatment session, Elizabeth was keen to tell me that she'd already solved her problem. After our first meeting, Elizabeth realised that she had let her deceased husband continue to abuse her in her memories, so she decided to take control. Whenever Elizabeth thought of her husband, she imagined that she was telling him to 'Go back to Hell where you belong' and Elizabeth clearly enjoyed that. A year later, she told me that the bad memories had not come back. For Elizabeth – and possibly for others as well – just hearing that she could control bad memories was all she needed.

The research confirmed that, for many clients, traumatic stress could be relieved quickly and gently. And I found an information processing model that brought it all together. It not only explained what it takes to create and to treat traumatic memories but also pointed to what a truly 'science-based', rather than 'evidence-based', approach to evaluating psychological treatments would look like. A therapy has to not only work but must also make sense in terms of a scientific model.

Natural Trauma Resolution and PTSD

During a traumatic incident, fight and flight reactions of arousal and avoidance protect us. When the acute crisis passes, the trauma survivor repeatedly thinks about what happened. This ancient survival mechanism lays down durable memories, for Nature wants us to well remember things that could have killed us.

Survivors then oscillate through alternating states of 'denial' and 'intrusion': swinging from feeling emotionally flat (denial) to a state of mental and physiological arousal in which they're bombarded by thoughts and memories of the event (intrusion). This normal, but intensely difficult time, eases gradually as equilibrium returns and new ways of thinking about the self, others and the world emerge.

When things go well after a trauma, the survivor's mind processes the experience as they sleep and dream on it, and think about what happened and what it means to them. But sometimes natural healing stalls.

Problems develop when the re-experiencing, avoidance and arousal reactions, which were protective during the traumatic event itself, persist long after the initial threat has abated. It then becomes a problem of memory. Posttraumatic stress disorder arises because memories of the trauma are frozen in time so they never change. This sets up a pathogenic cycle that endlessly recycles the horror.

Remembering a trauma creates a sense of threat which induces the affected person to avoid the memory and the things that bring it to mind. This protective avoidance inadvertently deflects attention away from the recollection so that it can never change. The memory is forever primed to reignite further repetitions of the cycle when it's next triggered into conscious recall.

An Information Processing Model

In their 1986 paper, Edna Foa and Michael Kozak described posttraumatic stress disorder as arising from three types of information that are embedded in networks of trauma-related memories: 'stimulus information' (what the person saw, heard and sensed during the incident); 'response information' (what they thought, felt and did); and 'meaning information' (the personal significance of the experience, and how the event and its aftermath affected the person).[14]

When a PTSD sufferer recalls a trauma, the information in the memory signals danger and they try to escape the memory by distracting themselves, using drugs or alcohol, or attempting to forget what happened.

For some, the memory of an event might be disturbing due to its gory nature and the way it bristles the senses. Memories are most disturbing if they're vivid, uncontrollable and recalled from the 1st person perspective. For others, it could be what they did or didn't do, whether they ran or found courage, which makes the memory stick. For many, it's what the incident means personally and the ethical issues it raises that give the memory its punch. Believing that you're going mad, you can't trust other people, or that the world's a dangerous place magnifies the emotional impact.

How Trauma Therapy Works

> If you are distressed by anything external, the pain is not due to the thing itself, but to your estimate of it; and this you have the power to revoke at any moment.
>
> Marcus Aurelius (121–180 AD)

Trauma memories protect us from danger. They only become a problem when they continue to operate after the real danger has passed and the intrusive recollections interfere with our lives.

Foa and Kozak proposed a basic two-step process for relieving trauma memories. First, you have to activate the memory, that is, bring it to mind. Then you add new stimulus, response or meaning information that changes the memory for the better. This restarts the natural healing process and the deep mind takes it from there. That's it – simple, but profound.

There are a few options for activating a memory, and many ways to change it by adding new information.

You can recall a memory from either the 1st person perspective as if you're in the event, or from a 3rd person perspective in which you look at what happened from a distance. Memories can also be accessed at unconscious levels, as when I worked with Sylvia's memories of childhood sexual abuse; during sleep, as was the case when David snored during phobia therapy; or in dreams, as we will discuss later.

The information processing model implies that there's no limit to the kinds of new information that can change memories for the better, or how this information might be imparted. Different therapies offer mixes of components for doing the same essential job of accessing and then changing memories by adding new information. The model made sense of reports of good outcomes from having clients recall distressing memories while simultaneously doing such things as singing 'Happy Birthday', tapping acupuncture points, counting backwards from 100, and performing all kinds of mental and physical exercises.

Gone was the old cookie-cutter approach which treated everyone in the same way. It was now clear that everything that goes on between a therapist and a client, from the first greeting to the last farewell, is loaded with new information that could potentially break the trance created by trauma memories. It can be enough when a therapist explains that there's nothing wrong with your mind and the problem is just an old solution that needs updating. And mindfulness and objective evaluation moved to centre stage in the healing process.

If you go to a psychologist, they'll probably assess all sorts of things before, during and even after they work with you. The information processing model explained why, in itself, this assessment process can be powerfully therapeutic. In the mid-1990s, researchers asked six patients with posttraumatic stress disorder to rate their disturbing memories on scales four times each day for two months.[15] That's all they did: repeatedly rate one symptom. Three months after the monitoring ended, four patients no longer had a diagnosable disorder, one had some symptoms, and one still had PTSD. I could now understand why. This simple assessment process added new information about all sorts of things, including the client's ability to voluntarily recall and rate problem memories.

For this thought experiment, I want you to become aware of where you are.

Pay attention to what you're seeing, hearing and feeling. Dwell with that sense of mindfulness.

Now rate what you feel on an Emot-o-Meter where '-10' is 'very unpleasant' and '+10' is 'very pleasant'. Record your rating.

What was it like to go from just paying attention to your surrounds to rating your feelings with a number on a scale? When I do this, I feel a kind of mental gear shift as I go from attending to what's happening to rating the emotional flavour of the experience. It's as if I mentally pull back to judge how I'm feeling, and then give it a number on a scale.

Almost all treatments for traumatic stress require clients to repeatedly rate their level of anxiety on a scale: it's an essential feature of exposure therapy, EMDR, EFT and Cognitive Control Training. Psychologists call it the 'subjective units of distress scale', or SUDS. For some, and perhaps for many, this is an important factor in effective treatments.

Over the past 30 years, I have seen an impoverished intellectual landscape with a few scrawny notions about how trauma works blossom into a field alive with potential solutions to the problem of bad memories. With the necessary groundwork in place, symptom-causing thoughts and beliefs, and even genetically determined One Thought Solutions such as phobia and post-traumatic stress disorder, can be relieved safely and gently, often in an hour or so. Colleagues who have used these techniques after attending my workshops tell me of similar outcomes. Recently I had the pleasure of catching up with a client I treated 25 years ago.

"Peter" was 47 years old when I saw him in 1992. Conscripted as a National Serviceman in 1965, Peter had witnessed the death of friends during combat in the Vietnam War. When I first saw him, Peter was severely traumatised and contemplating suicide. Across a dozen sessions spaced over a couple of years, Peter's treatment included hypnotherapy for a phobia of hospitals and surgery. Over lunch, I audio-recorded Peter's opinion of the work we did together a quarter of a century before. I asked, 'Was it worthwhile?'

Peter said, 'Most definitely, most certainly. It was a turning point in my life. I was walking around with feelings of dread. I got to the stage where I didn't want to open the mail. I'd become a hermit. And we did a session to prepare me for (gallbladder) surgery and recovery. That worked out just so well, and it's been there ever since, because I had a thing about dentists as well because I had a traumatic experience with it (field dental treatment in Vietnam).

And there were so many pluses. That's when I gave up smoking as well'.

From my work as a clinical psychologist, I learned that with new information and appropriate technique we can use our deep minds to creatively take on challenges and solve big problems. The knowledge and skills picked up along the way helped prepare Susan and me for the upcoming environmental challenges of native forest dieback and the gas field industrialisation of rural Australia.

Chapter 3

Native Forest Dieback

If you think in terms of a year, plant a seed; if in terms of ten years, plant trees; if in terms of 100 years, teach the people.

Confucius (551–479 BC)

IT WAS NOT OBVIOUS that morning in 1999 as we looked out across the Toonumbar Valley, but I was sure the forests were changing colour. The natural blue-green tinge of Australian eucalypts was turning an unhealthy-looking brown, and it was spreading in a front across the valley.

Creek's Bend and the Toonumbar Valley

Logging's Legacy

When we moved to Toonumbar in the 1970s, the eucalypt forests in the valley carved by the Iron Pot Creek were open with a grassy understorey. You could ride a horse for kilometres in any direction. But in the '80s, the weed lantana (*Lantana camara*) invaded where logging had broken the canopy and let sunlight in. You could no longer see through the bush; you certainly couldn't walk through it.

By the 1990s, lantana had replaced much of the forest understorey. The weed was out of control, trees were dying, and the forests rang with the pinging sound of native honeyeaters. Bell Miners (*Manorina melanophyrys*) had always been in pockets of Toonumbar's forests, but now they seemed to be everywhere.

An ecological catastrophe rolled across the landscape. Lantana thickets as tall as houses formed an impenetrable green desert where ticks and bush lice flourished, but not much else. Once abundant koalas, gliders, possums and other creatures were disappearing.

Fight a bushfire in the Northern Rivers and you'll find that lantana burns hotter than native undergrowth. Lantana ablaze scorches skin through overalls even when you stand well back. There was a risk that a lantana-fuelled firestorm, whipped up by summer's westerly winds, could destroy Toonumbar National Park's World Heritage Murray Scrub rainforest. At a mere 340 hectares, the Murray Scrub is the largest flatland, subtropical rainforest remaining in New South Wales.

As the 20th century ended, our concern turned to despondency. There was nothing that Susan and I could do to save our forests from lantana. The problem was too big for us to tackle, and we thought about leaving. Then Susan and a neighbour expressed their concerns to local National Parks management, and they asked ecologist John Hunter to take a look. Returning from a helicopter flight over the Toonumbar Valley, John said, 'It looks as if a bomb has gone off'. He saw native trees dying across the landscape in a sea of lantana. John's report triggered a problem-solving effort that continues to this day.

Lantana Understorey Choking Forest

The Hunters' Story

The government funded a dieback working group – Susan is a community representative – to address the problem. In 2005, the group convened a national forum at Lismore's Southern Cross University. The conference provided the science that helped us understand the problem, and John Hunter told a story that gave us the means to solve it.

Susan was sitting with a small group in a side room at the forum where John talked about a recent visit to his family's farm in Queensland. John said that when he arrived, he saw that the long-familiar lantana had disappeared. When John asked his father what happened to the lantana, his father said, in effect, 'We fixed that'.

John Hunter's father and his neighbours had heard about a Queensland forestry practice of spraying small lantana bushes with a strong dose of glyphosate. When they used handheld spray bottles to apply a concentrated glyphosate and water mix, the lantana died to its roots. We realised straight away that John's story had profound implications.

I took the nozzle off a cattle drench gun so it squirted a jet of large droplets, made up a mix, put some on a lantana hedge, and it worked a treat. We could kill lantana with what was, in effect, a water pistol. John Hunter heard about what we'd done and organised scientific trials of the technique on our property, in State Forests and in a National Park. Over subsequent years, with the support of a number of agencies, we adapted the method to treat large lantana hedges.

A decade on, we have refined the method, reduced the herbicide concentration, and treated hundreds of hectares of lantana-infested native forest on our property. Across the creek, a skilled team of indigenous bush regenerators, the Githabul Rangers, are using these techniques to regenerate the forests they have Native Title responsibility for. We have a paper published in a peer-reviewed journal and the method is used far and wide.[1] For this work, in 2013 Susan received the Northern Rivers Individual Landcarer of the Year Award and was a Landcare NSW State Finalist.

With this method, an individual can kill lantana in rugged country as fast as they can walk. Operators apply the herbicide in discrete lines of large droplets, so there's minimal chemical runoff. Native plants quickly regenerate through the lantana carcasses. The focused jet makes it possible to selectively remove lantana from around other plants.

We knew how to kill lantana on a landscape scale, but the challenge of understanding and responding to the dieback remained.

Family Therapy for Forests

At the 2005 forum, a review of the scientific literature on the dieback told us much about the cause and effect relationships between such factors as canopy disturbance, fire regimes, weeds, insects, soil chemistry, climate and bird populations.[2] But the review offered little advice about how the problem might be solved. The authors of the independent scientific literature review concluded:

> There is likely to be no single or simple management solution. In managing forests, it is necessary to recognise that there is a complexity of connections and interactions, many of which have yet to be deciphered. Because Bell Miner Associated Dieback is associated with interacting disturbances, concentration on particular management regimes in isolation is unlikely to resolve the problem. Rather, an integrated management program will be necessary.

The factors contributing to dieback are indeed many and interactive. And it's routine for research scientists to note that a problem is complex and further research is needed. But the forests couldn't wait for more research. We knew individual stands of 'flooded gum' (*Eucalyptus grandis*), 'blue gum' (*Eucalyptus saligna*), 'grey gum' (*Eucalyptus propinqua*) and other eucalypts that had already disappeared, and their seed would remain viable in the ground for only a few years. The regenerative potential of these areas would be long gone before scientists understood the ins and outs of the dieback process.

I was thinking about the relationship between trees, insects, birds and lantana when it occurred to me that a forest is like a big unruly family. That reminded me of my training in family therapy.

It was the late 1980s and my supervisor "Andrew" was briefing me for a family therapy session at a Community Health Unit. We were to watch through a one-way mirror while another psychologist worked with a troubled family in the next room. Andrew had a task for me. He showed me the phone intake notes and asked for seven hypotheses (possible explanations) about what could be going wrong with this family. Andrew added the caveat that none of these ideas might turn out to be right, but they would get me thinking.

This was our warm-up: a flexing of mental muscles for the creative effort of finding solutions to difficult social problems. As clinicians, we didn't enjoy a researcher's licence to note that the issue was complex and recommend further study. Our clients' needs were urgent.

As the psychologist in the next room interviewed family members, we tossed around ideas about what could be going wrong. Andrew was expert in what is known as systemic family therapy, a Milton Erickson-inspired approach that assumes problems serve a function. Andrew told us to think of the family as a system in which each member has a role. The family system was stuck in a way that was creating stress. Our job was to inject new information which would hopefully change the way members were thinking and interacting and shift the family towards better health.

If we had an idea, we phoned the psychologist in the other room and asked her to put a question to a particular family member. When we saw the family again a month later, the dynamics had changed, but that's another story.

Clinical psychologists get used to dealing with complex challenges. They think in terms of interacting systems, be they families, organisations or the human mind. I was comfortable entertaining a number of working hypotheses, even when little was known about the situation.

When I thought about forest dieback from a family therapist's perspective, the challenge was to figure out what was disturbing the natural equilibrium, and what we could do to trigger a healing response. Susan and I compared healthy and dieback-affected forest on our property and there were obvious differences. Dieback-free areas had little to no lantana, diverse bird life with few Bell Miners, healthy lower and mid-storey plants, and an intact canopy. Sick forest was just lantana interspersed with dead and dying trees, and abundant Bell Miners.

It seemed to us that, in a sense, lantana is a solution to the problem of an unnatural gap in the forest canopy. From Nature's perspective, it doesn't matter if native plants or lantana fill the hole. But it mattered to us.

Thinking of the forest as a system, I drew up the following model of a pathogenic feedback cycle that could drive forest dieback.

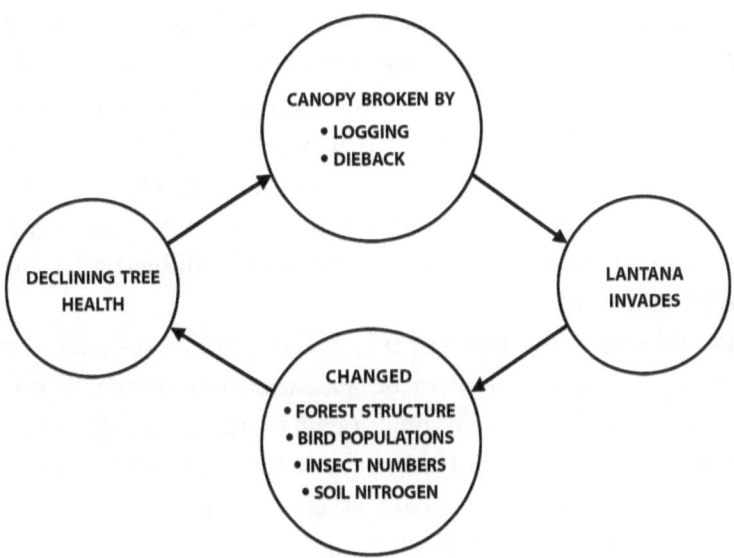

A Systems Model of Forest Dieback

When logging breaks the canopy, the forest system is fundamentally changed. Lantana invades, replacing the native ground cover and forest mid-storey. It adds humus and alters soil chemistry, drawing nutrients to the surface and increasing nitrogen, which eucalypts do not like. The increased nitrogen in eucalypt leaves attracts sap-sucking insects called 'psyllids'.

The lantana protects Bell Miner nests from currawongs, goannas and other egg predators. With this breeding advantage, Bell Miner populations expand, and this territorial bird chases away other birds that normally eat the insects.

For protection, the psyllid insects form 'lerps' (sugary coatings) over themselves. Birds like to eat the sugar and the insects. But due to a quirk of Nature, when the Bell Miners eat the lerps their beaks do not remove the underlying insects. So the psyllid lives on to form another sugary coating and insect numbers explode.

Trees repeatedly defoliate in a futile attempt to throw off the insects. Seed production fails, trees die and the forest ecosystem collapses.

We looked at our model and asked where the key to the problem could be. Where might we break the vicious cycle of forest decline?

It made no sense to change soil chemistry. You could perhaps mist net and kill thousands of Bell Miners, but the populations would rebound as soon as you stopped the cull. You could inject hundreds of trees with systemic insecticide to kill the psyllids. But even if these things were practical, you'd still have a landscape covered in lantana.

Psyllid insects and Bell Miners are native to the Australian bush. There are too many of them because the forest system is out of balance. Aside from the original logging and canopy disturbance, lantana is the only part of the dieback forest system that's out of place. We identified our villain as lantana and, thanks to John Hunter, we knew what to do about it.

Our hypothesis is that the forest will heal itself and Bell Miner numbers will decrease if you remove all the lantana from an appropriately large area and keep it out until the forest fully recovers its natural structure.

We believe that this is good science. The proposition is readily testable. To date, our hypothesis stands.

The Bell Miners left some areas a couple of years after the lantana was removed, and they have stayed away. Other birds and insect predators moved in to control the psyllids and these areas of forest are now resilient and safe from further lantana invasion. More severely affected areas require follow-ups over a decade or so.

But knowing how a problem can be solved doesn't mean that it has been solved or ever will be. Some potent One Thought Solutions could undermine efforts to save our native eucalypt forests.

Ill-suited Labels

John Hunter found that a herbicide applicator registered as a 'splatter gun' had been used to treat small bushes of lantana in pine forests. When we modified the method for large-scale bush regeneration work, we wanted to change the name to 'stream jet' because for some people the splatter gun label conjures an image of herbicide being splashed about willy-nilly. The name implied that the method was not suitable for use in ecologically sensitive areas when it's ideal for such work.

Unfortunately, the registered splatter gun name has stuck. We've also got a less than perfect name for the dieback itself.

The working group had to decide early on what to call the problem. This was no straightforward task. Little was known about this form of dieback. But one thing was certain: wherever you found dying trees there were plague numbers of Bell Miners.

The Bell Miner, or bellbird as it is more commonly known, is a much-loved forest creature. A longtime friend of Australians, Henry Kendall's poem celebrates the Bell Miner: 'And, softer than slumber, and sweeter than singing, the notes of the bellbirds are running and ringing'. But this was something else: an irritating 'ping … ping' noise that was anything but sweet. If you venture into lantana-infested forests, the Bell Miners mob and screech to drive you away. Calls that had delighted generations now signalled big trouble in the bush.

It was true that where you find dieback you also find Bell Miners, so it seemed appropriate to name the problem 'Bell Miner associated dieback'. And given the way people felt, the acronym BMAD was apt. No one anticipated the hidden implications of this One Thought Solution.

Our next thought experiment explores the implicit power of names.

> Say the phrase 'Bell Miner associated dieback' over a few times.
>
> Now rate your feelings about the Bell Miner on an Emot-o-Meter where '-10' is 'very negative' and '+10' is 'very positive'. Record the first number that pops into your mind. Clear your mind.
>
> When you're ready, say the statement, 'To solve the dieback problem we need to do something about Bell Miners'.
>
> Now rate how much you agree with this statement using an Emot-o-Meter where '-10' is 'strongly disagree' and '+10' is 'strongly agree'. Record your rating.

I'm guessing that in the first part of the thought experiment which associates Bell Miners with dieback, you had a somewhat negative feeling about the bird. But there's no right or wrong response here, and you might have reacted differently.

If in the second part of the thought experiment, you agreed that we need to do something about Bell Miners to treat the dieback, then you're not alone.

Many people intuitively sense that Bell Miners must be centrally important for any solution to the problem known as Bell Miner associated dieback. People have killed thousands of birds on the strength of this One Thought Solution. But Susan and I don't blame Bell Miners for the mess. We think of the birds as friends that help with our bush regeneration work. As we walk through our forests, their calls tell us where we'll find a lantana hedge and how big it's likely to be: the more birds, the louder the noise, the bigger the hedge.

The BMAD name solved the problem of what to call this form of dieback. Unfortunately, it also obscured the true nature of the challenge and what we need to do about it. The name implies that Bell Miners are the root cause of the disease, but lantana's the key. We'd like to call it 'lantana associated dieback' or LAD, but it's too late for that now. We'll talk more about this later, but we should be careful when choosing a name or label for big environmental challenges.

Let's look at some other One Thought Solutions that could derail efforts to save our native eucalypt forests from dieback.

Birds Nest in Lantana

Some people do not want to remove lantana because native birds live in it. It's true that Bell Miners nest in the hedges, and the image of lantana protecting bird nests generates positive feelings. Who doesn't want to protect native birds and their nests? But this supposed benefit comes at a great cost. The Bell Miner is an aggressive bird that chases other birds away, and lantana excludes many native animals and plants that would normally live in the forest.

Beyond that, there's a personal benefit from believing that you don't have to remove lantana. After all, it's a dirty, dangerous and difficult job.

But the One Thought Solution most likely to stymie efforts to save native forests relates to the use of glyphosate herbicide.

Glyphosate Should be Banned

In 2015, the World Health Organization classified glyphosate as 'probably carcinogenic to humans' and put it in the 'Group 2A' category that includes: lead and ultraviolet radiation; creosote and emissions from frying and household wood fires; and the circumstances of being a hairdresser or barber, working in the petroleum industry, or doing shift work.

The 'definitely carcinogenic' 'Group 1' category includes: the substances asbestos, benzene and particulate matter in air pollution; the mixtures of alcoholic beverages, diesel exhaust, processed meats, soot and wood dust; and the circumstances of aluminium production, glass making and tobacco smoking.

When it comes to managing risks to health, we need to take every precaution. Glyphosate is dangerous and must be used with care. We agree with the concerned citizens who don't want glyphosate used in public places, and especially where children play. We disagree with the use of glyphosate on herbicide-resistant crops.

Susan and I want to use as little herbicide and other chemicals as possible on our land. We wish the dieback problem could be solved without recourse to glyphosate. But we know of no effective alternative for removing hundreds of hectares of lantana in the rugged country we care for.

Glyphosate is no addictive drug that the bush has to rely on. We think of it as medicine for sick forests: a treatment that you administer a couple of times and stop using when the forest gets well. Operators use less and less herbicide during follow-ups. In many areas, we used splatter gun once for a good result. We have beautiful areas of forest that 10 years ago were dying. The natural forest structure has returned, and the shade will stop lantana from dominating again.

This is how we weigh up the costs and benefits of using the herbicide.

When settlers cleared our paddocks in the early 1900s, it took weeks to fell a single tree with axes and saws and to transport the timber with horses and bullocks. When fossil fuel technology arrived in the form of chainsaws, bulldozers and trucks, forest disruption went into overdrive. The bush is now scarred with tracks, logging dumps and clearings that are chock-full of lantana. Humans created the problem, and the native forest cannot rid itself of this invasive weed without our help.

Using glyphosate in splatter guns to regenerate native forests is like producing solar panels to generate renewable energy. Both processes depend on fossil fuel technology, involve dangerous substances, and come with a carbon footprint and a pollution debt. When we use solar panels, we accept the environmental cost of the pollution created by their manufacture and transport because it results in a greater good in the long run. It takes a few years to pay off the debt on solar panels, but then we have sustainable nonpolluting energy. Like our use of solar panels, we use glyphosate to regenerate dying forests because the benefits outweigh the costs.

Trees are Nature's irreplaceable and valuable gift. The leaves of the trees transform sunlight into life. Healthy forests sequester carbon. They're the lungs of the planet. Forests support biodiversity and filter precious water. They create environments that nourish the human spirit. A healthy forest is self-sustaining, potentially forever.

If we don't repair our forests, the environmental cost will be incalculable. Nature's not going to care if our grandchildren inherit nothing but lantana. It's up to us how much of Australia's once magnificent forest estate we pass on. Why allow our forests to degrade when we could repair and maintain them?

Postscript – June 2019

Governments need to connect their actions to what they know. They have declared lantana to be a 'Weed of National Significance', they've listed Bell Miner Associated Dieback as a 'Key Threatening Process', and their recent scientific review[3] lays out a clear case for removing lantana from native forests. Nonetheless, the NSW Government still plans to keep on logging native forests with no follow-up weed control. They even want to log dieback-affected areas to get whatever value they can before the trees all die.

The forestry industry and its political partners wrongly assume that saving dieback-affected forests would be difficult or even impossible. In reality, the disease is readily curable. This is a complex problem with a simple solution: remove lantana and keep it out until the forest recovers. It's as simple as that.

Forests are not like mines; productivity can't be increased by just cutting more trees and going further into old-growth areas. Forests have to be managed like gardens and farms. You can't grow vegetables if you never weed your garden. Farms can't produce if invasive weeds take over. And you can't get timber from a forest that's dead and gone.

Earlier in 2019, Susan and I made a 30-minute YouTube video about how we cure forest dieback on Creek's Bend (https://youtu.be/s4zINkKPESU). More folk are becoming aware of the problem and looking for solutions. We reckon it's time to create a lantana-free Northern Rivers. This is the first step to curing Lantana Associated Dieback along Australia's eastern seaboard. The challenge can be met. The job is doable. The economic, environmental and social benefits from taking action are compelling.

We now come to another big, man-made environmental challenge. Hold onto your Akubra, you're about to fall down the unconventional gas rabbit hole where the One Thought Solution goes to the 'dark side'.

Chapter 4

Unconventional Gas: The One Thought Solution goes to the dark side

> I see in the near future a crisis approaching that unnerves me and causes me to tremble for the safety of my country ... corporations have been enthroned and an era of corruption in high places will follow, and the money power of the country will endeavor to prolong its reign by working upon the prejudices of the people until all wealth is aggregated in a few hands and the Republic is destroyed.
>
> Abraham Lincoln (1808–1865)

THIS CHALLENGE BEGINS WITH ancient sunlight trapped in deep time, condensed into fossilised life, and cooked under the heat and pressure of kilometres of rock.

From the 'age of dinosaurs', some 200 million years ago (mya), methane – a greenhouse gas many times more potent than carbon dioxide – lay sequestered, safely locked away from the atmosphere three kilometres down in shale, two in sandstone, and one in coal seams, as life evolved overhead.

The gas was there when mammals (205 mya) and flowering plants (130 mya) first appeared. Then a meteor struck and dinosaurs departed (66 mya). The gas stayed put as continents drifted and Australia split off from Antarctica and South America (50 mya). Locally, the Wollumbin/Mt Warning volcano erupted (20 mya).

Ice ages came and went, as did the great woolly mammoth (*Mammuthus primigenius*) and our human relatives *Australopithecus*, *Homo erectus* and the Neanderthals.

Our kind, the self-named 'wise person' (*Homo sapiens*) has walked the Earth for 200,000 years. We invented agriculture, cities, armies, cooking, religion, technology, writing and science, while the methane from deep time did nothing. Then, everything changed.

A human subspecies, *Homo sapiens halliburtinus* (Latin for 'wise person too smart by half'), worked out how to unleash gas by drilling sideways to fracture the earth.

Welcome to the challenge of gas field industrialisation.

Down the Rabbit Hole

The gas industry invasion of the Northern Rivers, our slice of rural Australia, began by stealth. A friend said, 'You'd better look at this' and that led Susan and me down the rabbit hole. It was a hell of a hole and, like Alice, once we were in, there was no turning back, and as we fell deeper, things became 'curiouser and curiouser'.

By the time we woke up, gas miners had sealed the fate of Queensland's Darling Downs and were deep into the Pilliga State Forest and the premier farming region of the Liverpool Plains. They had drilled more than 50 gas wells in the Northern Rivers and planned thousands more. A gas pipeline connecting our region to the Gladstone liquefied natural gas export hub via the Border Ranges National Park looked a done deal. Government ministers and gas company executives were telling us that there was nothing the community could do about it.

That seems a long time ago now, though only about a decade has passed. I feel as if I've earned a Master's Degree in Gas that I never wanted, but am now grateful to have. I'll tell you what I know about the threat and how it fostered one of the finest examples of creative problem-solving on a grand scale that Australia has seen.

To grasp the nature of this challenge, you have to understand the scale and complexity of the impacts that unconventional gas mining have on the Earth and its people.

The Physical Reality

We'll begin with the drilling of wells and what it takes to get the gas out of the ground and processed. Then we'll look at the impacts.

Conventional gas mining uses a limited number of wells in unpopulated, remote areas to extract gas from naturally formed underground reservoirs. Unconventional mining for gas in seams of coal, shale and tight sands (gas-bearing sandstones) typically involves thousands of interconnected wells spread across populated, rural landscapes: 40,000 coal seam gas (CSG) wells are planned for the Darling Downs. All forms of unconventional gas mining share a common technology and involve the use and liberation of similar substances.

The Australian unconventional gas industry is most developed in Queensland's Darling Downs. This rich agricultural area in the drainage basins of the Condamine and Maranoa Rivers, west of Brisbane, is home to 5.5% of Queensland's population. About 20% of the residents are children 14 years or younger.

Coal Seam Gas Field in Queensland's Darling Downs (©2010 Google)

The depth of gas wells depends on the type and local character of the targeted gas-bearing seam. Radiating out in different directions, each vertical well can connect to kilometres of horizontally drilled, fractured, dewatered and depressurised gas-bearing strata.

Picture in your mind's eye the Sydney Harbour Bridge in profile, from the water to the top of the arch. To get a sense of the 1,000 m (3,281 ft) depth of a typical CSG well, imagine eight bridges stacked one on top of the other: that's how far down they drill the well. A shale seam gas well is three times as deep.

In gas wells, the diameter of the drilled hole and the inserted steel pipe narrows with increasing depth. At 1,000 metres the gap between rock and pipe is about 1.9 cm (¾ in). Miners have to seal the space between pipe and rock with cement for all eternity in order to prevent methane and other gases from escaping into the atmosphere via the borehole, and to block gases and liquids moving between rock layers, aquifers and depressurised gas seams. Steel pipes in gas wells come with a two-year warranty. There's no warranty on the cement.

In Australia, miners add about 18,500 kg of chemical additive per CSG well. Up to 40% (7,500 kg) of this is not recovered: drilling each well leaves about 7.5 tonnes of chemicals underground. Most of the chemicals used by the industry have not been assessed for their toxicity, persistence or long-term health impacts. Nor has there been any assessment of compounds that form when mining chemicals interact with other substances or with natural catalysts such as sunlight, water, air and radioactive elements.

When a well is 'fracked' (hydraulically fractured), water, sand and chemicals are forced down the well at very high pressure to fracture the gas-bearing seams. Gas is liberated when the added water and the water within the seam are pumped to the surface via the bore pipe. The gas is collected for processing, and the wastewater is stored in huge dams lined with sheets of plastic taped together to prevent leakage and contamination of surrounding soils.

To get an idea of how much underground water the industry extracts each year, bring to mind the ever-popular standard of an Olympic swimming pool. The low-end gas industry estimate of 61 gigalitres is equivalent to 24,400 Olympic swimming pools. It's hard to imagine what that would look like, but it's a big puddle. At the higher end of estimates, the Federal Government Water Group's range is equivalent to one to three times the amount of water in Sydney Harbour.

Gas miners have dumped untreated CSG wastewater into rivers and sprayed it on dirt roads to suppress dust. The industry claims that reverse osmosis filtration renders the waste water safe for human use and for discharge into the environment, but this form of filtration can't remove a number of dangerous chemicals. I never found out how they dispose of the contaminants filtered out of the wastewater: an issue that Emeritus Professor Chris Fell described as 'the elephant in the room'.

The water that's pumped from coal and shale seams is salty. The unconventional gas industry in Australia is projected to bring 31,000,000 tonnes of salt to the surface over the next 30 years. That's a lot of spice for your fish and chips. To make the incomprehensible imaginable, picture that amount of salt filling the Melbourne Cricket Ground 15 times over. The gas industry has no plan for getting rid of this much salt.

It takes a lot of energy in the form of electricity and diesel to pump water and chemicals into and out of kilometres of wells and fractured seams, and then to treat and transport the gas. These industrial processes create massive amounts of air pollution.

National Pollution Inventory data from 20 CSG facilities in the Darling Downs show that over a one-year period (2013–2014) the pollutants emitted into the atmosphere included: 1,383 tonnes of volatile organic compounds, 13 tonnes of acetaldehyde, 2.2 tonnes of BTEX (benzene, toluene, ethylbenzene and xylene), 241 tonnes of formaldehyde, 8,788 tonnes of carbon monoxide, 12,189 tonnes of oxides of nitrogen and 2,325 tonnes of particulates.[1] Much of this air pollution occurs in a narrow industrialised corridor.

Imagine that you store just the liquid volatile organic compounds released in one year in 20-litre plastic drums and stack them one on top of the other. The column would stand about 28 kilometres high – three times the height of Mt Everest.

A Fractured Earth Responds

Bringing water from deep underground to the surface frees up previously bound gases which, as intended, move up the well. But this has consequences. Fracking and removing water from gas-bearing seams create an unknowable network of new and previously existing cracks and faults that act as conduits for the liberated gas to vent into the atmosphere. As gas comes up fissures and cracks, water goes down. The most obvious effect of this geologic turmoil is lowered water tables and depleted farm bores; the gas mining company Santos predicted that by 2028 the level of groundwater in Bowen Basin gas fields would drop by up to 65 metres.[2] According to Dr Isaac Santos, coal seam gas mining could have catastrophic consequences in the Northern Rivers where sea water would likely inundate depressurised aquifers.

There are two World Heritage rainforests at the end of the Toonumbar Valley. Follow the creeks to the top of the ridges and you can find where the water first comes out of the ground. Aquifer-fed springs have sustained Toonumbar's rainforests for millions of years. These forests would be at risk if local water tables dropped by even a couple of metres.

How often would you expect that gas companies and regulatory authorities have measured methane concentrations in the air above gas fields? The answer is: not at all. They only estimate fugitive emissions with formulae that calculate leakage from valves and seals and such.

In 2012, Dr Isaac Santos and Dr Damien Maher recorded atmospheric methane concentrations as they drove the 500 kilometres from Lismore's Southern Cross University to the Tara gas fields in Queensland's Darling Downs.[3] Their instruments showed concentrations about the current global average of 1.8 parts per million until they approached Tara, where methane and radon readings increased threefold. Australia set a new world record with methane levels of 6.89 parts per million, exceeding the previous highest reading from a Siberian gas field. The methane to CO_2 isotope ratio indicated that these emissions were coal seam gases, as were the bubbles that have turned the Condamine River into a spa.

The scientists discovered that a blanket of methane of unknown thickness extends tens of kilometres around Tara. Why is there a landscape-scale venting of coal seam gases into Tara's air? According to the researchers, 'In natural conditions, methane is contained within the coal seam by water pressure ... (in CSG mining) we get lowering of the water table, horizontal drilling, fracturing, infrastructure leakage, but our evidence suggests that we also have leaks through the soil as well, and these leaks through the soil are not counted in any fugitive estimates'.

In 2016, US scientists found that the 'global burden of atmospheric methane has been increasing over the past decade'.[4] When they examined measurements of methane in the air above the US, they discovered that from 2002 to 2014 – the period corresponding to America's shale oil and gas boom – methane emissions had increased by more than 30%. The scientists concluded that this increase in methane emissions accounted for '30 to 60 percent of the global growth of atmospheric methane in the past decade'.

Methane is colourless and odourless. You can see it venting in the Condamine River because it bubbles through water. In 2016, NSW Greens MP Jeremy Buckingham clicked a stove lighter over the side of a boat and set the Condamine River on fire. The Condamine River has been bubbling methane since 2012 and, according to CSIRO's Professor Damian Barrett, the rate of gas flow had increased over the 12 months prior to Mr Buckingham's boat trip and near barbeque.[5] A spokesperson for Origin Energy, a local

CSG miner, advised that 'The seeps pose no risk to the environment, or to public safety, providing people show common sense and act responsibly around them.'

Australians will have to learn to not light fires near rivers.

The Human Dimension

People who profit from the industry see gas mining as a good thing because it generates income for company executives, shareholders and employees and the financial benefits ripple out to contractors, hoteliers and others. It's the people threatened or injured by gas mining who see it as a bad thing.

In Australia, rural landowners subject to a petroleum exploration license face the prospect of gas companies being legally empowered to forcibly enter their properties, build roads, set up camps, drill wells, dig dams to hold contaminated water, and establish noisy, brightly lit well sites that run 24 hours a day.

Susan and I were alarmed when we heard that gas wells could be drilled 100 metres from our house, which would be outside the kitchen window, over by the fig tree.

The sense of threat created by invasive gas development triggers the fight-or-flight response.[6] If this ancient protective strategy works to remove the danger, then all will be well. But if the threat persists and no effective problem-solving takes place, stress, anger and depression can set in.

For affected rural people, the diminished quality of their lifestyles and the loss of control over their land can create shock. Anxiety and grief, complicated by disturbed sleep due to noise and light pollution, can result in debilitating symptoms of psychopathology. A Tara woman told me that she visited a farmer friend to find him curled up on the floor, crying. The noise of a nearby gas compression station was driving him mad. He could not escape. He could not sell his land. He could not afford to move away.

Country people often feel a bond, a spiritual connection, to the land they work and care for. When miners damage the land they love, rural folk can suffer distress and 'solastalgia' (a loss of solace).[7] For people who care, grief and powerlessness to protect their land cut deep.

As I write this, rural communities grieve for the suicide death of George Bender, a well-known Darling Downs farmer. George fought for years to keep the gas miners off his land before he succumbed to the relentless pressure. A woman who attended George's funeral cried as she told me about the impact on local people. She spoke of gas companies intimidating and harassing citizens who resisted.

The unconventional gas industry harms the physical health of people who have to live in gas fields. The essential problem with liberating substances from gas-bearing seams is that we are made of similar stuff. We share a basic chemistry with our long-buried fossilised ancestors. Our complex, more evolved bodies are vulnerable to the effects of contact with even minute amounts of these organic compounds.

Dangerous chemicals used and liberated by gas mining expose communities to a mix of persistent, bioaccumulative, toxic, carcinogenic, mutagenic, teratogenic (agents that interfere with embryonic development), and hormone-disrupting pollutants. These can seriously injure health in very low concentrations, even down to parts per billion.

Of special concern is the release of great amounts of endocrine (hormone) disrupting chemicals. In our bodies, tiny amounts of hormones control basic functions such as digestion, growth, emotions, sexual development, reproduction, sleep and the immune response. About one hundred of the chemicals used in gas mining are known or suspected hormone disruptors. Exposure to tiny amounts of these substances can profoundly damage health and increase the risk of birth defects, cancer and neurological and other diseases, especially in children. Health effects can be unpredictable and delayed and can remain hidden for decades and span generations.

A medical survey found elevated levels of symptoms suggestive of nervous system damage in children in the Tara area.[8] Children are like sentinels because they're more vulnerable than adults to gas field pollutants and are likely to fall ill first. Relative to adults, kids are closer to the ground and are more often active outside. They drink more water, breathe more air and eat more food per kilo of body weight than do adults. And children have more years left to live, which puts them at greater risk of illnesses such as cancer that take decades to develop.

As was the case with thalidomide, children are particularly sensitive to gas field pollutants during critical stages of development. A mother's contact with pollutants during pregnancy – and even the exposure of the mother and father prior to conception – can affect a child's health.

In gas fields, dust and particulates produced by mining and burning diesel are especially dangerous because they hydrate and bind to toxic chemicals in the surrounding air. When inhaled, these particulates take chemicals deep into the body. If particles that fall to the ground are tracked into the house, people can inhale them after vacuuming. Exposure to particulates is implicated in a range of illnesses including autism, cancer and cardiovascular and kidney disease. There's no safe level, and risks are greatest for sensitive groups such as the elderly and children.

Unconventional gas mining damages underground water systems, vents methane and other gases into the atmosphere, and creates dangerous air, water and soil pollution where people live. But some want us to believe that these impacts are not risks worth considering.

One Thought Solutions as Risk Management

> You are not only responsible for what you say,
> but also for what you do not say.
> Martin Luther (1483–1546)

Are risk management principles and our legal and ethical obligations to protect others absolute, or do they depend on personal interests?

Risk management is the process of thinking systematically about all possible risks before they occur and setting up procedures to avoid problems or mitigate impacts. Proper cost-benefit analysis is a reasoned consideration of all the potential costs and benefits of a proposed development. 'Duty holders' are those who are legally obliged to exercise due diligence and to consider all risks: not just those for which regulations exist, but even hazards which they do not know about.

As members of the Toonumbar Recreation Reserve Trust, we were responsible for protecting the public's safety on the reserve. We were required to actively seek out risks and proactively deal with them. The NSW Lands Department officer was clear about what this meant. There was no ambiguity. The 'duty of care', that is, the moral and legal obligation to ensure the safety and well-being of others, was ours and ours alone. Ignorance was no excuse, and it was not the public's job to educate us. Such is the responsibility that ordinary citizens take on with even minor voluntary positions.

Most of us would agree with the NSW Chief Scientist and Engineer Professor Mary O'Kane that the CSG industry should be managed with 'eyes wide open, a full appreciation of the risks, complete transparency, rigorous compliance, and a commitment to addressing any problems promptly'.[9] We assume that managing the risks of operating gas fields in populated areas is about protecting people and the environment from harm. Most expect cost-benefit analyses to consider costs as well as benefits and think that the duty of care rests with politicians and company executives. So it comes as a shock to realise that the industry and its political supporters see things very differently.

The risk that gas industry promoters seek to manage is not the harm that gas mining might cause people and the environment. The risk they fear is that people might find out what they're up to and do something that impedes their operations. Their aim is to protect company profits and government revenue. For them, risk management translates to public relations. They extend their duty of care only to themselves and their shareholders. Consequently, they argue that gas mining is completely safe with no risk or cost worth thinking about.[10] To this end, they employ a raft of One Thought Solutions to manipulate opinion and obscure the truth about the unconventional gas industry.

Risk, What Risk?

A gas company executive explained to me that it was wrong for a NSW Premier to say we need CSG regulations because this suggested there was something that needed regulating. In this CEO's opinion, there are few human activities safer than gas mining; he saw no problem operating gas wells next to kindergartens.

For the industry it's simple. Their One Thought Solutions revolve around the theme that gas mining is unambiguously safe and good. Living amongst gas fields is great. Everyone and everything's a winner. All we need is a little trust, some vision and a positive can-do attitude. The industry is proven safe and should any problem arise, our world's best regulations will take care of it. Anyone who says otherwise is mistaken or crazy.

If regulators, politicians and executives can convince themselves that gas mining has only benefits and poses no risk, they feel free to ignore their responsibilities and duty of care to protect people and the countryside.

Relax, We've Been Doing This for Years

In the following One Thought Solution, an image of a long time period is used to engender a sense of safety. The logic goes: we've been mining gas for so long, it must be safe.

> On the subject of CSG in general, I do believe that much of the debate about fracking is driven by environmental scaremongering. Hydraulic fracturing has been around in the United States for at least 65 years with its origins believed to be much earlier (Senator Eric Abetz, 2015, email to author).

> Our industry has a proven and safe track record over a number of decades ... CSG in Australia has operated in Australia for nearly 20 years, without any health concerns (Metgasco CEO Mr Peter Henderson, 2013, email to author).

Could you feel the desired effect? Did you sense the implication that if something has been going on for a long time it must be safe?

But what's time got to do with it?

In 1898, the British Chief Inspector of Factories reported that asbestos had 'easily demonstrated' health risks. Many similar warnings followed, yet it was more than 100 years before Australia banned asbestos in 2002.

I Know Nothing

This One Thought Solution attempts to conjure evidence from nothing. The argument goes: if these good people know nothing, there's nothing to know, therefore gas fields are safe. But a lack of knowledge isn't evidence of anything other than ignorance.

Following is Metgasco's response to questions in the Northern Star newspaper of 17 March 2012:

> Metgasco is not aware of any farm bores drying up as a result of CSG operations ... Mr Mark Harris and Mr Brad Mullard have both stated that they are not aware of any cross-contamination of aquifers as a result of coal seam gas activity ... Mr Mullard ... invited participants to write to him and provide him with examples.

There's no reasoned assessment of risks to aquifers here, just declarations of ignorance as if that somehow assures safety. Could you feel the effect they were after?

From the statement, it's clear that these people are not actively looking for information about risks; Mr Mullard reportedly expects the public to do his risk assessment research for him.

A useful feature of the 'I know nothing' One Thought Solution is that such statements would be true even if evidence of contamination exists, provided that the person making the claim remains ignorant of the facts. This creates an incentive to avoid information that might compromise the cultivated state of not-knowing.

It's worthy of a scene from *Yes Minister* in which Sir Humphrey hides the truth about fracking and aquifer contamination so his minister can go on honestly claiming that he's not aware of any impacts.

Attack and Demean

When in 2012 Dr Isaac Santos and Dr Damien Maher made public their findings of landscape-scale methane emissions in Queensland gas fields, then Federal MP Martin Ferguson, who later took up an executive position with the Australian Petroleum Production and Exploration Association, accused the scientists of 'a cynical attempt to grab headlines'. Mr Ferguson called for 'a factual, scientific debate, not an emotional debate'. He said the scientists were 'trying to score political points without proper consideration of the best interests of the broader community'.[11]

This One Thought Solution confected an image of irresponsible, self-serving scientists to engender feelings of disapproval and doubt about their findings. The aim was to distract attention from the profound discovery that methane is venting into the atmosphere across the Darling Downs.

Mr Ferguson's logic goes: the scientists are selfish, therefore what they say is rubbish and, of course, gas mining is safe; no patriotic Australian would think otherwise.

In the following One Thought Solutions, the image of a despicable enemy – in this case, citizens who care for their country – engenders feelings of disapproval. The argument runs: these critics are bad people and the gas miners are good guys, so it's all right to mine gas in populated areas. Examples of the tactic range from ridicule to the ridiculous.

> In my opinion, mental health issues were only likely in the future if dishonest, disreputable activists manufactured anxiety (NSW MP Scot MacDonald, email to author).

> The truth is this: Digging coal is no threat to anyone, except the green ideologues who want to enfeeble our economy and enslave our bodies (NSW MP Dr Peter Phelps, speech to parliament).
> (© State of New South Wales through the Parliament of New South Wales)

Could you feel the intended effect? Did these words make you feel more, or less, inclined to believe that activists and greenies are the problem?

Activists and scientists attract heavy-duty attacks from gas industry promoters. MP Dr Peter Phelps made the following statement in a parliamentary debate in August 2015:

> This ignorance has been fostered by misinformation from green extremists. That is the nature of the contemporary green movement in Australia and in many other places in the western world. It is a pyramid structure. At the base is the vast majority of people who would be described as ordinary, concerned citizens. They are sincere but ill-informed people who are pulled along by emotion and who know little about the technical aspects of coal seam gas extraction. They believe what they hear in good faith, but at the same time they must rely upon the often tainted evidence of so-called green experts. That is the broad base of the modern environmental movement. The middle group are fewer in number and I would call them the lunatics or the activists. They are people who would have a tubal ligation rather than

bring another filthy human into the world. They see humanity as a scourge and dream of a great plague that will wipe out 90 percent of humanity.[12] (© State of New South Wales through the Parliament of New South Wales)

I assure you, country people who don't want to live in gas fields mean you no harm. They're no threat to you or your ability to breed.

The following comments made in 2014 by MP Dr Peter Phelps come with a warning. If you read them, you might not invite a scientist to dinner again.

> At the heart of many scientists – but not all scientists – lies the heart of a totalitarian planner. One can see them now, beavering away, alone, unknown, in their laboratories. And now, through the great global warming swindle they can influence policy, they can set agendas, they can reach into everyone's lives; they can, like Lenin, proclaim 'what must be done'. While the humanities had a sort of warm-hearted, muddle-headed leftism, the sciences carry with them no such feeling for humanity. And it is not a new phenomenon. We should not forget that some of the strongest supporters of totalitarian regimes in the last century have been scientists and, in return, the state lavishes praise, money and respectability on them.[13] (© State of New South Wales through the Parliament of New South Wales)

Befriending Rocks and Gases

Pro-gas politicians pretend that rocks and gases come to life as good friends who need their protection. What could be nobler than defending a mate against bullies? If it could speak for itself, coal would thank Dr Peter Phelps for organising 'friends of coal' functions at the NSW Parliament House.

The image in these One Thought Solutions is of friendly rocks and gases. The intended emotion is bonhomie and sympathy. The logic runs: anyone who criticises rocks and gases must be ignorant and nasty, therefore it's all right to mine coal and gas.

MP Mr Rick Colless worries that 'carbon and carbon dioxide have been demonised'. Mr Colless declared that carbon and its sibling carbon dioxide 'are not foes or demons; they are very much our friends'. As Mr Colless said:

> Members who learned about the carbon cycle at school would know that the carbon cycle is also termed 'the cycle of life'. Carbon is a friend. The carbon dioxide in the atmosphere is taken up by green plants; photosynthesis occurs. That carbon dioxide is turned into sugars and energy, which other animals need in order to go about their daily business ... It is the cycle of life.[14]
> (© State of New South Wales through the Parliament of New South Wales)

To maintain this One Thought Solution, Mr Colless has to ignore the broader reality while keeping attention fixed on a few cause and effect relationships in the carbon cycle.

Except for the occasional addition of new carbon from volcanic activity and the weathering of rocks, the carbon cycle was once a relatively closed system. Sunlight and chemical energy drive the recycling of carbon on the surface of the planet. For carbon, this was a zero-sum game. Sunlight and photosynthesis grow grass that a cow eats, the cow burps methane, cow manure rots, and so on and on forever, but the total amount of carbon in the system stays much the same over time.

Mining and burning gas and coal add massive amounts of new carbon to the cycle that operates on the planet's surface. This is no longer a closed system. Newly liberated gases from coal seams supercharge the cycle of life, change chemical processes and overheat a destabilised climate system.

Regulation to the Rescue

You can try to calm concerns about the safety of gas mining by chanting a roll call of regulations. The One Thought Solution goes: look at all the regulations, marvel at the protection, feel the security, therefore gas mining is safe.

Consider the emotional effects of repeating 'regulation' and related words in the following passages. Can you feel the sense of security that the industry promoters want to engender?

Metgasco recognises the need for a strong and effective regulatory body and seeks regulations that are based on sound risk management principles and science (Metgasco's submission to the NSW Parliamentary CSG Inquiry). (© State of New South Wales through the Parliament of New South Wales)

The NSW upstream gas sector is well regulated and must comply with a number of acts including: Petroleum (Onshore) Act; Environmental Planning and Assessment Act; State Environmental Planning Policies; Native Titles Act (both State and Federal); National Parks and Wildlife Act; Native Vegetation Act; Rivers and Foreshores Improvement Act; Rural Fires Act; Water Management Act and Water Act; Fisheries Management Act; and Threatened Species Conservation Act (Metgasco's reply to questions in the Northern Star newspaper).

Current NSW Government regulations for the industry are based on the NSW Chief Scientist and Engineer's review of coal seam gas operations. But Professor O'Kane's report is fundamentally flawed because she inexplicably overlooked the prodigious amounts of air pollution created by the industrial processing of unconventional gas. Beyond that, what happens when regulations, sound or unsound, have to contend with reality?

If people always obeyed the rules, there would be no crime and no negligence. In the real world, the protection afforded by regulation is only as good as the intent and skill of operators, the regulator's zeal to protect the public, and the effectiveness of law enforcement. When illegal and unethical things occur, regulations only provide for possible recompense.

If regulations ensured safety there would be no accidents due to human error, and regulators would reliably act to protect the public from predictable risks. On 14 July 2013, an explosive build-up of pressure in Metgasco's Kingfisher E01 well – the company's first attempt at mining gas from tight sands – ejected some 200 metres of steel drill pipe high into the air, endangering workers and providing spectacular photos. According to the Mine Safety

Investigation Unit, the well had leaked since it was first drilled, creating 'continually rising pressure ... around the production casing'. With the investigation ongoing, Minister Anthony Roberts approved the infamous gas well in Bentley, which would have been Metgasco's second attempt at mining tight sands, before anyone knew why their first go at it had failed so dramatically.

Double Standards for Proof

Gas industry spruikers set the bar low for proof that unconventional gas mining is safe, but demand an Olympic high jump standard of evidence from citizens concerned about risks. Their One Thought Solution seeks to foster reassurance with a false claim that there is evidence that gas mining is safe, while engendering doubt about claims that gas field pollutants are a risk. The logic of the argument goes: we can prove that gas mining is safe, you can't prove it's harmful, therefore it's all right to operate gas fields where people live.

MP Mr Scot MacDonald wanted the highest standard of scientific evidence – peer-reviewed proof of causation – before he would entertain the possibility that there is any risk involved in gas mining. As Mr MacDonald asked of me in a 2014 email:

> I would be very interested in any peer reviewed work demonstrating a link between Australian gas extraction and/or Fracking and harm to the environment or human health ... As gas extraction had been underway for about 2 decades in Qld without problems, I think it is reasonable for those making unsubstantiated claims to prove harm. Can you point to any causation with confidence?

But when I asked Mr MacDonald for scientific evidence to back his claim that gas mining is safe, he offered only the following personal anecdote:

> I specifically and very clearly asked one (Camden) farmer who raised 400 head of cattle had there been any impact (of CSG mining) on his stock or sale prices. He confirmed there had been

> none and he said gas and agriculture were co-existing successfully ... I sincerely hope you are approaching this issue with no biases. It would be a great shame for the community if Gas extraction was debated without a solid foundation of evidence.
>
> I asked him (the farmer) a range of questions that will help you. No impact on property values or livestock. No human health problems. No mental health problems ... No environmental problems ... No negative impact on amenity (emails from Mr Scot MacDonald to author).

One farmer's observations cannot prove that gas mining is safe. Nor should the opinions of tradies, smokers or motorists determine the way governments manage the risks posed by asbestos, tobacco or leaded petrol.

Double standards also operate in the way that gas industry promoters apply the 'burden of proof', that is, the obligation to provide evidence to back a claim.

In regulatory contexts, the burden of proof is usually understood to rest with those seeking to profit from doing something that exposes the public to potential risk. For instance, when a pharmaceutical company wants to sell a new medication to the public, they have to demonstrate the safety and efficacy of their product with studies that compare health data taken before and after people use the medication. It's not up to the public to prove that the new medication is harmful.

Dr Peter Phelps took a different view in a May 2014 parliamentary debate:

> At every stage the opponents of technological progress argue that just because there is no evidence of harm that does not mean that something is not harmful. We have to prove that it is not harmful before we embrace it. This form of pre-scientific thinking presents a serious obstacle to rational discussion. The absence of an effect can never be proved in the way that I cannot prove that there are no fairies at the bottom of my garden. I say two things: First, sustained observation over the past 20 years

has revealed no evidence of their presence; and, secondly, the existence of fairies in my garden or elsewhere is very unlikely on a priori grounds.[15] (© State of New South Wales through the Parliament of New South Wales)

Dr Phelps seems to be saying that we should embrace new technologies without first testing that they are safe. Do you think that gas companies should have to show that their operations are safe before approval is given to build a gas field where people live? Or do you think that the gas industry is entitled to the presumption of innocence, as if it's a defendant in a criminal trial, and it's up to the community to prove beyond all reasonable doubt that living in a gas field is dangerous?

Demonstrating the safety of the gas industry would once have been easy. Companies and regulatory authorities had only to collect baseline health and environmental data before drilling began, and compare this to data obtained after the gas fields were operating. And even if they failed to collect baseline data, they could have obtained evidence from any subsequent years to use for comparison. But they never did this. Consequently, they have no evidence that their operations are safe.

You Can't Prove It

There has been no baseline testing of health and the environment for Australia's currently operating gas fields. If there's no measure of conditions before drilling began, then regardless of how dirty and dangerous things become later on, the industry can deny responsibility and claim that there's no proof that people weren't as sick, or the countryside as polluted, before they turned up.

Some industry promoters use the lack of baseline data as a One Thought Solution to criticise scientists who argue that gas field pollutants pose a risk to health. The logic runs: scientists don't even have a baseline, so they can't prove anything, therefore gas fields are safe.

In areas such as Queensland's Darling Downs, the lack of baseline data insures companies against legal actions and provides a perverse incentive to pollute. With no baseline data and multiple companies mining in the same area, the risk of adverse litigation diminishes as the scale and complexity of the pollution increases.

Scientific proof is not what most people think it is. Philosophers of science understand that you can't even prove beyond all doubt that the sun will come up tomorrow morning. Sure, the sun has come up every morning for the past 5 billion years or so, and we have no reason to think it will do otherwise tomorrow. This gives us reasonable grounds for expecting the dawn to arrive as it always has, but it doesn't prove that it will.

The power of science doesn't stem from it yielding absolute truth, but rather that its claims are capable of being confirmed or disconfirmed. Scepticism, open-mindedness and a willingness to test ideas against reality are the hallmarks of good science.

I can't prove and I have no peer-reviewed research to show that the average daily dose of 3.8 tonnes of volatile organic compounds and 6.4 tonnes of particulates that the CSG industry vents into the air above the Darling Downs is a risk to children. But I have good reasons for thinking that it could be. What do you think? Does the lack of data that compares air quality and human health before and after drilling takes place, bolster or diminish your confidence that it's safe to raise children in gas fields?

I can't prove that smoking causes cancer. I can't even prove that jumping out of an aeroplane without a parachute will kill you: some have done so and survived. Nonetheless, I have good scientific reasons for believing that smoking tobacco, inhaling asbestos fibres and operating gas fields in populated areas are risky things to do.

When there's no baseline data, health scientists have to rely on epidemiological studies which look for statistical correlations between past exposures to something and subsequent harm. Such research is difficult and time-consuming. The Vietnam War ended in the mid-1970s, but the health problems of war veterans and their families were not scientifically studied until the 1990s. It takes time for epidemiological research to catch up.

Nonetheless, a rapidly growing body of research points to potentially serious health impacts from gas field pollutants, and major epidemiological studies are underway. Findings include a correlation between birth defects and how close the mother lived to a gas field during pregnancy, and a relationship between gas mining and hormone-disrupting chemicals in the Colorado River and aquifer systems used for human consumption.[16,17]

This is not the first time that dangerous industries have argued that a paucity of evidence means there is no risk. In the 20th century, the leaded petrol, asbestos and tobacco industries were well entrenched before the community woke up to the dangers associated with their products. Executives actively suppressed research as they touted their products as safe, well-regulated and good for the economy. They attacked scientists and lied repeatedly that there was no credible evidence that tobacco was harmful or addictive, or that breathing asbestos fibre causes cancer, or that ethyl lead accumulates in the bodies of children.

Profits reaped over decades by these industries have never been discounted to reflect the true costs of suffering, illness and death borne by the community. And today, the unconventional gas industry promotes itself without any evidence that it's safe and with no proper assessment of risks to people and the environment.

Misrepresenting Information

This thought experiment examines how the gas industry misrepresents information to suggest that gas mining is safe.

> Ask yourself how dangerous you feel it is to work in the petroleum industry, say in an oil refinery or a gas processing plant.
>
> Rate your feeling on an Emot-o-Meter where '-10' is 'very dangerous' and '+10' is 'very safe'. Record your rating.
>
> Now read on.

In a 2013 letter to the author, Metgasco CEO Mr Peter Henderson wrote, 'There are numerous studies available to show that CSG operations represent a low health risk to the community'. In the following passage, Mr Henderson suggested that the Australian Institute of Petroleum's (AIP) Health Watch program shows that the gas industry is safe.

'The people most exposed to petroleum are healthy. The people probably most exposed to hydrocarbon gases and liquids, including substances such as BTEX which are naturally found in crude oil, are those who work in oil refineries and conventional natural gas processing plants. The AIP Health Watch program, which has been in operation since 1980 and is run by Monash University, shows that workers in the petroleum and natural gas production industry have better health than the general Australian community and are less likely to die of the diseases commonly causing death – including cancer, heart and respiratory conditions.'

Now that you've read about the Health Watch program, make a second rating on the Emot-o-Meter of how dangerous you feel it is to work in the petroleum industry. Record your rating. Compare your two ratings.

Did your feeling about the safety of working in the petroleum industry change after you read what Mr Henderson had to say about the AIP Health Watch program? Did gas mining seem safer to you? If petroleum workers are healthier than the average Australian, doesn't that show that 'CSG operations represent a low health risk'?

The AIP's study did not find that working with oil and gas is good for your health. As the study's authors explained, the relatively better health statistics for industry workers compared to age-adjusted figures for the Australian population were due to 'selection bias': subjects in the study were healthier than the average from the start. Pre-employment health checks are mandatory in the petroleum industry, and subjects smoked less tobacco than the general population, hence the better health statistics. But what did the study actually find about the health impacts of working in the petroleum industry?

According to the 14th AIP Health Watch report, for male employees, 'Two cancers, mesothelioma and melanoma, have been and are still occurring at statistically significantly higher rates than in the general population'. Prostate cancer was 'also in statistically significant excess'. For women employees, the incidence of melanoma 'is slightly higher than in the general female population', as is the rate of lung cancer. And a case-controlled analysis provided 'strong evidence for an association between previous benzene exposure in the Australian petroleum industry and an increased risk of leukaemia'.

Let's revisit our earlier thought experiment.

With the new information you've just read, how safe do you now feel it would be to work in the petroleum industry?

Rate your feelings on an Emot-o-Meter where '-10' is 'very dangerous' and '+10' is 'very safe'. Record your rating. Compare it to your earlier responses.

Did the new information change the way you felt about working in the industry?

Mr Henderson also directed me to Australian Gaslight's (AGL) 'environmental health impact statement' (EHIS) which he said 'covers the full spread of potential health risks' and 'concludes that its proposed Camden Northern Expansion would have posed low and acceptable risks to community health and to air, groundwater and surface water'.

I read AGL's report and could find no evidence that CSG mining in Camden is safe. There was no data comparing health prior to and after establishing gas fields. In fact, there was no reference to any health data collected during 13 years of operations in Camden. As the authors explained, this was a 'desktop assessment', not a real-world study.

The AGL document noted that for many gas field pollutants only very limited information and no suitable human health guidelines are available. Beyond this lack of data, the exercise assumed that there are no cumulative or interactive effects from exposing people to mixes of dangerous substances.

Mr Henderson also cited the Queensland Government's 'coal seam gas health report', but again this contains no evidence that gas mining is safe. Although its data was too limited to establish a link between gas field pollutants and illness, the report does conclude that there was 'some evidence that might associate some of the residents' symptoms to exposures to airborne contaminants arising from CSG activities'.

Mr Henderson said he had other evidence that CSG mining is safe, but he would not provide chemical assays to support his claims that: there is no benzene in coal seams; CSG in the Northern Rivers is 'almost pure methane'; and that 'there is absolutely no reason for concern in terms of metals, volatile organics or BTEX chemicals'. Government ministers also ignored my requests that the assay data be made publicly available.

By comparison, AGL's EHIS stated that their gas contained above 'limit of reporting' (the arbitrary concentration deemed worthy of note) quantities of ethanol, dichloromethane, hexane, cyclohexane, heptane, styrene, benzene, toluene and ethylbenzene. Where Mr Henderson claimed that his CSG was 'about 98% methane', methane made up only 90% of the Camden gas. And contrary to Mr Henderson's claim that coal seams don't contain benzene, AGL's wastewater contained benzene at a level ten times greater than the drinking water standard. AGL attributed this to a CSIRO finding of 'the likely presence of low levels of BTEX in the target coal seam aquifer'.

In a 2013 letter to the author, Mr Henderson claimed that his company's untreated CSG wastewater was safe:

> A thorough analysis of our CSG produced water shows that it meets Australian Drinking Water Guidelines, apart from its salt levels, which are about 1/10 of the level in sea water. Bioassay (acute toxicity) testing has provided further and broader confirmation that the CSG water is not toxic. We have a range of studies to demonstrate that our water, after some salt removal, is suitable for irrigation. It is suitable for stock watering, even without salt removal.

If gas companies can eliminate concerns about health risks, CSG wastewater becomes a profitable product. It's a creative business plan: build gas fields, export the gas, and then sell the untreated waste water back to farmers who lost their bore water because of the gas mining.

Mr Henderson would not show me the wastewater analysis he referred to, so I again turned to AGL's report. AGL's wastewater in Camden contains arsenic, strontium, barium, nickel, lead, bromine, iodine, fluoride, methane, naphthalene, benzo(b)fluoranthene, benzo(a)pyrene, benzene and 'total petroleum hydrocarbons' (TPHs C_{10} to C_{36}) at levels which all exceed Australian drinking water guidelines.

Should such a product appear on your supermarket shelf, perhaps it would be a good idea to avoid GasCo's Mountain Mist Spring Water.

Let's look at some other deceptive One Thought Solutions involving water and gas mining, but this time the issue is whether gas mining is a threat to aquifers.

Ignoring Evidence

Some combine an allegation of lying with the false claim that there has been no case of aquifer contamination due to drilling chemicals. This is used to foster doubt about concerned citizens' integrity and to imply that gas mining is safe.

According to MP Dr Peter Phelps:

> This is the big lie which every one of them believes and which is propounded by the green movement time and again; that is, that there is aquifer cross-contamination. We have evidence to prove that that is a lie. We have had coal seam gas mining operations in Australia for 20 years and there is not one instance of proven aquifer cross-contamination ... That is hardly surprising when one looks at the structures used on boring operations. There is a steel pipe covered by concrete and then another steel pipe, which is a sure-fire way of avoiding cross-contamination.[18] (© State of New South Wales through the Parliament of New South Wales)

Dr Phelps' image of a steel pipe covered by concrete – in reality, cement – and then another steel pipe suggests a sense of security, but is it really adequate protection against cross-contamination?

Gas wells extend laterally beyond the sections of pipe joined together, and connections leak, steel rusts and cement crumbles. Some wells leak from the start. All wells fail eventually. And in the real world, things don't always go to plan.

The following Metgasco drilling notes from the NSW Department of Industry, Resources and Energy's Digital Imaging of Geological Systems (DIGS) website give us an insider's peek at what can happen when you try to seal the 'anulus', the ringlike space between pipe and rock, in a gas well.[19]

> Issue #14 – Riflebird E4 (Lost Circulation; Loss of integrity). Pumped 2200 litres of grout into annulus but did not get a return to surface; took another 3000 lt without any return to surface; another 400 l with swelling pellets; 'It is obvious we have very little if any grout seal around the casing'; grouted; added Tuff swell, bran etc; still no returns to surface; used 'lost circulation material'; pumped bentonite and shredded paper to penetrate cracks; gas metre went into alarm mode 'off scale'; hole spurting air and water; volumes of gas. (© State of New South Wales through the Parliament of New South Wales)

> Issue #15 – Riflebird E5 (Lost Circulation; Intercepted large water flows; Borehole collapse). Early problems with sand &

gravel; lost circulation completely @ 98–100m; losing drilling mud to the formation; broke suction due to mud pits collapsing and losing mud; The site is a mess. The mud pits are a mess. See what tomorrow brings. Caving clay & sand well collapsed ~96m; Large water flow 25 lt/sec @ 92m; unable to air drill; hole blockage@716 m. (© State of New South Wales through the Parliament of New South Wales)

In a 2015 email to the author, MP Mr Scot MacDonald also used the One Thought Solution that there is no evidence of aquifer contamination:

> I note one of the statements you have repeated refers to Aquifer interference and negative impact for farmers ... I have asked you for evidence, but none has been forthcoming. From a purely integrity point of view, at what point do you stop making claims that you can't verify? I wish I had your freedom to make baseless statements. Do (you) make a habit of this in your occupation? Your(s) in envy. Scot.

In reply, I asked Mr MacDonald, 'Are you not aware that the NSW EPA confirmed contamination of an aquifer by a faulty Santos holding pond? This was reported in both industry and public media'. In this incident, CSG waste water leaked through a torn plastic pond liner to contaminate a distant aquifer with high levels of lead, aluminium, arsenic, barium, boron and nickel, and uranium levels 20 times higher than safe drinking limits.

Mr MacDonald wrote back that he was aware of this incident; in fact, he was on the inquiry investigating the Pilliga aquifer contamination. Mr MacDonald said that I was 'correct to point this incident out'. But he added, 'You must also be fair and acknowledge the scale of the issue'. He noted, 'EPA fine of $1,500 reflecting the damage; no long-term impact; perched aquifer; not connected to systems used by people or industry'.

Not all politicians are as sanguine about the risk to aquifers as Dr Phelps and Mr MacDonald. In a 2012 letter to the author, Federal Senator Bill Heffernan wrote, 'I am most alarmed about the contamination of aquifers ...' And in 2015, MP Reverend Fred Nile stated in parliament that, 'Recently we have seen contaminated leaks from coal seam gas projects in the Pilliga State Forest and in Gloucester'. (© State of New South Wales through the Parliament of New South Wales) Rev Nile was referring to a January 2015 report that mono-ethanolamine borate, a fracking chemical, had been found in water samples near AGL's pilot CSG gas field at Gloucester.[20]

Economics of Gas Mining

Should proposed developments be evaluated solely on the basis of the money and jobs they create, or should costs and the common good be taken into account?

The One Thought Solution 'CSG brings jobs' is based on truth – the gas industry has employees – and the claim taps into people's desire to see their communities prosper. But this one carriage train of thought does not mean that it makes economic sense for gas companies to industrialise populated, productive areas of rural Australia.

The unconventional gas industry cannot be integrated into functioning regional economies. Turning rural landscapes into gas fields compromises established farming, tourism, forestry, fishing and rural residential industries. In areas like the Northern Rivers that trade on a reputation for exceptional environmental qualities and agriculture, gas mining would inflict considerable costs, including lowered land values. For farmers, their home and land is often their major asset and the legacy they leave their children. The gas field induced loss of land value represents a compulsory transfer of intergenerational wealth from farming families to mining companies.

Is increased economic activity necessarily a good thing? Burning a town to the ground would generate income for builders, brickies and Bunnings, and boost the 'gross national product' (the total market value of goods and services produced during a given period). But does that mean such an act would be in the community's interests?

Was it progress when gas industry activity brought Chinchilla on the Darling Downs its first brothel? If money's the only standard, such a development ticks all the boxes. The sex industry's been around even longer than fracking. Brothels are legal and well-regulated: a growth industry whose services are always in demand. And the benefits to the community go beyond taxes and rates, to training and employment for local women and men, and a flow-on economic benefit to local businesses.

Beyond such considerations, how is it that Australia will be the world's largest exporter of liquid natural gas when the gas industry in Queensland can't turn a profit or repay its billions of dollars of debt? Why were gas companies surprised by the low yields from Darling Downs' gas wells? Why did Martin Ferguson as minister negotiate tax deductions for gas companies that mean taxpayers will get little by way of royalties for decades to come? Why do Australians now have to pay record high prices for their gas? How are we to understand AGL's thinking that it makes economic sense to import gas from overseas for their domestic customers? It's difficult to characterise the psychological processes that led to this situation.

One Thought Solutions – 'We must join the gas revolution', 'China will drive our resources boom for 100 years', 'Gas royalties will bring prosperity for all' – justified the rapid development of the unconventional gas industry in Australia. The promise of profit and the image of wealth flowing from wells fostered great optimism and driving desire.

Can you think of any situation where it would be a good idea to go deeply into debt to invest in a business on the assumption that record high prices will last forever? It's risky business to bet heavily that any commodity will be worth as much next year when others are likely to cash in on unusually high prices.

The New York Times in 2011 quoted gas industry sources as saying 'shale plays are just giant Ponzi schemes' and 'this is an industry that is caught in the grip of magical thinking'.[21] In the same year, Don Voelte, then the chief executive officer of Australia's largest petroleum producer Woodside said, 'Come back and check four or five years from now ... I think one of the greatest things I will have achieved is not taking my company into coalbed methane'. When he checked in again in September 2014, Mr Voelte said, 'Queensland LNG doesn't add up'. He described the industry as 'a big bet' and a process 'with no pilot and no test'.[22]

The reasons for the gas industry boom and bust go beyond irrational exuberance, gambling and poor management. Rather, the fervour of gas industry proponents resembles a 'cargo cult'.

In the South Pacific during World War II, islanders saw the wealth – clothing, medicine, food and other goods – that aeroplanes delivered for the Japanese and American troops. The islanders based their One Thought Solution on an accurate observation: when the foreigners built runways and did certain things, treasures arrived from the sky.

So the islanders abandoned their gardens. Why work when cargo from the sky makes you rich? They set about building crude landing strips and planes made of straw. They paraded with rifle-shaped sticks, wore replicas of headphones carved from wood and made aeroplane noises. They lit fires to mark makeshift runways.

The Australian gas cultists didn't look to the sky for wealth because they knew the cargo comes from holes in the ground. Their belief was also based on a true enough observation: a lot of gas was issuing from wells in the United States. Their One Thought Solution saved them the work of building a genuinely safe and profitable business. Like the islanders, they could see the obvious but didn't understand what was really going on.

The gas cultists were willing to sacrifice their country's best agricultural land. Why farm when drilling for gas will make us rich, they reasoned. They set about building replicas of what they had seen overseas. They only needed one export facility in Gladstone Harbour, but they built three to be sure they'd get their share of the treasure. They drilled and drilled, built pipelines and factories, chanted magic mantras – 'We want CSG', 'Rivers of gold', 'Jobs, jobs, jobs' – and paraded around at conferences and on television. Politicians crafted word spell legislation. Then, as they waited for the cargo to arrive, gas and oil prices fell with increasing worldwide supply and diminishing demand, and the truth got out.

An Activist's Journey

> When our leaders fail us, ordinary people
> have to become heroes.
> Drew Hutton (1947–)

I think I understand how Spike Milligan felt when he titled his 1973 book *Hitler: My part in his downfall*. Like Spike, I want to talk about something of historical importance in which I played a very small part: the campaign to protect rural Australia from gas field industrialisation.

The Northern Rivers community responded to the gas field threat with creative problem-solving on a grand scale. Susan and I were privileged to witness some of the kaleidoscope of ideas, personalities and events that fired a great social and environmental movement. A full history is not for me to give. But for people looking to improve the way they take on challenges, the Gasfield Free campaign is a rich source of inspiration.

Susan and I scaled back my clinical practice and our farming operations and worked full-time getting information to the community and politicians. We hoped that once informed, those with the power to solve the problem would do so.

At the 2011 NSW parliamentary inquiry into CSG, I expressed my fears to a panel that included Dr Peter Phelps, Mr Scot MacDonald, Mr Rick Colless, Mr Jeremy Buckingham and others.

> I am deeply concerned that if this industry is allowed to permanently change the land and country life, then the result will be widespread emotional distress, social disruption and political turmoil ... There is great anxiety and fear in the community. If governments perpetuate the deliberate destruction of property, lifestyle and prospects for country Australians, many will become depressed, some will suicide, but some will respond with anger, revenge and violence ... I do not want to see what it is going to do to this community when we have scenes of elderly women being dragged away from bulldozers. (© State of New South Wales through the Parliament of New South Wales)

Queensland Premier Newman's ban on gas mining in the Scenic Rim, on the other side of the border from the Northern Rivers, was a reminder that a problem such as gas field industrialisation would ultimately be solved by a political decision. So in February 2012, Susan and I sent an open letter to NSW Premier Barry O'Farrell. The letter was endorsed by 24 organisations in the Northern Rivers, and read, in part, as follows:

> You and your government confront a dilemma. You must choose either the extreme, radical plan ... to turn the Northern Rivers into gas fields, or the conservative, responsible option, supported by the majority of citizens, of protecting this area's thriving rural communities and World Heritage natural environments.
>
> There is a rapidly growing, powerful, community-wide opposition that is determined to block CSG activities in the Northern Rivers. These citizens will not back away from their responsibility to protect the country they love. Their opposition is non-violent but non-negotiable. For the sake of their families, their country and their future, they will stop CSG in the Northern Rivers.

To tackle such a challenge, like so many others, we spent years attending meetings, making submissions, writing letters and going to actions. I ran resilience training workshops and prepared reports on gas field health impacts and other issues.

Along the way, I learned how some people use One Thought Solutions to manipulate others and obscure the truth. But shallow thinking can affect even well-meaning people.

Reluctant Health Professionals

It seemed important to bring health professionals up to speed regarding the potential impacts of exposure to gas field pollutants. So, in March 2012, all general medical practitioners and other Northern Rivers' health professionals were invited to a seminar on the health impacts of the CSG industry. Except for a medical specialist who was on the panel, not one medical practitioner turned up. A similar seminar on mental health impacts held later that year attracted a few psychologists, but again no medical practitioner.

To drum up support for baseline health testing of people at risk, I sent local health professionals a discussion paper on the need for a coordinated response to CSG-related health impacts, but there was no interest. An associate professor of psychology told me that collecting baseline data would be too time-consuming and expensive.

Blocked by my One Thought Solution that we needed medical professionals to respond to the looming health threat, I tried to live with doing nothing more. Months later, I realised that if medicos and academics weren't interested, then the community would have to protect itself. Those most at risk from having to live and raise families in gas fields needed information, and if no one else was going to do it for them, they would have to collect baseline data themselves.

A savvy medical practitioner agreed to co-author the literature review I was working on and to help prepare the self-administered symptom checklists. Unfortunately, our collaboration fell apart not long before the material was published. With a series of One Thought Solutions, a prominent professor of medicine pressured my intending co-author to drop out of the project.

As conveyed by my exiting colleague, the professor offered the following reasons why people should not receive my review and questionnaires.

The professor argued that medical practitioners have an ethical obligation to do no harm, and giving people information about symptoms of exposure to pollutants could harm through the 'nocebo effect'. This occurs when a person thinks they've been injured by something and feel ill even though they have not been exposed to anything dangerous.

There was truth in what the professor said: some people living in gas fields could falsely conclude that pollutants had harmed them. If I told people about the symptoms of exposure to pollution, some of them might think that they were sick for no real reason.

As laudable as it is, does a doctor's ethical obligation to do no harm justify a veto on informing people about risks and giving them the tools to protect themselves? If the principle of doing no harm is paramount, how could doctors warn patients about breast cancer symptoms when they know that some women will find a breast lump, be unnecessarily concerned and seek treatment for what is a benign symptom? How could people be educated about heart attacks when, for some, this advice will result in unnecessary distress and presentation to a doctor for indigestion or anxiety?

How could you protect yourself and your family if you don't know that something is potentially harmful, don't know what symptoms to look for, and can't identify dangerous situations? If you don't know that the fibro you're breaking up contains asbestos, you'll have no idea that you're being injured. And if you develop lung cancer years later, you won't know why this has happened to you.

The professor's next One Thought Solution was that my health questionnaires would encourage people to waste doctors' time. Again, there was some truth to that. But is it really a waste of time for a doctor to deal with an anxious patient's concerns, even when it turns out that they have not had a heart attack or stroke, do not have breast cancer, or have not been injured by gas field pollutants?

Some level of false alarms is an indication that a health advertising campaign is working. Unnecessary presentations could be considered an acceptable cost of raising awareness about important medical problems.

The professor also argued that my report and questionnaires would violate research ethics. If researchers conducted a study in these areas, their data would be contaminated. Again, there was some truth to that: research is always best done with naïve subjects. It's not right for an academic to violate research ethics, but in this case, the ethical concerns went beyond the interests of researchers.

That's why a clinical psychologist, rather than a medical practitioner, authored a review of the literature on gas field health impacts.

A Community Protects Itself

During the Gasfield Free campaign, there was always an urgent need to write to some politician, authority or inquiry. The Northern Rivers community generated thousands of letters and submissions: a prodigious intellectual effort that diverted untold hours from farms and businesses. Any accounting for the work, donations and lost productivity that citizens put into tackling this challenge would run to many millions of dollars. But the effort was worth it.

It became clear early on that no matter how well written, no submission, petition, letter or email was going to change the government's support for gas field industrialisation of rural areas. In the 1960s, the philosopher Herbert Marcuse argued that in a democracy political activities such as writing submissions and signing petitions can function as 'repressive tolerance' because they divert energy away from effective actions. This was not the case with the Gasfield Free campaign.

As people researched the issue, the community educated itself, not just about the gas mining threat, but about the impacts of vested interests on parliamentary democracy and the potential of ordinary people to make things right.

The truth was out and spreading fast. The people discovered what the gas miners were up to, and they were not going to stand by and watch. They knew what they had to do, and they set about doing it.

Protectors, not Protesters

Pro-gas politicians stereotype 'protectors', those activist citizens opposed to harmful developments, as extremists and radicals, but they have no idea who they are really up against.

Known by the moniker 'GAG', Groups Against Gas formed across the region. The Keerrong Gas Squad, Kyogle GAG, Lock the Gate Northern Rivers Regional Alliance, Rock Valley Gas Rangers, Richmond Valley GAG, Lismore GAG and the Gasfield Free Ballina Shire Group, allied with pre-existing organisations such as the Northern Rivers Guardians and Neighbourhood Environment Centres. Meetings brought together people of diverse political, religious and cultural backgrounds, united in opposing invasive gas development. Groups set about making banners, printing T-shirts and raising funds.

The campaign took to the streets. 3,000 people marched against CSG in Murwillumbah, 750 in Kyogle, and thousands participated in anti-CSG marches in Lismore, Sydney and elsewhere.

The Gasfield Free movement was soon the largest, and probably the most motivated, organisation in the Northern Rivers. Activated citizens envisaged what success would look like and worked to make their vision come true. Those with business acumen helped investors, shareholders, banks and the Australian Stock Exchange understand the risks inherent in forcing the gas industry onto a resistant community. A media group issued press releases, gave interviews and responded to news. Legal practitioners offered advice, planned legal actions and represented people who were arrested. A regional alliance of GAG groups coordinated actions and set up networks and support services for protectors.

Workshops across the region trained people in 'non-violent direct action' as practised by Mahatma Gandhi and Dr Martin Luther King. They emphasised that the local police were neighbours, caught up in a problem that threatened everyone. A senior officer told me that many local police supported the campaign.

Documentary makers recorded history and created moving images to inspire. Musicians and singers showed up to lift spirits. I'll never forget hearing a choir sing as a bulldozer worked high above them on the wall of a CSG wastewater dam, or being at Don's Party at Doubtful Creek where music beamed across the valley to a drill rig working in the dark of an approaching storm. We laughed along as *CSG the Musical* reworked *Oklahoma* into a choral dancing story of community resistance.

The Knitting Nannas Against Gas (KNAG) knitted and purled and inspired their global audience of fans as they took care of protectors, prodded politicians and stitched up the front lines. The Nannas' creative use of humour, imagery and message has redefined environmental activism. And the Girls Against Gas with their black leotards and golden-yellow capes radiated youth, smiles and love in some dark and difficult times.

Practical People Power

Electronic webs bind our world, streaming information everywhere; for entertainment and gossip, we now turn to video rather than the village. Gas company advertising projected an image of power, but in February 2012 the Gasfield Free Communities campaign hit back.

At country hall meetings across the region, citizens voted on whether they wanted gas fields on their roads. Volunteers followed up to survey every household in the district. These community surveys broke down the isolation of neighbours. It took courage for the mostly female surveyors to go door-to-door, but as they went their confidence grew. It seemed remarkable at first, but then it became obvious and inevitable. The vast majority of people in the Northern Rivers did not want to live in gas fields. Only a few were for the industry. The pro-gas advertising had failed. Celebrations across the region proclaimed Gasfield Free Communities determined to protect themselves.

An Electoral Commission poll conducted during Lismore's local government elections in 2012 found 86.9% against CSG and only a tiny minority in favour. Polls held on federal election day 2013 confirmed the king tide of anti-CSG sentiment in Lismore and Casino. The opposition was not confined to the Northern Rivers. A 2015 Fairfax Media/Nielsen poll found that in NSW 75% of Coalition voters and 73% of Labor voters opposed coal seam gas exploration on agricultural land.

The gas miners were losing, and the time came when the industry's advertising only worked against them.

Democracy's Pointy End

Local actions to block gas mining began in March 2012 at Kerry, near Beaudesert on the Queensland side of the Border Ranges. Three months later, protectors blockaded Metgasco's Shannonbrook CSG waste water site for a week. In November 2012, with the Knitting Nannas in attendance, locals and supporters from the Glenugie and Pillar Valley communities blockaded a drilling site near Grafton.

2012 ended with a meeting in the Lismore Town Hall arranged by local MP Thomas George and attended by NSW Government Minister Mr Brad Hazzard and a party of officials. The audience of 1,000 locals made clear their dissatisfaction with the Government's CSG policy.

The year 2013 began violently. In January, riot police arrested 18 protectors at the Glenugie blockade. A 65-year-old grandmother told me how her legs went like jelly as a riot police officer manhandled her. She was singing 'Advance Australia Fair', the officer thought she was resisting, so he threw her to the ground and held her there with his knee in her back. Weeks later her shoulder and arm were still raw.

In my practice, I have treated many members of the police and military services. These dedicated personnel deserve respect for the work they do. But when politicians order specialist police forces to act in the interests of mining companies and harshly subdue peaceable citizens, both the officers and the community pay a high price.

There are two general forms of illegal activity associated with the unconventional gas industry.

On one hand, there are people such as Wallaby rugby union international David Pocock and his wife, and hundreds of others, who put themselves at risk and are arrested for 'locking on' (fixing oneself to equipment) to impede mining operations. Such actions break the law but are not criminal in intent. The protectors act in public and do not conceal their lawbreaking or try to avoid arrest. They accept the consequences of their actions. They do not profit from breaking the law, and they pay a high personal price for their stand.

On the other hand, gas companies act with criminal intent when they do things such as illegally dumping wastewater into sewerage treatment plants and rivers. They hide what they have done, and if they're found out, the companies deny responsibility and seek to minimise their crime. They perpetrate illegal acts for profit with no regard for the potential harm to others or the environment.

The ethical issues cannot be reduced to a One Thought Solution prohibition on all acts that break the law. What should responsible citizens do when governments enact unjust laws that disadvantage the community in favour of vested interests? Is complying with an unjust law ethical behaviour or complicity in a wrong? Would it have been right to support the gaoling of civil rights workers who protested against segregation in the US South during the 1960s? Was it ethical to support South Africa's apartheid laws? Were Germans morally obliged to comply with Hitler's laws to report Jews to the SS?

The Christian ethic of nonviolence championed by Dr Martin Luther King during the 1960s US civil rights movement serves an important function in modern democracies. The principled behaviour of protectors in situations of extreme provocation sets an example that works to diffuse underlying anger which could spill over into violence.

During the Glenugie action, police arrested 28 people, Metgasco drilled its well, but resistance grew. When the drill rig arrived at Doubtful Creek near Kyogle, a few hundred protectors delayed the company's entry and a near two-month campaign began.

It takes a large crew to maintain an extended action. Someone has to liaise with police, talk to media, counsel distressed people, shovel gravel on muddy roads, run the camp kitchen, haul drinking water, maintain toilets and sanitation, direct traffic and parking, ensure safety and support arrested people. But perhaps the most demanding role is that of the 'Simmo' or 'bunny'.

Everyone who locks on is Simmo. They're also known as bunnies because they lock on without knowing how to get free. Their ignorance is essential because if police suspect that Simmo knows where the key is, the officers can use pressure points or capsicum spray to force compliance. When police realise that Simmo really doesn't know how to unlock the device, they usually don't inflict pain.

In March of 2013, the police had a tough time getting the miner's trucks back out of the Doubtful Creek drilling site. Soon after, Metgasco suspended drilling activity when NSW Premier Barry O'Farrell announced a two-kilometre coal seam gas exclusion zone around residential areas.

The story gets murky from here. No one's sure why events panned out as they did. Some say it was an act of arrogant stupidity. Others believe it was a clever, even brilliant plan that went wrong. Some think they can detect the shadow of an embedded deep undercover activist. After all, they ask, who did most to unite the Northern Rivers and foster one of the greatest social and environmental movements in Australia's history?

Metgasco's 2014 plan to drill for gas in a sandstone layer two kilometres below Bentley seemed smart because the problematic CSG exclusion zone didn't apply to tight sands wells. But, as Sir Humphrey would say, the idea was 'courageous' – they would be drilling in the very heart of the Northern Rivers. A history-making showdown was on the way.

The 'Bentley blockade' drew thousands to the campaign and created memories to last lifetimes. I want to share a couple with you.

During a shift as a lock-on buddy at Bentley, my job was to keep a lookout. I struck up a conversation with a young woman who was ready, if need be, to lock on. She was afraid and worried about what the police could do to her. She had never been involved with anything like this before, but she felt compelled to do what she could to end the gas field threat. We talked about her sadness for the children who lived in Queensland's Darling Downs. She was a brave young protector: the kind of person this world will need aplenty to solve the big challenges ahead.

Bravery is not the absence of fear, but rather doing what is right regardless of how you feel. At Bentley, the hundreds prepared to lock on included an Anglican minister, indigenous elders, farmers and adults of every age and from every walk of life and political persuasion. These were the Northern Rivers' protectors – the people who would not let the miners pass.

In April 2014, an alert called people to Bentley to confront an expected 800 to 900 riot police. As Susan and I drove up the hill in the dark, we came upon thousands of people gathered at the blockade to greet the dawn. They were smiling and singing and getting ready for whatever was coming their way that day.

The police riot squad did not show on that day or on any other day. Senior police had earlier visited the Bentley site, and in a 5 May 2014 briefing to the minister, Assistant Commissioner Jeff Loy reported that police had never before seen 'the sophistication of strategies' employed by protectors. He described the situation as an 'unprecedented public order challenge' with a 'high to extreme' 'risk to public and police safety'. Assistant Commissioner Loy said that the 'community groundswell of support' was 'strong and becoming stronger every day', with 'open support' from neighbouring local government mayors. (© State of New South Wales through the Parliament of New South Wales)

Final Dawn at the Bentley Blockade
(Photo courtesy of R J Poole, www.rjpoole.com)

The NSW Government suspended Metgasco's drilling approval and court cases followed. At the March 2015 NSW state elections, all four previously safe National Party seats on the North Coast became marginal, and for the first time Ballina fell to the Greens. In November 2015, Metgasco agreed to give up their licences for a $25,000,000 settlement.

Since then, the NSW Government has introduced a draconian maximum seven-year gaol sentence and huge fines for locking on at gas mining sites. At the same time, they reduced to trivial levels penalties for gas company breaches of the law.

In August 2016, the Victorian government announced a permanent ban on unconventional gas in the state. The government said that they took this action to 'protect our farmers and preserve Victoria's reputation as a world-leading producer of clean, green, high-quality food'. They concluded that 'the risks and lack of community support outweigh the benefits for Victoria'.

In 2016, Richard Deem published *Gasfield Free NSW Northern Rivers* and Brendan Shoebridge's movie *The Bentley Effect* told how the Northern Rivers resisted the gas industry.[23,24]

Postscript – June 2019

It's five years since the Bentley Blockade, but few are celebrating – worldwide, these are the hottest years on record. Catastrophe looms as governments deal and citizens dream of rescue.

In 2019 the UN-sanctioned Permanent Peoples' Tribunal (PPT) found that the 'mega corporations' of the unconventional gas industry have gone beyond 'regulatory capture' to 'state capture' and created a 'new form of sovereignty' that 'does not derive from the people' or serve the interests of citizens and nature.[25]

Not all Australian governments are captured. The miners rule Queensland. In 2019 the Northern Territory (NT) was opened to fracking. Western Australia and South Australia banned fracking in some areas, while Tasmania's ban runs until 2025. In NSW no new licenses have been issued and a decision on Santos' Narrabri project is due soon. In 2019, a NSW gas import terminal was approved and the Deputy Premier said that imported gas is cheaper than CSG. In 2017 Victoria reinforced its permanent ban. In May 2019, the federal election pitted a coal-spruiking Liberal/National Coalition against a Labor Party that proposed a $1.5 billion subsidy to help develop massive new gas fields in the NT and Queensland. The Labor politicians knew what they were doing.

In 2018 I responded to two cases of ignorance in people who should have known better.

In June 2018, Mr Mark Butler, then Federal Labor's spokesperson on energy and climate change, told me that he didn't know about landscape-scale methane emissions from gas fields. I sent Mr Butler the relevant research. I don't know how Mr Butler reconciles knowing about methane emissions with his policy of subsidising new gas fields. The second case of ignorance was more unexpected.

In January 2018, I sent an open letter to Dr Alan Finkel, Australia's Chief Scientist. Speaking on the radio, Dr Finkel broke from urging scientists to read more science-fiction to offer some fictional science of his own. He said that citizens' concerns about 'fugitive emissions or contamination of aquifers' were examples of 'wiki net', anti-scientific thinking that was 'rampant through many communities' even though 'there's actually no data to support those concerns'. Dr Finkel didn't reply to my letter or the research I sent.

The PPT says that the gas industry is waging a 'silent war' 'directed at Mother Earth' and people are 'collateral damage'.[25] A key strategy in this war is the intentional ignoring by government inquiries of massive air pollution from CSG processing.

Exposure to air pollution causes increased rates of birth defects, autism, low intelligence, cancer, stroke, dementia, autoimmune disease, and much more.[26] We've known for a decade that expectant mothers living in areas of higher air pollution in Brisbane have smaller foetuses.[27] Brisbane isn't heavily polluted and the air looks clear. Pity families who raise children in Darling Downs gas fields.

In 2018, Dr Geralyn McCarron found that from 2007 to 2014 annual admissions to Darling Downs hospitals increased 133% for circulatory and 142% for respiratory symptoms. Across the same period there was a huge increase in annual CSG air pollution: nitrogen oxides up 489% to 10,048 tonnes, carbon monoxide 800% to 6,800 tonnes, PM10 particulates 6,000% to 1,926 tonnes, and more.[28] The risks from such pollution cannot be 'managed'.

For the PPT, 'the future of the planet' depends on the 'mass movement of the people in the streets'.[25] But a new Bentley Blockade is unlikely: anti-Protector laws are severe, pro-gas forces are organised and we can't recreate the circumstances that led to success.

That, Dear Reader, sets up our greatest challenge. How do we counter the casual cruelty, intentional ignorance and amoral bastardry of those who put personal greed above the common good?

Part 2

Using the Deep Mind

Chapter 5

The Key Mental Processes

> Knowing others is intelligence;
> knowing yourself is true wisdom.
>
> Lao Tzu (Circa 5th century BC)

THE THREE BIG CHALLENGES in Susan's and my life seem different, but they share instructive common features. They all took years to resolve. Shallow thinking contributed to each problem and One Thought Solutions acted as spells, inducing trances that impeded deeper thinking and creative problem-solving. In each case, solutions became possible as we understood the nature of the problem and enlisted the deep mind to work out what we could do.

Our genetic inheritance gives us humans the capacity to respond flexibly and intelligently. Even rigid, biologically based One Thought Solutions such as phobia and posttraumatic stress disorder yield to new information, training and a resolve to do things differently. With right knowledge and technique, we can successfully tackle life's challenges.

From here, our focus is on the workings of the human mind. We look at how our mental processes operate and how we can use them to go beyond shallow thought to the deep mind.

The Problem-Solving Mind

What mental abilities do all warm-blooded vertebrates need to survive and successfully take on the challenges of life?

Imagine that we're building a basic plan for all mammalian and avian minds: a layout that describes the essential mental machinery that a hare, a heron and a human all need to solve problems. I'll name our generic creature 'bob creadur', from the Welsh for 'all creatures', but I'll refer to her as 'Bob'.

Bob is going nowhere if she can't perceive the world around her and the sensations that come from within. Being able to see, hear, smell, taste and touch, connects Bob to the outside reality. Sensations of balance and movement enable her to orient and get around. Bob has to feel hungry and thirsty and short of breath at the right times, be able to satisfy these needs, and know when she's had enough.

No creature gets far if it can't learn from things that happen to it and recall what it has learned. Bob has to remember not just events from the past, but also the facts, skills and lessons she picked up along the way. Bob also has to imagine the future. Her prospects dim if she can't plan ahead or anticipate what could happen if she goes into the cave that looks like the one where her mother disappeared years ago.

Bob needs a store of beliefs and functional understandings about herself, others and the world. This knowledge, built from life's lessons, helps Bob to make sense of her surrounds and respond appropriately.

Bob lives with others, so she has to be able to communicate, be it by speaking, squeaking, singing or some ritual involving feathers. Bob has to get on socially, at least well enough to find food and to reproduce. She has to sense and manage her feelings of friendliness, empathy and belonging.

But it's a battle out there, what with surviving 'Nature, red in tooth and claw' and passing on one's genes and all, so Bob has to sense and react appropriately to negative as well as positive emotions. She has to feel the anxiety and fear that signal danger. She also needs to identify and deal with the actions of others that indicate aggression and dominance.

Bob cannot attend to everything at once, so she needs unconscious mental processes to take care of many things automatically. A well-tuned intuition alerts her to important matters that are not immediately apparent. When Bob sleeps, dreams consolidate recent things she's learned and work through unfinished emotional business.

That's about it. Those are the basic mental processes that warm-blooded creatures need to meet the challenges of life: perception, memory, imagination, beliefs, language, emotions, intuition, sleep and dreams.

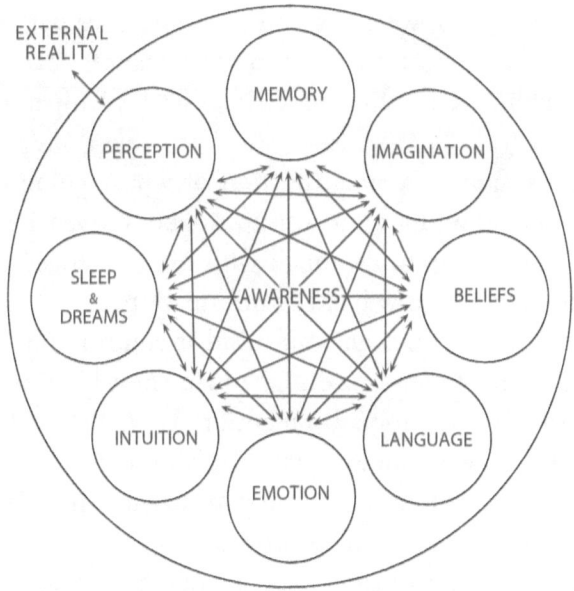

Awareness and the Key Mental Processes

There are refinements and add-ons, especially when it comes to *Homo sapiens*, but our generic plan for Bob's mind lays out the Key Mental Processes for problem-solving.

Why 'key'? Because understanding and knowing how to use these processes unlocks the power of the creative deep mind.

Awareness

We'll begin with awareness, the familiar but mysterious ability that dominates our lives.

When awake, we are aware of whatever we attend to at any moment. But conscious awareness is limited in capacity, and its focus is narrow.[1]

Awareness appears seamless to us, but it arises from diverse mental operations which we're largely unaware of. Just as we can enjoy an orchestra's music without knowing about the instruments that create the sound, we can savour an experience without knowing how our mind creates it. But to break trances that bind us to shallow thought, we need to understand what's happening behind the show.

We only attend to a small portion of what's going on in our minds and bodies and around us: up to about seven items at any time. We're not going to do much with big challenges if we limit ourselves to such a narrow band of information.

Notice what goes through your mind as you read on.

Are you aware of your breathing? You are now because I brought breathing to your attention by mentioning it. Before I did that, you were breathing, as indeed you were automatically monitoring all your bodily sensations, adjusting your balance and posture, and controlling your physiological processes.

Let's add more information about your breathing. Notice the way your body likes to breathe. Each time you inhale, bring in a good feeling. And as you breathe out, let go of any tension in your muscles. Bring in a good feeling. Relax with each out breath.

Now notice the sensations in your left leg. Focus on the back of your knee. Attend to the feeling of pressure. Is your skin touching clothing, or perhaps a chair, or maybe you can feel the air?

Are you still aware of your breathing? I know you are now because I just mentioned your breathing again. But before I did that, were you still aware of your breathing while you were attending to the sensations in your leg?

Awareness is not like daylight that illuminates everywhere. It's more akin to a spotlight that we shine on this or that, pointing it at things we're interested in. But the beam of light is only so wide. When we aim it at something new, what we were previously looking at recedes into shadow.

Awareness runs on automatic, but we can direct it with fine precision, as can others. Consider how my written words steer your focus. And what you are aware of depends on much more than where you or I point your attention.

Behind the Scene

Awareness arises from the simultaneous interaction of all our Key Mental Processes operating at high speed and out of sight. In real time, the distinctions between mental operations disappear as they synchronise. The process is complex and subtle, even when we do something as simple as understanding a single word.

What goes on in your mind as you read the word 'regret'?

You know what 'regret' means because you have a definition of the word stored in the internal mental dictionary you built up as you learned to speak. But the word has more than just a literal meaning attached to it.

When a word flashes by it is embedded in the context of a sentence, a paragraph, a book and your past experience. If you take the time to notice, hearing or reading the single word 'regret' might bring to mind sad feelings, poignant memories, a resolve to do better, or beliefs about what kind of person you are and the fairness of life. In real time, we process such information automatically as we hear and read words. This is mundane, the kind of mental activity we perform effortlessly at an unconscious level all the time.

When we take on big challenges and problems we need to process prodigious amounts of information. To do this we have to go beyond shallow thinking and One Thought Solutions to a deeper level.

The human mind is a wondrous system, but it's too fast and fluid to get a handle on while it's in full flight. I will slow things down and artificially separate the Key Mental Processes so we can look at them one at a time. But remember, there is no distinct separation between perception, memory, imagination, belief, language, emotions, intuition, and sleep and dreaming. Throughout our lives these processes act as one to create our reality.

Later on, we will bring all that you learn about the Key Mental Processes back together again so you can practice working with your unified deep mind.

Chapter 6

Perception:
Where mind meets the world

> If the doors of perception were cleansed every thing would appear to man as it is, Infinite. For man has closed himself up, till he sees all things thro' narrow chinks of his cavern.
>
> William Blake (1757–1827)

IT SEEMS SIMPLE ENOUGH – our vision works like a camera, what we see is real, and things are pretty much as we perceive them. We interact effectively with our environment, so reality must be orderly and predictable. But are things as straightforward as they seem?

The Key Mental Process of perception connects us to reality. Our senses of sight, hearing, touch, taste, smell and proprioception (sense of bodily position, location, orientation and movement) let us know what's happening now, in the present.

According to Einstein and the theories of physics, the arrow of time moves only in one direction, from the past to the future; you can't put Humpty Dumpty back together again. English speakers read words from left to right, so if I depict the relationship between past, present and future by drawing a straight line on this page, it seems natural to put 'present' about the centre of the line, with 'past' to the left and 'future' to the right.

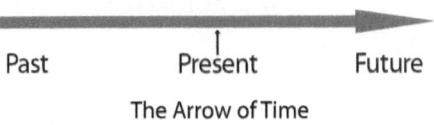

Past   Present   Future

The Arrow of Time

What exactly do we mean by 'now'? How long does the present last? Put another way, when does the present become the past and the future become the now?

The closer you look at the present, the briefer and briefer it becomes until it seems to disappear altogether. No matter how refined our sense of mindfulness, it's as if the present is an infinitely brief moment that's forever receding into the past, and we are moving into the future at the speed of time, whatever that is. No matter how quickly our neural networks process information, we can only ever be aware of a representation of what just was, not what actually is at that moment.

Perception becomes even more mysterious if things don't go as expected. That's when we get clues to how our mind works. Psychologists learn much about normal functioning by studying the effects of brain injuries. You're more likely to learn how an engine works when your car breaks down than when it's running well. When our senses deceive us with perceptual illusions, we can gain a deeper understanding of how our minds and reality interact.

In this graphic, how do the long diagonal lines look to you?

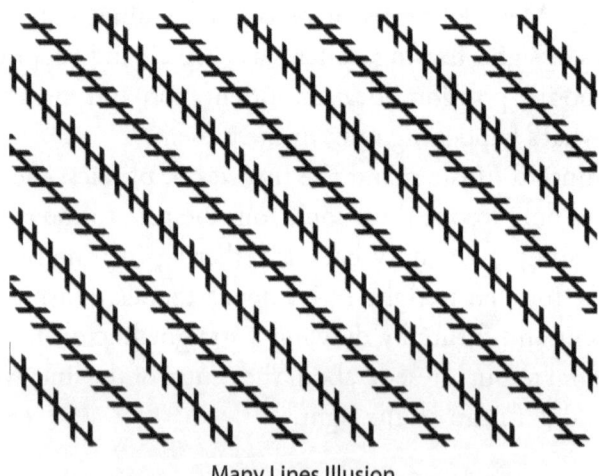

Many Lines Illusion

Check with a ruler and you can see that the long lines are parallel and straight. Knowing this does not change how they look to me. It doesn't matter what I know to be true; the lines appear wavy and nonparallel. But a friend of mine sees it differently. For her, the lines look straight but not parallel.

The next illusion seems to say something about the way that context distorts how we judge obstacles. In this graphic, the logs across the road are the same length. Now that you know that, can you make the logs look the same length?

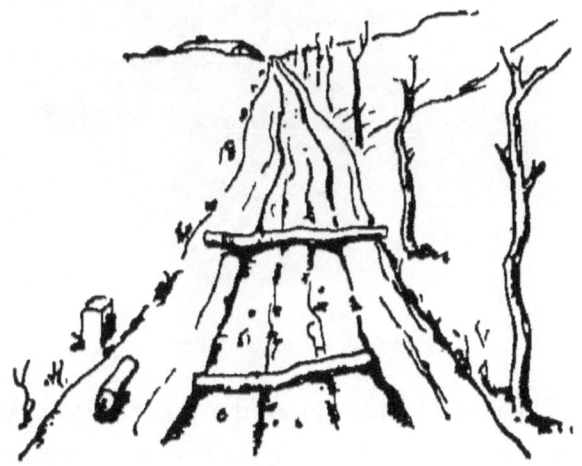

Logs on Road Illusion

The two long lines in the following illusion are the same length.

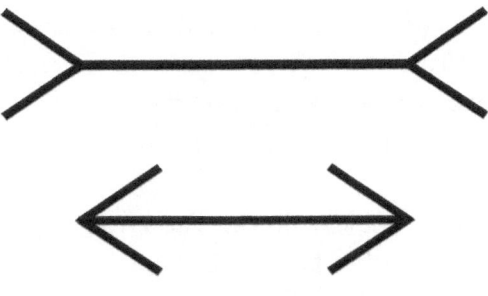

Mueller-Lyer Illusion

Knowing that the lines are the same length makes no difference to how they appear to me. I can only see the top line as longer than the bottom line.

In the next illusion from Professor Edward Adelson, the squares on the chequerboard marked A and B are exactly the same shade and colour.

Adelson's Shadow Illusion

Check. Do what I did. Cover the other squares with your fingers, or cut holes in a piece of paper, so you only see the two squares labelled A and B.

What are we to make of these and other optical illusions? These are no mere tricks. They're clues to the way our minds work.

There's no deception or sleight of hand involved, no magician's misdirection of attention at a crucial moment, or clever use of mirrors. It doesn't matter what we know beforehand or how long and intensely we stare, we just can't see the truth that's in front of us.

So where's the illusion? Where does the mistake in perception occur?

Let's break the problem down. The error of perception takes place either outside or inside us: there's nowhere else it can be. The lines, logs and squares look like they're on the page out there, but the illusion can't be in the figure itself. We know that the lines are straight, the logs are equal in length and the squares are the same colour. Nor can the illusions be occurring in the space between us and the picture. There's no force that bends the light as it travels through the air from the figures to our eyes.

We have to conclude that the illusion is somehow taking place inside us, in our minds. But how can that be? How can the illusion be in our minds when we plainly see it over there? So where and how are the illusions created?

Let's begin at the boundary where we end and the external environment begins: the two-dimensional sensory systems that connect us to the three-dimensional world around us.

When photons, the massless elementary particles that make up electromagnetic radiation, vibrate with a frequency that human eyes can detect, they pass through the lens and fall in an upside down pattern onto the back of the eye. They land on the retina, a flat sheet of light-sensitive cells, and the optic nerve registers them as a hit. This is the essential interface. Our mind constructs everything we see from this two-dimensional pattern of photons striking a thin layer of cells at the back of our eyeballs.

It's a similar story for all our senses. Our mind builds what we hear from two-dimensional patterns of vibrating air particles that hit our eardrums. A sensitive arrangement of tiny bones behind the eardrum transmits the impact to the auditory nerve. Sensations of taste and smell arise from cells in the nose and on the tongue that register contacts with substances. But illusions are not in the pattern of photons, air particles or chemicals that stimulate our senses – they are generated in our minds.

Consider a pencil that you hold in your hand. If you look at the pencil and rotate it every which way, the pattern of photons striking the back of your eyes changes constantly, but you always see a pencil. From an infinite number of possibilities, your mind makes an informed guess of what the pattern of photons hitting the back of your eye represents and that choice is what you perceive as being out there. When your mind decides wrongly, you experience an illusion.

Determining the colour of things has been important for human survival, and our perceptual system evolved to detect differences in a world that has lots of shadows. In the chequerboard illusion, the task for our mind is to determine the colour of the squares, but that decision can't be based solely on the actual light that's reflected off the chequerboard.

In the real world, shadows vary the intensity of light coming from a particular colour. To cope with this, our mind has evolved strategies to identify and compensate for the effects of shadows. And that explains the chequerboard illusion. Our mind expects a regular pattern of squares, takes the shadow into account, and makes a sophisticated decision about what the pattern of photons means. It's the mind's best guess that we perceive to be differently coloured squares on the chequerboard.

It follows that there are as many versions of what's out there as there are nervous systems to perceive them. Many creatures have visual systems that register frequencies of infrared and ultraviolet light and bass and treble ranges of sound that are beyond our sensory capabilities. For instance, bees can see blue, green and ultraviolet light, but not red. Birds can perceive the spectrum from red through to violet, and some can see ultraviolet. Birds can also distinguish subtle differences between shades of colour that humans can not see. Like many insects, the housefly's vision is good at detecting movement, but not stationary detail. It's almost impossible to swat a fly with your open hand, but move very slowly and you can grab the fly.

I can see the colour red and my horse can't. Birds and bees can see ultraviolet light, but I can't. Does that mean that I have a more advanced ability to see what's really there than my horse, but an inferior ability to bees and birds, or are we all creating different realities?

PERCEPTION: WHERE MIND MEETS THE WORLD

Wayne, Katie and Rainbow

Rainbows are real. How else could one be captured in the above photograph? You won't find the pot of gold at rainbow's end because as you walk, the rainbow moves. So the rainbow's position is somehow connected to where you are. If a rainbow moves for everyone, where is the rainbow?

Rainbows come into being when light separates into different frequencies as it passes through droplets of water in the air and then strikes our eyes. Photons have no colour. Colour only comes into existence when photons of a particular frequency contact a sensory system that interprets them as a colour and then projects the image so it appears to be out there. When you look at the above photo, your mind interprets the light coming off the page as an image of me, my dog and a rainbow.

Colour, like beauty and all other sensory qualities, is not so much in the eye but in the mind that evolution bestowed on the beholder. And what we perceive is directly affected by our expectations. Sometimes, what someone tells us determines what we see.

You might have seen this drawing of a duck.

Duck Illusion

Can you also see the rabbit?

Now that you know it can be both, can you make the picture switch between the duck and the rabbit? I see the rabbit when I think that the animal is facing to the right, and the duck appears when I assume the animal is facing to the left. It's harder, and might be impossible, to see the two animals simultaneously.

Can you see the elegant young woman in the following drawing?

Young Woman Illusion

Can you also make out the very old woman? Again, it's easy to see each woman in turn, but not both at the same time. Perception tends to be an all or nothing affair.

Like seeing a glass as half empty or half full, what seems obvious might just reflect the beliefs we hold and the way we use our mental abilities. Some see nothing but bad news and portents of catastrophe, while others, with exactly the same information, see grounds for hope and green shoots of promise everywhere.

Before we move to memory and imagination, the Key Mental Processes which inform us about the past and the future, I should give you my answer to the earlier question about what the study of perception tells us about the nature of 'now'.

The present is like a rainbow. You'll never be able to find where it begins or ends because you can't think of it that way. Rainbows and the present exist, but only when there's a mind to create them.

Chapter 7

Memory and Imagination: Visions of past and future

> Remembrance of things past is not necessarily the remembrance of things as they were.
>
> Marcel Proust (1871–1922)

> The world of reality has its limits; the world of imagination is boundless.
>
> Jean-Jacques Rousseau (1712–1778)

MEMORY RE-CREATES THE PAST, but with our imaginations, we can conjure up events that never were, things that can never be, and possibilities that are yet to arrive. With memory and imagination, we can learn from the past and craft the future.

Picture in your mind's eye a unicorn with black-and-white zebra stripes wearing a bejewelled tiara. You know you're indulging in an act of creation as your mind effortlessly draws on concepts of 'zebra stripes', 'unicorn', 'jewels' and 'tiara' to form what you imagine. But it's less obvious that when you remember something, you're actively generating what comes to mind.

Our mind builds images of the past from stored mental traces of experience. Memory is not like a library of pictures, videos and stories that accurately record what happened. Rather, recollections are reconstructions, not factual replays.[1] And sometimes, all it takes is a single word, picture or story to create a memory of something that never happened.

Psychologists showed people a video of a traffic accident and asked them one of two versions of a question about what they'd seen.[2] The researchers asked one group, 'About how fast were the cars going when they hit each other?' The others heard exactly the same question except that the word 'hit' was replaced with 'smashed into'. There was no broken glass in the video, but a week later when they were asked, 'Did you see any broken glass?' the people who originally heard the word 'smashed' were twice as likely to remember seeing broken glass as those who heard the word 'hit'. For them, the words 'smashed into' created a false eyewitness memory of broken glass. Hearing a story can also create a false memory.

Using what is known as the 'lost-in-the-mall' technique, psychologists gave subjects a booklet containing four short stories about events from their childhoods.[3] Each subject's family prepared the stories, but one of the accounts was a fake. The researchers inserted a fictitious story about how, when they were five years old, the subject was lost in a shopping mall until an elderly person came to their rescue and returned them to their family. Over the next six days, subjects wrote down all they could remember about the four events. At a follow-up interview, 25% of the subjects remembered the false event as having really happened. When told that one of the four events was a fake, about 20% of the subjects picked a real event from their family history as the fake.

Sometimes, just seeing a picture can create a memory of something that could not have been. Subjects looked at fake advertisements for Disneyland that featured Bugs Bunny – a Warner Brothers character that you'd never see at Disneyland – and researchers asked them to rate the advertisement on various scales.[4] In one study, seeing a single fake picture led to 16% of subjects later remembering that they had met Bugs Bunny when they visited Disneyland as a child. And fake advertisements with a picture of Bugs created more false memories than ads that only mentioned him.[5] It seems that adding a picture enhances the 'truthiness' (seeming to be true without necessarily being so) of things we read.

So even if a memory seems real, things might not have been just as you remember them.

Beyond that, the creative nature of recollection makes it possible for clinical psychologists to relieve suffering. Each time you recall a memory, it becomes possible to change it. When I help clients with their problematic memories, my aim is to add some new information, insight or perspective that alters their previously rigid recollection. As Sigmund Freud described the process, a troubling memory is resolved when it 'is subjected to rectification by other ideas'.

Psychological therapies can heal because the internal worlds of memory and imagination operate according to rules similar to those that govern the way we interact with external reality. When we remember or imagine an event, we use similar neural networks to those activated when we actually experience such things. That's why a memory or an image can make us feel genuinely sad or happy, and why clinicians and coaches teach clients to control imagery to improve their health, emotional well-being and physical performance. But when they are undisciplined, memory and imagination can be a curse, automatically recreating past suffering or conjuring disturbing prophecies of the future. And our own minds are not the only source of dangerous imagery.

Media Hypnotists

We live with an invasive media that peddles violence to an entranced audience that's increasingly desensitised to the suffering they see. If you want jaded people to notice an advertisement, you need to arouse them, and sex is not the only way to wake someone up. Every evening the television news broadcasts disturbing images and stories into homes and then cuts from scenes of grief and terror to pitch products. All the while, the fantasy industry churns out ever more violent material.

We tried, but Susan and I couldn't stay with some movies and television series that friends – gentle people all – recommended.

The tale of a high school teacher turned methamphetamine dealer seemed quirky for a while, but then the remains of a murdered body soaking in acid came through the ceiling. We watched a few episodes of *Game of Thrones* for the intrigue and baby dragons, but then the gratuitous sexual torture of women became *de rigueur*. We enjoyed *Vikings* until the heroes indulged in extreme cruelty. How much further can entertaining with violence go?

Fox Studio executives were surprised by complaints about a billboard for their movie *X-Men: Apocalypse* which featured a female character being strangled. They said, 'We didn't immediately recognise the upsetting connotation of this image in print form'.[6]

Years ago I ran a *Lara Croft* game on my computer. The goal was to keep Lara alive by having her dodge, jump and weave until she inevitably met her end. I never mastered getting Lara to jump over a pit of sharp spikes. I'd then reboot and off she'd go to another grizzly death. A couple of times I got Lara to where she drowned.

We know that practising an action in imagination improves actual performance, so how could it be a good idea to encourage people to enjoy vivid imagery of a woman's violent death? Most young men can distinguish fantasy from reality, but what about socially alienated adolescent males who live with mental illness, poverty and bleak futures? What worthwhile life skills do they pick up as they practice killing people?

In a radio interview, I heard a commentator with military experience express surprise that a child was able to get off half a dozen accurate headshots as students ran for their lives during a high school shooting incident in the US. Such accuracy is usually associated with the armed forces. The commentator did not appreciate that shooter games are, in effect, military-grade training exercises.

After the '9/11' attacks on New York's World Trade Centre, 24-year-old "Charles" came to see me. Charles hadn't slept for days as he trawled the media for images of people jumping from the collapsing infernos. Charles was not alone in his obsession with violent imagery. Around the world, endless replays seared the event into memories. For months after 9/11, parents across the US reported symptoms of distress and post-traumatic reactions in their children, and researchers found that kids who watched more television after the attacks experienced higher levels of distress.[7] The effect was international. During the first six months after the 9/11 attacks, schoolchildren in England, who had only seen the incident on television, experienced intrusive imagery and moderate to severe levels of post-traumatic symptoms.[8]

There was a time when you would never see a grieving mother interviewed on television; traumatised people were treated with respect and their privacy protected. But those times have gone.

When Talking Harms and Silence Heals

Watching violent imagery can harm, and so can talking about thoughts and feelings soon after a traumatic event.

During natural disasters like the 2010–2011 Queensland floods, television reporters poke microphones at distressed survivors and ask them to describe such things as how they felt when floodwaters swept their child from their arms. Such questioning is an emotional assault, and the harm can be severe and long-lasting.

The notion that it helps to talk about distressing experiences first appeared in the 1890's work of Freud and Breuer. It was re-packaged by 'new age' therapies in the 1960s, and later became a core component of counselling. But it's now understood that during post-trauma debriefing, you should not ask people to relive and recount what happened.

During the 1980s and 90s, when I debriefed police officers, bank staff, train drivers and others exposed to life-threatening situations, the then-standard procedure was to have survivors publicly tell their story and describe how they felt. This made sense if you thought that distressing emotions were like pressurised steam that needed venting.

For two years after the 9/11 attacks, researchers monitored the health of people who were invited to express their reactions on the day of the attacks and soon after.[9] The people who chose not to talk did better than those who talked. For people who expressed their feelings after the trauma, the more they talked, the worse they subsequently fared.

Why would discussing a distressing event cause harm, and keeping things to yourself be helpful? Perhaps there are clues in the way we sometimes remember but usually forget dreams.

During the two traumatic incidents in my life, and for some time afterwards, I felt as if I was in a kind of dream. Dreams are experiences dense with meaning, but they are not meant to be routinely remembered. Have you ever woken from a vivid dream and thought that you'd never forget it, only to have it disappear a few minutes later? If you want to remember a dream, describe it out loud as soon as you wake. That's what subjects did in my sleep laboratory 40 years ago, and friends who took part in that study still remember their falling asleep dreams from that night.

Dreams are generated in intuitive and visual areas of the mind and brain, separated from processes that control daytime reason and language. When you describe it out loud, the dream story and its images become available to daytime consciousness and thus are remembered. Similarly, when a trauma survivor talks about what happened, their dreamlike fragments of impression, feeling and meaning consolidate into a vivid memory.

For some unfortunate folk, telling their story on national television transforms personal tragedy into public history. Their suffering is forever preserved on video that can be endlessly replayed but never erased.

There are other reasons why the media's fascination with violence is dangerous.

Lure of the Unfinished

If you've ever had a catchy song keep going over and over in your mind, you probably heard some of the song but not the ending. A natural desire for completion can set up a repetitive replay of an incomplete melody, thought or action. When you find yourself stuck with a looping tune in your head, bring it to an end by singing it all the way through to a rousing finale.

Like a half-heard song, unfinished stories can draw us into compulsive repetition. And the media is chock full of horror stories with no endings. Television news punches out emotionally charged fragments of imagery and events that usually end abruptly when things are at their worst with no resolution in sight. You see the carnage of a car crash, explosion or earthquake, but never find out how things turn out in the long run for the people involved.

For some war veterans, giving up the nightly news rapidly reduces their anxiety. My generation saw the first televisions. When people my age developed the habit of watching the news, pictures were in black and white and there was much less graphic portrayal of suffering. Over the years, few noticed the incremental increase in the dose of violence being injected into households.

My media prescription is simple. Break the trance. Don't watch the news. Take back control of the imagery and ideas that go into your mind. If you need to, read newspapers or listen to the radio; they'll keep you informed without exposing you to inflammatory visual imagery.

But there are times when we can't look away. There are some challenges that, if you take them on, will necessarily expose you to extremely disturbing stories and imagery. You need to learn everything you can about such problems, but you will reach a point of diminishing returns. When you know pretty much all you need to know about an issue, you can safely shift to looking only for practical information that takes you towards a solution.

Mastering Memory and Imagination

We will now practice techniques for controlling and using your memory and imagination. The methods come from the scientific literature and all are useful beyond the clinic. These practical skills are suitable for anyone who wants to better manage their imagery. They are particularly useful when you take on big challenges.

The training is in two parts. First, you will experience what happens when you change sensory aspects of your imagery. Then we will move beyond simple changes to more complex techniques for mastering memory and imagination.

Working with Imagery

There's no right or wrong way to go about this work. The important thing is your experience: what it means to you and what you take from it. When I ask you to imagine something, allow the images to form in your own way and in your own time. Some images might come quickly and clearly, some could remain faint and indistinct, and it really doesn't matter. The training will work if you just make believe that you're imagining the things I describe.

As we've been doing, I'll get you to rate your feelings on Emot-o-Meter scales. The first number that pops into your mind is fine.

You can use the techniques to change the emotional impact of both good and bad memories and images. They can enhance your enjoyment of the good and reduce the impact of the unpleasant.

Set and Setting

Set yourself up to succeed. Cultivate the right frame of mind and find a good place to work. Adjust your 'set' (attitude and mental state) and 'setting' (your physical surrounds) so that you feel comfortable and secure and are unlikely to be interrupted. Explain to your partner, friends or family what you're doing and ask them to take care of phone calls and other interruptions.

Learning is best done with relaxed ease. Be patient with yourself; there's no place here for hypercritical coaches. Work at your natural pace. If you feel rushed or your heart isn't in it, pull back, remember that you have all the time you need, and take a break.

Begin and end sessions gently and smoothly. This will give you time to consolidate what you've learned. A gradual return from inner work strengthens the connections between your experiences and normal day-to-day awareness.

Using Training Memories

For the training, you'll need a set of good memories, a set of bad memories, a set of pleasant images and a set of unpleasant images. Carefully select the personal material you use. Each training memory or image should satisfy the following criteria.

Pick good memories that are happy and relatively uncomplicated. Do not use memories that feel good because they're about resolving a difficulty or feeling relieved that something bad didn't happen. For example, memories of making up with your partner after an argument, or feeling good that you avoided an accident, are not suitable.

Do not work with good memories that are precious or especially meaningful to you. Avoid memories that involve family members or close friends. Rather, for the training, look for less important good times in your life.

Take care when you choose training memories that involve unpleasant feelings. The ideal training memory is of a relatively unimportant event that was only mildly to moderately irritating or unpleasant. For me, my childhood memory of Miss Dowdy outing me as tone-deaf would suit. Perhaps you can think of a time when someone unimportant made you feel cranky: maybe a rude person in a shop, a picky boss, or an aggravating politician on television.

Check that each memory involves only a mild to moderate level of irritation or distress, say about a '3' or '4' on an Emot-o-Meter where '0' is 'no distress' and '+10' is 'extremely distressing'. The memories should not involve anyone suffering trauma or injury. Avoid memories that involve family members, friends or anyone you can't make fun of. It's best not to use recent memories related to ongoing stressful situations; you can take these on for real after you've practised the techniques.

Apply the same criteria when you create your cache of pleasant and unpleasant images. Again, look for imagery that only creates a mild to moderate level of feeling.

As always, check with your intuition and ideosensory signals that it's appropriate to use a particular memory or image for training. If it doesn't feel right, work up alternatives and keep checking them until you find some that are suitable.

It's up to you whether you adopt a systematic approach and experiment with each transformation using all four types of training imagery: good and bad memories and pleasant and unpleasant images. Or choose as you wish, perhaps using only one type of training memory or image for each technique.

However you go about the training, your deep mind can develop the skills that you need. And remember, it really doesn't matter if you can't find any suitable training memories or images at all. The training will work if you just think about what you read.

Sad Imagery, Happy Imagery

Sensory Qualities and Perspective

We'll examine the effects of altering such qualities as distance, size, colour, volume and voice, switching from a 1st person to a 3rd person perspective, and changing content by adding new people, altering settings and creating new endings.

Before each exercise, check that it feels all right deep down for you to do this work. Be attentive to any negative feeling. If it's not the right time for you to do the exercise, respect the wisdom of your deep mind and go on reading. You can come back later to practice any technique.

Distance

We begin with a thought experiment that explores the effect that distance has on your imagery.

Bring to mind a negative or positive training memory or image that involves another person. Imagine it as if you're actually there.

Notice the emotion that comes with the image. Rate the feeling on an Emot-o-Meter where '-10' represents 'very unpleasant' and '+10' is 'very pleasant'. Record your rating.

Now bring the person in the scene up very close, so they're right in your face, saying and doing the same things.

Notice the emotion. Rate the feeling on the Emot-o-Meter. Record your rating.

Now imagine that you're pushing the person away, over there. You have to crane your neck to see them because they're so far away.

Notice how that feels, and rate the emotion on the Emot-o-Meter. Record your rating. Then allow the image to gently fade away.

Many people find that their feelings change as they vary the distance between themselves and the person in the image. If you used a negative training memory or image, you might have found that bringing the antagonistic person closer intensified the discomfort, while pushing them away felt better. Conversely, if you used a good memory or image, your pleasant feelings might have strengthened as you drew the friendly person closer. And the good feelings might have dissipated as you pushed the person further away.

But that's not always how it works when you change the distance in an image. Like all the transformations we will be working with, it's your personal reactions that matter.

For subjects in my Doctor of Psychology research (from here referred to as 'my study'), changing the distance in their training memory between themselves and a person who made them angry markedly altered their level of distress.[10] As the person got closer, distress increased, and as the person moved away, distress levels decreased. A month after the study, 30% of subjects rated the imagery transformation of 'increasing the distance' as strongly helpful in controlling their actual traumatic memories.

It's unsurprising that we feel edgy if an antagonistic person comes close: it's as if they are invading our personal space. If they come too close, our sense of threat can go off the scale. A psychologist friend likened this critical zone of comfort to the length of our arm held out with a clenched fist. If someone we see as a threat gets this close, our fight-or-flight emotions of fear, anxiety and even anger are likely to intensify. But if the person is family, a friend or a lover, bringing them closer will probably increase positive feelings.

As in real life, so it is in the realm of imagination. Similar rules apply. When we remember or imagine something, the distance we maintain between ourselves and the people and events in our mind's eye affects our emotional experience. Traumatised and anxious people too often remember their tormentors and horrors up close. This makes their distress personal and intense and increases a perpetrator's power to harm them again. It feels much better to take control and push the hurtful person away.

A Matter of Size

We now look at the effects of size on your imagery. Take heart, this routine will become easier as we go on.

> Bring to mind your training memory or image involving a person. Imagine it as if you're really there.
>
> Notice the emotion that comes with the image. Rate the feeling on an Emot-o-Meter where '-10' represents 'very unpleasant' and '+10' is 'very pleasant'. Record your rating.
>
> Now imagine that the person is getting bigger and bigger until they're about eight foot tall, towering over you.
>
> Notice the emotion. Rate the feeling on the Emot-o-Meter. Record your rating.
>
> Now shrink the person down, way down, until they're about four foot tall standing in front of you, doing whatever it was they were doing before, but now they're tiny.
>
> Notice how that feels and rate the emotion on the Emot-o-Meter.
>
> Record your rating. Then allow the image to gently fade away as you open your eyes.

Size mattered a lot for the trauma survivors who participated in my study. When they made the irritating person in their training memory larger, they felt more threatened and angry. Conversely, when they shrank their provocateur down, they felt more relaxed and in control.

A month after working with their training memory, 37% of subjects found that 'making the person smaller' was strongly helpful in managing their real trauma memories and nightmares.

If you used a negative training memory or image, perhaps you had a similar experience, but not necessarily. And the effect of changing the size of someone we like is less predictable than altering the size of someone we don't like.

For me, it doesn't seem relevant to imagine friends or loved ones as larger or to shrink them down, and doing so doesn't much affect my feelings. But then, if my training image involved a chocolate cake, perhaps making the cake bigger would feel better.

Colour versus Black and White

If your training memory is getting messed up with the things we've been doing to it, this might be a good time to get another one from your kit bag for the next thought experiment.

Get set and bring your training memory or image to mind. Imagine it as if you are actually there.

Notice the emotion. Rate the feeling on an Emot-o-Meter where '-10' represents 'very unpleasant' and '+10' is 'very pleasant'. Record your rating.

Spruce it up. Give it rich, sumptuous colour. Maybe add some sparkle and sharpen the contrast. Notice the feeling and rate it on our Emot-o-Meter. Record your rating.

Now leach the colour out until it's a black and white scene, like you see in a newspaper or, if you're as old as me, like you used to see on a black and white television.

Notice how that feels. Rate it on the Emot-o-Meter. Record your rating.

Then allow the image to fade away as you open your eyes.

For most subjects in my study, changing their training memory from colour to black and white and back again made little difference. But for two Vietnam War veterans, the switch from colour to black and white increased their anxiety because it reminded them of watching black-and-white television, which was how images of the Vietnam War were broadcast at the time. Another war veteran later told me that it felt better when he changed to black and white a recurring traumatic memory of seeing burned bodies after combat.

For me, enhancing the colour of a good memory or image increases its pleasantness. It feels good to add a bit of sparkle to a happy memory.

Changing Viewpoint

We can recall the past and imagine the future from two possible viewpoints.[11] When we imagine or remember something from a 1st person perspective, it's as if we're actually there. When we view imagery from a 3rd person perspective, it's as if the event is happening over there and we're looking on from a distance.

Most people naturally remember things from a 1st person perspective, but researchers find that no one has trouble switching memories to a 3rd person perspective and back again. Each point of view is as easy to maintain as the other.

We'll wrap up our work on the effects of changing the visual qualities of imagery by playing with perspective.

Bring to mind one of your training memories or images. Imagine it as if you're actually there, taking in everything that's going on.

Notice the feeling. Rate it on an Emot-o-Meter where '-10' is 'very unpleasant' and '+10' is 'very pleasant'. Record your rating.

Now imagine that you're drawing yourself out of the scene. Pull back so that you're watching yourself and what's going on over there, as if you're an observer looking on from a distance. Watch and listen to everything that happens.

Notice the feeling and rate it on the Emot-o-Meter. Record your rating.

When you have learned all you need to learn, allow the training image to fade away and open your eyes.

For subjects in my study, prior to their Cognitive Control Training, about 90% remembered their trauma memories from a 1st person perspective. A month after training, 80% reported that they now took a 3rd person perspective when they recalled their traumas.

The 1st person perspective comes with physiological, behavioural and emotional responses that resemble those of the actual event. Changing from a 1st to a 3rd person viewpoint usually lessens the intensity of these associated emotions.

Taking the observer point of view in imagery is akin to 'observational learning', the process whereby we gain new skills and attitudes by watching others. Clinical psychologists use the 3rd person perspective to reduce stress, enhance learning and promote mastery during potentially stressful work with memories and imagery. Sports psychologists get clients to imagine actions from a 3rd person perspective if they want them to objectively analyse their sporting performances.

Did you notice such effects when you shifted your training memory or image from the 1st to the 3rd person perspective?

For the subjects in my study, changing the perspective of an anger-inducing training memory moderately reduced their distress rating. But for five subjects, the change to an observer perspective increased anxiety. As one woman explained, 'I looked back on myself and felt that wasn't fair'. Nonetheless, when interviewed a month later, 39% of subjects rated changing to a 3rd person perspective as strongly useful for managing their intrusive trauma memories.

As a general guide, take the 1st person perspective when you imagine the good things that you want for the future. Let the feelings come and enjoy them. But when you use your imagination to plan how you'll go about achieving your goals, the 3rd person perspective can help you think more objectively. Then switch to a 1st person perspective to see how it would feel in reality.

If you need to imagine or remember distressing things, you might take the observer viewpoint to reduce the emotional intensity. This could make it easier for you to remain calm and absorb the lesson.

Like horses, people learn best when they're relaxed and alert. When you need to learn from good and bad things that happened in the past, the 3rd person perspective can help you maintain an optimal state of mind. You don't have to relive unpleasant feelings. A simple switch of viewpoint can free your mind for creative thinking about a challenge. You might be surprised at how easily you can switch perspectives.

Feel free to explore the effects of other changes to the visual qualities of your imagery, such as making things brighter and duller, or sharpening the focus and making the scene go fuzzy. You get the idea. Take the work from here as you see fit.

Don't Shout, This is My Memory

In the next thought experiment, we look at what happens when you change the way that memories and imagery sound.

Bring to mind a training memory or image that involves someone speaking to you. Imagine the scene as if you're actually there. Listen carefully to what's being said.

Notice the feelings that come with this scene. Rate your emotion on an Emot-o-Meter where '-10' represents 'very unpleasant' and '+10' is 'very pleasant'. Record your rating.

Now turn up the volume so that the other person is shouting at you, saying the same kinds of things, but very loudly.

Notice the feeling and rate it on the Emot-o-Meter. Record your rating.

Now turn the volume way down so the person is whispering. You can see their lips moving, but you have to pay close attention to make out what they're saying.

Notice the feeling. Rate it on the Emot-o-Meter. Record your rating.

Allow the imagery to fade away and open your eyes.

For subjects in my study, of all the transformations, changing the volume of the voice of the aggravating person in their training memory had the greatest effect on emotions. Lowering the volume reduced their level of distress, on average, from '8' to '2' on a '0 to 10' scale.

Some sounds, like a favourite piece of music, are better turned up. Such auditory images warrant tweaking to make them richer and more resonant. But if you remember unpleasant sounds such as shouting, explosions or a crash, turn the volume down and muffle the noise so it no longer startles you.

The Power of Elmer, Goofy and Donald

Carefully select the training memory or image for this thought experiment. Pick imagery that involves someone you don't like and can make fun of, at least in the privacy of your own mind. Please don't use this technique with imagery or memories that involve people you care for.

> Bring to mind a negative training memory or image that involves someone unpleasant speaking to you. Imagine the scene as if you're really there. Listen to what's said.
>
> Notice the feelings. Rate your emotion on an Emot-o-Meter where '-10' represents 'very unpleasant' and '+10' is 'very pleasant'. Record your rating.
>
> Now give the irritating person a cartoon voice that suits them: Elmer Fudd, Donald Duck, Goofy or any other cartoon character you like.
>
> Listen to them saying whatever it is they say, but with their new cartoon voice.
>
> Notice how that feels. Rate it on the Emot-o-Meter. Record your rating.
>
> Allow the imagery to fade away and open your eyes.

Did the change of voice affect the impact of the person speaking in your training imagery?

Changing voices has variable effects for different people and for different kinds of imagery. For subjects in my study, giving the person in their training memory the voice of a cartoon character dropped the level of distress, but only 15% of subjects rated this method as strongly useful for controlling actual trauma memories.

We next see what happens when you change the elements in memories and images.

Adding New Elements

Psychologists sometimes reduce distress by getting clients to add, remove or alter elements in their disturbing memories. They ask them to do such things as put tape over an abusive person's mouth, remove the action to a neutral setting, tie up assailants, create protective shields, use a one-way mirror to watch what happens, or put violent perpetrators behind bars.

I haven't included exercises that explore the effects of recalling a memory while your eyes are open and you add new elements by moving your eyes side to side or by tapping your skin. In Chapter 2, you'll find descriptions of how EMDR and the emotional freedom technique use these methods to affect a recalled memory.

Here we look at the effects of adding new characters – first a monkey and then a person – to your training memory or image.

A Circus Monkey

In this thought experiment, we add a monkey to your memory.

Bring to mind, as if you're there, a training memory or image that involves someone unimportant saying something annoying to you.

Notice the feelings. Rate them on the Emot-o-Meter where '-10' represents 'very unpleasant' and '+10' is 'very pleasant'. Record your rating.

Now picture a circus monkey standing on a box behind the person. You can see the monkey, all dressed up, jumping around, but the other person can't. Watch the monkey imitate what the person is saying and doing, as it parodies their movements and expressions.

Notice how that feels. Make a rating on the Emot-o-Meter. Record your rating.

Allow the imagery to fade away and open your eyes.

Humour can reduce the emotional impact of some negative memories and images. Even though it might sound callous to an outsider, 'black humour' can help emergency, medical and police service personnel cope with horror.

For subjects in my study, adding a monkey reduced the impact of the aggravating person in their training memory, on average, by about four points on a '0' to '10' distress scale. I think all subjects smiled when they first imagined the monkey on the box. A month later, 26% of subjects rated 'adding the monkey' as strongly useful for controlling real trauma memories.

Extra Characters

We next examine the effects of adding another character to your imagery, but this time it's a human.

Bring to mind a positive or negative training memory or image. Imagine it as if you're actually there.

Notice the feelings. Rate them on an Emot-o-Meter where '-10' represents 'very unpleasant' and '+10' is 'very pleasant'. Record your rating.

Now change the scene by adding another person. If it's an unpleasant situation, you might like to add a good friend or a real or imaginary strong person to support you. Or perhaps, if you're working with pleasant imagery, you will choose a friend to share a happy time with. You might like to try the technique with both positive and negative imagery.

Notice how that feels. Rate your emotions on the Emot-o-Meter. Record your rating. Allow the imagery to fade and open your eyes.

If you added a friend to negative imagery, did you feel an enhanced sense of support? Or, if you were working with positive imagery, did adding a friend increase your enjoyment of a good time?

Children don't have the physical strength or maturity to defend themselves against hostile adults. Consequently, adult survivors of childhood abuse often experience feelings of powerlessness when they recall what happened to them when they were young. Every time a memory recreates the lonely isolation and stress they endured as a child, the perpetrator's power is reinforced. So it's not surprising that a month after they added another person to their training memory, 48% of the subjects in my study rated this transformation as strongly useful for controlling their actual traumatic memories.

Powerlessness feeds on isolation. Enduring hurt and pain alone amplifies suffering, but knowing that someone cares counteracts despair. Children can survive even appalling circumstances if they know that someone loves them.

Effective action becomes more difficult if we feel unsupported, and strength is found in the fellowship of community and connection with others.

'All's well that ends well'

We next look at what happens when you give a memory a new ending. For this thought experiment, choose a relatively short positive or negative training memory.

> Bring the memory to mind from the perspective of being there.
>
> Review what happened. Notice the emotions. Rate the feeling on an Emot-o-Meter where '-10' represents 'very unpleasant' and '+10' is 'very pleasant'. Record your rating.
>
> Now give your training memory a new ending, and run it through to see how it feels.
>
> Rate the feeling on the Emot-o-Meter. Record your rating.
>
> When the time is right, allow the imagery to fade away, open your eyes and take a deep breath. Compare your two ratings. What effects did changing the ending have on how you think and feel about your memory?

A memory is a re-created story that seems complete in itself. But the ending, the final scene we remember, is an arbitrary point in time. Whatever the event, no matter how terrible or wonderful it was in reality, our lives continued from that point on without interruption. After even the most dreadful times, life did go on. Beyond the end of any memory, the rest of our life provides a rich source of material for updating and changing the way we think about things that happened in the past.

Clinicians typically ask clients to change the endings of distressing memories so they feel more powerful and in charge. Instructions range from a simple request to visualise a more positive ending, to complex processes such as imagining saying goodbye to a deceased friend.

Imagining different endings can relieve recurring nightmares. It doesn't seem to matter if the new ending is sensible or bizarre, or even favourable, so long as it's different. The therapeutic effect of giving a nightmare a new ending stems, at least in part, from the sense of mastery and control that it creates.

In my study, when they gave their practice memory a new ending, subjects' average rating of distress fell by more than four units on a '0' to '10' point scale. A month later, 43% of subjects rated the method of changing a memory's ending as strongly useful for managing real distressing memories.

Before we end our work with changing the nature and content of memories and imagery, let's put together all that you've practised thus far.

Adjusting Imagery for Best Effect

In the first thought experiment, we will use a negative memory or image. In the second, we will work with a positive training image or memory.

> Bring to mind, as if you're there again, one of your negative training memories or images.
>
> Notice the feeling. Rate it on an Emot-o-Meter where '-10' is 'very unpleasant' and '+10' is 'very pleasant'. Record your rating.

MEMORY AND IMAGINATION

Taking all the time you need, think of each transformation we have worked with, and adjust your training imagery to reduce its power to cause distress.

Perhaps you'll push the people in the scene back to a comfortable distance, shrink them down in size, adjust the volume and maybe give them a cartoon character's voice. You might like to switch the colour to black-and-white, or change perspective from being there to watching from a distance. You might add some friends for support. Maybe you'll add a monkey or two, and give it a new ending.

When you have the imagery adjusted so it has lost its power to cause distress, notice the feeling and rate it on the Emot-o-Meter. Record your rating.

Then ask your intuition if your deep mind is willing to adjust other unpleasant memories and images so they also lose their power to hurt you.

When the time is right, allow the newly adjusted memory or image to fade away.

Now bring to mind a pleasant training memory or image. Notice the good feeling and rate it on an Emot-o-Meter where '-10' is 'very unpleasant' and '+10' is 'very pleasant'. Record your rating.

Adjust the imagery, but this time to maximise the good feelings. Change the way things look and sound. Add what you want. Make changes that enhance the positive.

When you have the imagery adjusted, rate your feeling on the Emot-o-Meter. Record your rating.

Drift back to your surroundings, bringing those good feelings with you. They're worth keeping.

You can use what you have practised to learn from the past, enjoy the present, and to enhance the future. You might do this consciously by deliberately using the techniques to alter memories and imagery, or perhaps your deep mind will tap into these new skills to automatically change the way you think. Your deep mind can draw on all the things you are learning.

Dear Reader, this might be a good place for you to take a break. Across the past dozen or so pages, you've done a lot of work changing the qualities of your imagery. If you were in my office, I'd stop here to give you time to think about what you've been through. You can return to the book and the thought experiments later when you're feeling refreshed.

Multistage Imagery Techniques

The following thought experiments show how you can resolve problematic memories, learn from the past, set goals to script the future, stimulate deep mind problem-solving, change habits, and generate new ways of doing things.

First up, we'll work with methods that add you as an extra character. I'll get you to take on the roles of being your own coach and then your own counsellor.

Your Inner Coach

Find a training memory in which you reacted or behaved in a way that you weren't happy with at the time and would like to do differently should you confront a similar situation in the future. Check with your intuition that the memory is suitable.

> Run your training memory from beginning to end from a 1st person perspective, as if you're really there.
>
> Notice your feelings. Rate them on an Emot-o-Meter where '-10' represents 'very unpleasant' and '+10' is 'very pleasant'. Record your rating. Allow the training memory to fade away.
>
> Now imagine that you're taking on the calm, competent and confident attitude of a good coach. Then, in your mind's eye, picture a large blank screen up there in front of you.
>
> Run your original training memory again, but this time on the screen as if you're watching a movie. Watch and listen carefully to

everything that happened, all that you did and said from beginning to end.

When you've heard it all and seen it all, let the imagery fade away until the screen is again blank.

Now with the attitude of a good coach, reconstruct the memory until you see and hear yourself up there on the screen speaking and behaving in a way that does you proud: a performance you'd be happy with.

Remember that you're in control. Talk to and coach the 'you' up there on the screen. If you see or hear something you don't like, stop the action, rewind the memory and rework it until you're satisfied.

When you've rescripted the training memory, it's time to test your work. It looked and sounded good from a distance, but now you need to make sure it works.

Allow the screen with your rescripted training memory to fade away.

Now run your new improved version of the memory from the perspective of actually being there. If the changed memory does not feel right, or it creates unwanted consequences, draw yourself out of the image, return to the coach's perspective, and use what you have learned to again remake the memory. When it looks and sounds right, test it again from the perspective of actually being there. Recycle this process until you have created a tried and tested new way of doing things.

When you've confirmed that the new version works well, notice how that feels and make a rating on the Emot-o-Meter. Record your rating.

Ask your intuition if your deep mind is willing to try out the new ways of acting and feeling that you've created. Explore any reluctance you might feel and, if appropriate, use what you learn to again rework the training memory.

When the time is right, allow the newly minted memory to fade away. Bring the good feelings with you as you reorient to your surrounds.

Draw on your inner coach when you take on a challenge. Pull back from the immediate situation, adopt your coach's attitude, take control and work out how you will achieve your goal.

In summary, the steps for the Inner Coach procedure are:
1. Review the memory from a 1st person perspective.
2. Imagine a blank screen.
3. From a 3rd person perspective, review the old memory on the screen.
4. When you understand what happened, fade the memory.
5. Take on a coach's attitude, and remake the old memory up on the screen until you see yourself acting in a way that makes you proud.
6. Let the imagery on the screen fade away.
7. Test your work by running the reworked memory as if you're actually there.
8. If it doesn't feel right or work well, return to the screen, modify the imagery and then test it as you did before.
9. When you have a tried and tested new memory, check that your deep mind is willing to try out these new ways of doing things.

Supporting Your Younger Self

In this technique, you take on a counsellor's role to support the 'younger you' in a memory.

Find a memory of a mildly unpleasant event that occurred during your childhood or youth. The memory should not involve any trauma, assault or other very unpleasant experience.

Before you work with this technique, double-check with your intuition that your training memory is suitable. From an adult's perspective, a childhood memory might seem like no big deal, but it can still deliver an emotional punch when it's brought to awareness.

Imagine that you're looking at a blank screen in front of you.

Then, as an adult observer looking from a distance, watch and listen to everything that happened to the 'younger you' up there on the screen. Remind yourself that you're safe. Remember your adult strength as you let the 'younger you' go through the incident again.

Take all the time you need with the next step.

When you sense that you now understand what happened back then, give all your adult wisdom, understanding and support to the 'younger you'. You might imagine giving the 'younger you' a hug. Reassure them that they'll never have to go through that again. Talk about what happened. Assure them that you'll protect them from now on.

When you sense that the 'younger you' feels comforted, ask them if they still need to keep the old tensions. If your ideosensory signals indicate that the 'younger you' is not ready to let go of the old emotions, ask why it's important to keep the feelings. Does the 'younger you' still need them for protection?

When your ideosensory signals confirm that the 'younger you' no longer needs the old emotions, use your adult strength to help the 'younger you' let go of the unnecessary feelings once and for all.

When you sense that the 'younger you' has let go of the old tensions, ask for a 'yes' signal to confirm that they have indeed let go of the old emotions. If you get a 'no' feeling, talk with the 'younger you' about why the old feelings are still important. Use what you learn to reassure the 'younger you'.

You'll know when the 'younger you' lets go of the old emotions because it feels very good.

As always, end your session gently, and let the imagery fade gradually as you return to your surroundings.

This and other imagery techniques that transfer adult resources can gently ease distressing childhood memories. The subjects in my study ranked this as the most helpful technique for managing their intrusive thoughts, memories and nightmares.

In summary, the steps for the Supporting Your Younger Self procedure are:
1. Imagine that you are looking at a blank screen.
2. As an adult observer, review what happened to the 'younger you' on the screen.
3. Give your adult wisdom and support to the 'younger you'.
4. When the 'younger you' seems comforted, check if they still need the old tensions.
5. When ideosensory signals confirm that the 'younger you' is ready, use your adult strength and understanding to help them let go of the unnecessary feelings.
6. Test your work. Do more if your 'younger you' needs further help. Enjoy the feeling when your 'younger you' lets go of the old emotions.
7. Gently reorient to your surroundings.

Envision the Future

This technique begins with an image of the future and then works backwards through time to end at the present.

You can use this technique to plan how you'll take on a big challenge. But for now, let's practice with a less ambitious task.

Think of a goal that's worthwhile, but not too complicated: something that you could potentially achieve in the near future.

Create an image to represent your ultimate success, something like imagining yourself looking pleased after you've aced a job interview, enjoying the applause as you finish a public speaking gig, or looking fit and trim as a result of the healthy changes you've made in your daily routine. Find an image that represents a future you want to create.

When you have a suitable image to work with, imagine that you're looking at a blank screen in front of you. Then create the image of the outcome you desire up there on the screen. You might use the methods we worked with earlier to generate a vivid, compelling picture of the future you'd like to see.

Beginning with the final scene on the screen, work backwards from your vision of the future to the present. In reverse, create scenes to represent each step that you'll take to achieve your goal until you arrive back at an image that depicts where you are now.

When you've done that, you will have the scenes for a 'mind movie' that depicts all the steps you need to achieve your goal.

Test your work by imagining that you're in the new mind movie, and run it forward from where you are until you arrive at your destination. If you encounter problems, use what you've learned and go back to the 3rd person perspective to rework your first-cut version. Then test your work again.

When you have your mind movie looking good, begin a fine-grained editing by imagining in detail what you will have to do to realise each scene.

When you're ready, open your eyes and reorient to your surroundings. Bring with you all the images and lessons that you've learned.

The Envision the Future technique was inspired by treatments for phobia that ask clients to imagine time running in reverse. For instance, if you're afraid of flying, you can begin by imagining yourself arriving safely at your destination, and then visualise the entire journey in reverse, until you arrive back at your house before you set off.

Sometimes, all you have to do to plan how you're going to tackle a challenge is to clearly imagine what success will look like. If I imagine that I have delivered a workshop that I'm planning, it's easy to work back from that to think about all the things I'll have to do to make that happen.

When we imagine the process of tackling a challenge in its entirety in a mind movie format, it's easier to see the steps we'll have to take and get them in the right order.

To the Future

A journey is a popular metaphor for thinking about the planning process: one step leads to another until we arrive at our destination. But the metaphor is incomplete unless we have a map to guide us on the journey. It needs to be a good map. If you've got the wrong map, it doesn't matter how long or hard you work, you won't get to where you want to go. When we start by imagining our ultimate destination, we 'begin with the end in mind'.[12] Make that image clear and concise, and the steps you need to take will fall into place.

In this ever-quickening age, it's easy to get caught up in the day-to-day busyness of life so we never lift our heads up, take stock and think about where we're headed. The danger is that we can work hard only to find years down the track that we're no closer to where we want to be.

The Envision the Future method is not for making a life movie that you store on the shelf. Keep on improving and refining your mental maps as you work towards long-term goals. Your story is far from finished. Think of where you want to end up so you can plan the steps that'll get you there.

We finish our chapter on memory and imagination with a couple of guided imagery exercises for dealing with obstacles that can get in the way when we take on a challenge.

Guided Imagery

There are many guided imagery exercises for enhancing relaxation, health and creativity. Here's a thought experiment that's useful when we take on challenges. Use or modify it as you wish. Create your own personalised imagery to inspire and guide your creative work.

> Imagine that you're walking along a path in a tranquil garden on a fine day. The air is clear. The world around you is quiet and beautiful. You might like to enjoy the light as it plays off the flowers and plants.
>
> As you stroll along the path through the garden, you come to a clearing where there's a small, well-contained campfire burning. This is a special fire. You can use it to dispose of the things in your life that you don't want.
>
> Imagine that you're holding a piece of writing paper and a pen in your hands. Write out a list of all the things that you'd like to get rid of – old habits, fears, doubts, worries, bad memories, regrets, guilt – anything at all that you no longer need or want.
>
> When your list is complete, scrunch the paper into a ball and toss it into the fire. Watch the flames consume the paper. Enjoy the sense of satisfaction as the smoke wafts upwards and away.
>
> When you're ready, continue along the path in your special garden until you come to a fallen branch that blocks the way. Contemplate the barrier. Let it represent all the things that limit your life: the negative thoughts, mental blocks and other things that get in your way.
>
> When you're ready, muster the strength you need to remove the obstacle and toss it aside. Continue on your walk along the path. Feel the spring in your step. Enjoy knowing that you can master your memory and imagination to unlock the power of your deep mind.
>
> And as you open your eyes, bring the good feelings with you.

Chapter 8

Beliefs to Limit or Liberate

> We can complain because rose bushes have thorns,
> or rejoice because thorn bushes have roses.
> Abraham Lincoln (1808–1865)

WE NOW COME TO the Key Mental Process of belief, where attitudes and the ideas we take to be true can power us towards success or guarantee failure.

Some people always use an avoidant strategy. They routinely believe that they will fail, feel fearful and inadequate, and think and say negative things about themselves. Their One Thought Solution protects them but ensures that they never take on a challenge.

Beyond such extreme strategies, through life, we acquire beliefs and attitudes that affect our prospects for success. Of particular relevance for problem solvers are certain beliefs about the self and the world, assumptions about what it takes to succeed, and some biggies to do with the fate of humanity and the nature of suffering and evil.

First up, we'll look at liberating and limiting beliefs about who we are and what we're capable of.

Optimism and Pessimism

When you take on a demanding task, do you believe deep down that you're more likely to succeed or to fail? Do you expect the worst to happen, or do you subscribe to Monty Python's advice and always look on the bright side of life?

Such attitudes matter. Pessimistic beliefs focus us on failure, encourage despondent feelings and sap enthusiasm for making an effort. Optimistic beliefs foster positive feelings, increase energy and make success possible.

Which Do You Choose?

Our next thought experiment explores the emotional impact of optimistic and pessimistic One Thought Solutions.

> Imagine that you're thinking about joining a campaign to oppose invasive mining where you live. Then say the following passage over a few times.
>
> 'The miners always win. They're all powerful. There's nothing we can do.'
>
> Now rate how enthusiastic you feel about joining the anti-mining campaign on an Emot-o-Meter where '-10' is 'very unenthusiastic' and '+10' is 'very enthusiastic'. Record your rating. Let those thoughts and feelings fade away.
>
> Now say the following passage over a few times.
>
> 'The people will win. We're on the right side of history. We'll never give up.'

> Notice the feelings that come with these statements. Rate on the Emot-o-Meter how enthusiastic you now feel about joining the anti-mining campaign. Record your rating.
>
> Let those thoughts fade away, but you might like to keep any resolve you have to oppose invasive mining.

Did the different statements affect your enthusiasm for joining the campaign?

Optimists expect good fortune to last and bad times to pass. They take credit for their successes and the good things that happen to them: 'I really know my stuff'. When optimists fail, they tend to blame external circumstances, not themselves: 'You can't win them all'.

Pessimists believe that good luck is fleeting and bad things last a long time. They put their wins and the fortunate things that happen to them down to luck: 'I guess I was in the right place at the right time'. They take setbacks and failures as proof there's something wrong with them: 'See, I never get it right'.

Optimistic and pessimistic thinking both have a role to play when we take on challenges. During the early stages of a project, think negatively to ferret out all the things that could go wrong. When you've thought through the risks and possible negative consequences, switch to an optimistic perspective to bolster your morale and energy.

Self-esteem and Efficacy

> They can because they think they can.
>
> Virgil (70–19 BC)

Depressed people can suffer from the belief that there's nothing they can do to improve their lot. When the trance is dense, this belief guarantees failure and it quashes any interest in taking tasks on. This One Thought Solution lessens the chance of disappointment, but only by diminishing prospects for a happy, fulfilling life.

If we believe that we're controlled by what happens to us, we give away our power to change things. This belief makes people think they're buffeted by life, pushed this way and that by forces they can't control. They feel vulnerable and weak, blame others for what happens and accept no responsibility for finding solutions.

We can't determine what comes our way, but we can choose how we react to what happens and think about how we can change things for the better.

The antidote to thinking that limits us is to break the trance. Bring negative beliefs out into the open, challenge them and add more carriages to your train of thought. For instance, to counter a belief such as 'I never get anything right' ask yourself, is it true that you've never succeeded or done anything worthwhile? Challenge yourself to come up with ideas to make things different.

We now look at some beliefs about problem-solving itself and what it takes to succeed.

Learning New Things

> Failure is the foundation of success,
> and the means by which it is achieved.
>
> Lao Tzu (Circa 5th century BC)

It takes time and effort to learn anything worthwhile. We build knowledge and expertise incrementally, from the ground up, as we acquire new information and skills. 'I bought a guitar, practised for a week, but it was too hard so I gave up.' 'I went to a typing course but I kept hitting the wrong keys so I stopped going.' These folk failed because they didn't understand what it takes to learn new things.

Do you remember how hard it was to learn to drive a car? I recall fumbling with the gear lever as the car kangaroo-hopped down the road. Learning was difficult at first, but after a few weeks of practice, driving became easier. Practice is essential, as is a willingness to make and learn from mistakes. You'll never ride a bicycle if you're not willing to wobble. If something doesn't work, do it differently. Persist and you'll succeed.

Look to the Big Picture

Just because a problem is complex doesn't mean that the answer won't be straightforward. And you can work towards solutions before you understand all the details of a challenge. Healthy systems are in equilibrium. When they're out of balance, look for where they might be compromised. Compare a system that's working well with one that's out of kilter. Look for the differences and ask how these contribute to success or failure. This will give you clues to where you can intervene and what you need to do to make a difference.

If Susan and I had waited for scientists to fully understand native forest dieback, our bush regeneration work would be a decade behind. When we compared healthy and sick forests on our property, the obvious difference was lantana, and removing lantana is the key to curing our local dieback. Scientists continue to flesh out the details of the problem while our forests are already recovering.

The presence of persistent memories of horror is the crucial difference between trauma survivors who develop posttraumatic stress disorder and those who remain healthy. The problem can be solved when these memories are calmed down. By doing this, I could help my clients even though it was many more years before I properly understood PTSD and its treatment.

The gas industry wants people to focus on details and ignore the big picture of how gas fields damage country and communities. Citizens can't afford to wait for scientists to study the health impacts of gas field pollutants because, by then, it will be too late to protect their families. If you compare healthy rural communities and landscapes with those blanketed by gas fields, you won't know where to begin your list of the differences. In the case of such a vast and destructive industrial development, prevention or escape might be the only truly safe solutions.

Truth and Lies

> If you tell a big enough lie and tell it
> frequently enough, it will be believed.
>
> Adolf Hitler (1889–1945)

My 1970s philosophy professor's rule seems quaint now: 'Make any case you like, but you have to defend it against all criticism with reason and evidence. If you can't do that, you must abandon your claim'. From my professor's point of view, reason demanded scepticism about one's own beliefs, openness to being proved wrong and a willingness to change opinion. He believed in truth.

In this post-truth era, complex scientific, social and environmental issues are debated with selected facts, appeals to emotion and personal belief, and distortions that make whatever case vested interests pay for. Lying has become a popular strategy in politics and business, but it's unlikely to lead to genuine solutions to big challenges. Even the 'thousand year Reich' lasted only 12 years and four months from Hitler's appointment as Chancellor to his suicide.

Lying is not a legitimate problem-solving strategy. Integrity is essential for long-term success. And this means more than just telling the truth. After all, even dangerous and misleading One Thought Solutions often employ true statements.

Trust is fragile and easily destroyed. Could you trust someone who has lied to you about something important? Trust and rapport break down if a client senses that a psychologist is not acting with integrity. The gas industry's tactic of lying worked for a while, but then the truth got out and there was no going back. They fell foul of the 'emperor has no clothes' effect.

In the story, a tailor cons a vain emperor that he's wearing clothes that only intelligent people can see. A boy calls out the truth, breaks the emperor's lie-induced trance and suddenly everyone can see the reality. It now doesn't matter how much the gas and coal industries spend on advertising. Promotions such as 'friends of coal' and 'coal is an amazing little rock' create only mirth and mockery.

Attitudes to Time

Developments were once judged on whether they would have a positive or negative impact on our children and grandchildren. Policy is now based on short-term thinking with little to no regard for future generations. But successfully tackling big challenges will always call for long-term commitment and effort.

Problems spawned by the Vietnam War continue across generations. There's still no coordinated effort underway to save Australia's native forests from dieback. The campaign to save the Franklin River ran a decade or more. The Gasfield Free Australia battle will take longer.

If we allow them to, beliefs about time can prevent us from working towards the future we desire. I recommend a country attitude; we have to make an effort now to achieve things we can only imagine. Bush regenerators envisage a forest as it will be when it's restored, a decade on. Before planting a tree, a farmer imagines how it will look and throw shade in 30 years and then she puts the seedling in the ground. But there are more subtle ways that our beliefs about time can block or bolster progress.

In what direction would you point to indicate where the future lies? In which direction is the past for you?

For me, the future seems as if it's in front and the past is behind. When I asked Susan, she pointed to the left for the past, to the right for the future, and said that she was looking directly ahead at the present. For some clients, the past is directly in front of them while the future is either behind or too vague to point at.

Let's see what it feels like when you change your time perspective.

> Whether or not you do so naturally, point in front of you, and imagine that the future is in that direction and that the past lies directly behind you.
>
> Still pointing at the future out in front, imagine that you're about to take on a new big challenge.
>
> Now rate how confident you feel about your prospects of success on an Emot-o-Meter where '-10' is 'very little confidence' and '+10' is 'very confident'. Record the number that first comes to mind. Clear your mind.
>
> When you're ready, reverse your sense of where the past and future lie. Point in front of you, but now imagine that the past lies directly ahead and the future's behind you.
>
> As before, keep your finger pointing at the past out in front of you and imagine that you're about to take on a big challenge.
>
> Now rate how confident you feel about your prospects of success on the Emot-o-Meter. Record your rating. Clear your mind.

Did it make any difference when you imagined that the future or the past was in front of you? For me, it feels as if the task would be more daunting if I thought that the past was in front; it would get in my way and make it harder to think about what I needed to do next. For traumatised people, their horrendous histories seem to fill their past, present and future.

We now come to some profound beliefs about the world, the future and the nature of suffering.

The Predictably Unpredictable

History only reads like a story when we look back. When the future's yet to play out, we're actors in an unscripted drama and surprises are inevitable. No one can anticipate the twists and turns in a long-haul campaign or know how things will ultimately turn out when they take on a big challenge.

No one in 1939 could foresee the flow of fate that would see Hitler dead in 1945. With 70 years of hindsight, history records a series of crucial events during World War II that still seem improbable: the Battle of Britain, Germany invading Russia in the winter, an atomic reactor under bleachers at the University of Chicago, and Alan Turing cracking the Enigma Code and inventing the digital computer while riding his push-bike.

Success requires work and some luck. I could never have anticipated how certain clients would change the way I thought about trauma. The breakthrough with forest dieback came when Susan heard a story. There were many unforeseeable factors that contributed to the success of the Gasfield Free campaign.

Expect unexpected events – you can count on them occurring, but you won't know what they are until they arrive. You might as well look forward to the exciting times that'll be coming your way and enjoy the ride.

But why bother at all if the Earth is doomed, and suffering and evil have no end?

Trance of the Terminal

> Even if I knew that tomorrow the world would go to pieces,
> I would still plant my apple tree.
> Martin Luther (1483–1546)

Forecasting apocalypse is a perennially popular pastime. There are catastrophes aplenty to choose from: climate destabilisation, pandemics, ecosystem collapse, pollution, asteroids, nuclear war, terrorism, the World Wide Web unravelling, coffee bean rust – a list of horrors as long as a piece of string.

If you imagine any particular demise as inevitable, you might lose interest in doing anything. For some, the response to an imagined Armageddon is to stay in bed. Others opt for variants of 'Eat, drink and you be Mary, for tomorrow we die'. To succeed, we have to find other, more productive attitudes than fatalism and despair.

List all the ways that the world could end and catastrophe will look like a done deal. So what's the rational response? What should we think and do in a time when the future seems so grim? But first, just how good are we humans at predicting what's going to happen?

Global nuclear war seemed imminent throughout my teenage years in the 1960s. I read that it was a close thing. The world bristled with thousands of nuclear weapons but did not blow up. No one predicted the end of apartheid in South Africa, the fall of the Berlin Wall, the attacks on New York's World Trade Towers, or Donald Trump.

Did anyone foretell that on the stroke of New Year 2000, Y2K would turn out to be a dead bug? Contrary to the predictions of legions of experts, when the clock struck midnight, no plane crashed, no nuclear reactor melted down and pacemakers kept ticking. Was any computer even inconvenienced? A tech-savvy friend of mine argues that computer upgrades forestalled Doomsday, but I'm not convinced.

Such unforeseen events prompt the question, why are humans such poor soothsayers? Like Chicken Little, some seem primed to see the sky falling when it isn't, while others are blind to genuine disasters and blithely ignore obvious risks. For people inclined to have a go at challenges, what are the implications if the world does or doesn't end?

Doing nothing because we believe there is no future guarantees that we will never solve problems. Our inaction would make more likely the very outcomes we wish to avoid. It would seem a shame if the world goes on and we had done nothing to make things better when we had the chance. But then, if we take on problems only to have the world disappear, would it matter?

Humans are tough, resourceful and resilient. History is forever a story being written. Reasoned optimism and believing that we can solve problems is a sensible strategy, whether or not it turns out that the world ends. What other approach could lead to success?

The Challenge of Suffering and Evil

> To remain indifferent to the challenges we face is indefensible. If the goal is noble, whether or not it is realised within our lifetime is largely irrelevant. What we must do therefore is to strive and persevere and never give up.
>
> The 14th Dalai Lama, Lhamo Dondrub (1935–)

"Peta", a compassionate young activist, told me that she can't celebrate the success of the Gasfield Free campaign while so many others suffer the impacts of coal and gas mining. "Jan", a 45-year-old client, felt deep sorrow and guilt because no matter how hard she worked in her soup kitchen, she could never care for the many more who needed her help. For Peta and Jan, their beliefs about the nature of suffering and evil deplete their energy and rob them of satisfaction from the good they do.

Suffering and evil vex every human generation. How do we enjoy life while accepting that they can never be eliminated?

The Christian impulse to help others in need does not depend on the problem of suffering being solved. Our friend "Gail" raises funds to restore eyesight in poor countries. Gail knows that she can't save the eyesight of every blind person. Her goal is to make enough money to save the eyesight of 1,000 people and she's up to 900.

Buddhists understand that good and bad go together. Lantana is a valued ornamental plant, but it devastates the bush. Meeting a problem can make us stronger. The gas field threat unified the Northern Rivers and stimulated a great environmental and social movement.

As Buddhist philosopher Alan Watts explained in *Tao: The watercourse way*, 'Thus the art of life is not seen as holding to Yang and banishing Yin, but as keeping the two in balance, because there cannot be one without the other.' The practical problem of life is to not let the 'wrestling match' between good and evil get out of hand.[1]

With or without religious beliefs, we need to find meaning in our lives while accepting that evil and suffering can never be eliminated.

We're off now to explore the wonders that words work, and the very human Key Mental Process of language.

Chapter 9

Language:
The wonders that words work

> The people of that age were phrase slaves ... There was a magic in words greater than the conjurer's art. So befuddled and chaotic were their minds that the utterance of a single word could negate the generalizations of a lifetime of serious research and thought.
>
> Jack London (1876–1916)

LIKE MUSIC, WORDS HAVE rhythm, harmony and meaning that play on our neural networks. Words convey more than their dictionary definitions. They communicate information that we intend to share, as well as things we're not even aware of. And words bring with them emotions and images that unconsciously influence how we react. The effect is known as 'priming', and the research is startling.

Priming occurs outside of conscious awareness: a person hears or reads something and, without them knowing, this affects how they think, feel and act.

Researchers gave male and female university students a test involving advanced mathematics.[1] In the instructions, they told half the students that in the past men had scored higher on the test than women, and they told the other half that the test had never shown gender differences.

What do you think the study found? Tell students that men have done better on the test and that's how the results turn out: men score higher. Tell the subjects that women perform as well as men and the finding that men are better at maths disappears.

In a 1996 priming study, university students thought they were taking part in a test of language ability.[2] Their task was to make a grammatically correct four-word sentence such as 'he finds it instantly' from the scrambled set of five words 'he it hides finds instantly'. Afterwards, as they left, the students whose test included some words relevant to stereotypes of the elderly (e.g., 'lonely', 'grey', 'wise', 'bingo', 'retired') walked more slowly down the corridor than did the students who had not read these words. When asked later, no student had twigged that the words they read had anything to do with the elderly. None could believe that reading such words could affect how fast they walked, but it apparently did.

Priming with words can affect behaviours, the impressions we form and our motivation, but the underlying mechanisms are not well understood. With more recent research, the priming effect became even more curious and controversial.

When a 2012 replication of the original study on priming and walking speed used automated timers instead of people with stopwatches, the priming effect seemed to evaporate.[3] Then they re-ran the experiment, again using automated timers, but with a crucial difference. This time they manipulated the beliefs of the 'experimenters', the people who conducted the fake language test with the subjects. Half of the experimenters were led to think that subjects would walk slower, and the others were led to expect the opposite. What do you think happened? The walking speed effect returned, but only if the experimenters believed subjects would indeed walk slower.

This was not the first time that psychologists have found that what a person is told can change the measurable behaviour of others, and the effect is not limited to adult humans. What you tell student scientists can make rats run faster or slower, and what you tell teachers can increase the IQ scores of children.

In a classic 1963 study, researchers asked psychology students to time how long it took rats to learn to run a maze – that's the sort of thing psychologists did in those days.[4] They divided the rat testers into two groups who heard different things. One group was told that the rats were bred 'maze dull', the other that the rats were 'maze bright'. In reality, the rats were all just rats. I think you already know which rats the students found ran faster. Researchers followed up with another study of what they called 'demand characteristics' (the subtle cues that make subjects aware of what an experimenter expects) but this time the research involved children and teachers.

The researchers told eighteen teachers that about 20% of the children in their classes had performed well on a test of academic 'blooming'.[5] The teachers were given to expect that these children had an unusual potential for intellectual development during the year to come. Sure enough, when tested eight months later, the IQ scores of the 'unusual' children had increased markedly more than the scores of the others. But the teachers had been tricked. The test of academic potential was a fake. The children had been randomly assigned and there was no difference in the initial IQs of the children in the two groups. This was why one of my professors told us psychology students to not give out IQ scores when we tested a child's intellectual abilities: the number can change lives.

As ephemeral words that disappear with our breath as we speak, or as written ideas that might be preserved for generations to come, language changes minds, societies and history. Words can attract, heal and strengthen. But they can also be used as weapons, to repel, harm and weaken.

This chapter explores word spells and how the Key Mental Process of language operates in shallow thought and the deep mind. We'll begin with words that affect everyone, for we all have a name.

Names and Labels

In the balcony scene of Shakespeare's play, not knowing that Romeo is in the orchard below, Juliet leans out of her upstairs window and says:

> Tis but thy name that is my enemy; thou art thyself, though not a Montague ... O, be some other name! What's in a name? That which we call a rose by any other name would smell as sweet; so Romeo would, were he not Romeo call'd, retain that dear perfection which he owes without that title (Act 2, Scene 2).

I reckon Juliet got it wrong. A rose by any other name would not smell as sweet, not if you called it 'skunk weed', 'rotting corpse flower', or worse.

Names matter. People tend to see males with ever-popular Biblical names such as Matthew, Mark, Luke and John as more credible, but not so for Judas and Jehoshaphat. I'm thinking of adding my middle initial to my name since I read that displaying it increases positive evaluations of a person's intellectual capacities and achievements. What do you think? Do I sound smarter as 'Dr Wayne Somerville' or as 'Dr Wayne R Somerville'? Hmm. Look at the cover to see what I decided. But the power of names goes beyond affecting our impressions of things, other people and ourselves.

In clinical psychology, the label 'evidence-based practice' conveys a sense of scientific rigour, but does not accurately portray what the practice involves. Calling the disease that affects our forests Bell Miner associated dieback slanders a native bird, obscures the true villain and impedes efforts to save the forests. And in political debate, the implicit power of names and labels influences opinion on important environmental and social issues: 'clean coal' sounds friendlier than calling it 'slightly less polluting coal'.

Our next thought experiment looks at how names and labels affect one of the biggest environmental challenges we face.

Say the word 'change' over a few times.

Now rate your emotional impression of the word 'change' on an Emot-o-Meter where '-10' is 'very negative' and '+10' is 'very positive'. Record your rating. Clear your mind.

Now repeat the phrase 'climate change' a few times.

Rate your emotional impression of the 'climate change' label on the Emot-o-Meter. Record your rating. Clear your mind.

Now repeat the phrase 'global warming'.

Rate your emotional impression of the label on our Emot-o-Meter. Record your rating and return to the book.

How did you rate your impression of the word 'change'? For me, the word elicits neither positive nor negative but mostly neutral feelings. After all, change can be good or bad, an opportunity to make things better or worse.

How did the ratings of your emotional reactions to the two labels 'climate change' and 'global warming' compare? Did you rate either label more or less favourably than the other?

The fossil fuel industry sought to derail debate about human impacts on climate by attacking the 'global warming' label. They argued that the buildup of atmospheric carbon dioxide can't be making the planet hotter because we're having record-breaking blizzards and cold snaps. Unfortunately, in response to this reasoning, climate scientists changed the name and made things worse.

Can you think of a more innocuous and inaccurate label for what's happening to global weather systems than to call it 'climate change'?

Imagine the spiel: 'Who knows? We might get more rain, even if somewhere else becomes drier. If the Arctic melts the Northwest Passage will open and we can drill for more oil and gas. Humans are adaptable, regulations and policies will protect us. Let's leverage climate change to our advantage'.

The problem is not that the climate is changing. Climate varies, to a degree, over time. The threat we face in the Anthropocene, the epoch in which human activity impacts Earth's geology and ecosystems, arises not from change per se, but from the dangerous destabilisation of the Earth's weather systems.

Human civilization with its agriculture and growth of cities and states was only possible in the period of stable climate our species has enjoyed during the 12,000 years since the last ice age. But now, escalating levels of energy in weather systems approach tipping points and threaten life as we know it.

'Global warming' is a more accurate label than 'climate change', but still does not properly describe the problem. For me, the word 'warming' connotes a gentle, tactile image, and doesn't sound so bad.

A better label for the problem might be 'climate chaos' or 'climate destabilisation'. These bring to mind things we hear in the news: the regular resetting of records for land and ocean temperatures; storms, droughts and floods; rising levels of atmospheric methane and carbon dioxide; and glacier and polar ice retreat. Beyond the destabilised climate, names and labels feature in debates about other environmental issues.

Some politicians slander citizens opposed to gas fields and coal mines as 'dishonest and disreputable', 'green ideologues', 'extremists', 'lunatics', 'radicals' and 'eco-fascists'. But by any accepted definition, people who want to conserve the water, air and soil that have served us well in the past are properly labelled 'conservative', and those who seek to forcibly introduce new, harmful and irreversible changes to social and natural systems are 'radical' and 'extreme'.

Standout examples of effective names such as Lock the Gate, Gasfield Free Northern Rivers, and Knitting Nannas Against Gas are accurate statements of what the groups stand for. The label 'protector' clearly portrays the motivations of those who oppose invasive mining.

Australians have traditionally thought of the poor and those doing it tough as 'down on their luck' and deserving of compassion. But today, a hard-hearted attitude labels those not well off as 'losers' and 'leaners' who deserve their misfortune and warrant no regard.

For some, wealth, not character, determines a person's worthiness. If you're rich, you are worthy. If you're poor, you're unworthy. A former Australian Federal Treasurer accused the poor of wasting their money on beer and cigarettes and argued for 'price signals' (increased fees) to dissuade them from too often seeking medical attention. For him, the rich and powerful are 'lifters' who do the work that makes Australia great; they deserve the tax breaks and government support. The divisiveness that such labels create complicates some of our biggest challenges.

Putting Words Together

The way words are arranged affects their power. Presenting words and ideas in pairs can create sounds and a rhythm that make them pleasing to the ear, memorable and persuasive. Using the same letter at the beginning of each word can enhance the effect. Word pairs have entered everyday language as evocative phrases such as 'life or death', 'birds and bees', 'bread and butter', 'forgive and forget', 'signed and sealed', 'cloak and dagger' and so on. But two is just one number that you come across in language that's designed to persuade.

Complete the following line from Winston Churchill's famous first speech as England's wartime prime minister, 'I have nothing to offer but blood …'

Did you remember the line as 'I have nothing to offer but blood, tears and sweat'? Or perhaps with a nod to the rock group, 'I have nothing to offer but blood, sweat and tears'?

If you did, you're demonstrating the mind's curious preference for word triplets: phrases that group concepts into threes.

Why do so few people remember Churchill's actual words 'I have nothing to offer but blood, toil, tears and sweat'?

Unlike blood, tears and sweat, 'toil' is not a bodily fluid, but that's likely got nothing to do with our remembering a word triplet here.

A similar fate befell Thomas Hobbes' comment that without community, life would be 'solitary, poor, nasty, brutish and short'. This is now usually remembered as the triplet, 'nasty, brutish and short'.

Known as the 'rule of three', the idea is that words and phrases that come in threes are more noticeable and easier to understand and remember. In Latin, the rule is known as *'omne trium perfectum'*, which translates as 'Everything that comes in threes is perfect.'

The rule of three works at all levels of language, from words, phrases, sentences, to chapters and even books. Some suggest that the desirable effect arises from the rhythm of the words. Triplets sound natural to the ear, but this does not explain why we *Homo sapiens* like word triplets. But like them we do. They pop up everywhere.

The Olympic motto 'faster, higher, stronger' reproduces the Latin *'citius, altius, fortius'*. In law, we swear to 'tell the truth, the whole truth, and nothing but the truth'. In politics, the French national motto *'liberté, égalité, fraternité'* inspires, and the United States Declaration of Independence declares 'life, liberty and the pursuit of happiness' as inalienable human rights. Lincoln's Gettysburg Address memorably referred to 'government of the people, by the people, for the people'. From the wasteland of recent Australian politics, we have 'debt and deficit disaster' and 'jobs, jobs, jobs'.

Word Spells

Words have defined meanings, but come packed with implicit emotions, images and memories. When we string words into sequences, we hope that their explicit meanings and subtle associations work together to communicate what it is we want to say. The study of how words create impressions, change beliefs and initiate actions informs the healing art of the psychotherapist. But word spells also underpin advertising and the darker uses of language to persuade and deceive.

This thought experiment explores a popular word spell used in advertising.

Say the word 'natural' a few times.

Rate the feeling that comes with the word 'natural' on an Emot-o-Meter where '-10' is 'very negative' and '+10' is 'very positive'.

Record your rating. Clear your mind.

Now say the word 'gas' over a few times.

Rate your feelings on our Emot-o-Meter. Record the number. Clear your mind.

Now say the words 'natural gas' a few times.

Rate your feelings on our Emot-o-Meter. Record the number. Then clear your mind.

Did the word 'natural' by itself give you a positive feeling? The word suggests Nature and is the opposite of 'artificial'. For me, it conjures mainly positive feelings.

How did you rate the emotions associated with the word 'gas'? I guess with what you've been reading, 'gas' might induce some negative feelings, but not necessarily so. For me, 'gas' as a generic term still conjures mostly neutral to slightly negative feelings.

When the words were combined to make 'natural gas', could you sense positive feelings engendered by the word 'natural' transfer to the word 'gas'?

Did you rate 'natural gas' more positively than you rated 'gas' by itself?

'Natural' gets attached to many words: 'natural foods', 'natural lifestyle', 'natural horse training', to cite a few examples amongst thousands. Early on, the gas industry branded CSG as 'natural gas'. Advertisements featured the words paired with pictures of paddocks, horses, and actors acting like happy farmers, with ne'er a gas well in sight. The idea was to link their product to the positive feelings associated with such images and the word 'natural'.

The gas industry's One Thought Solution worked for a while, but the spell was easily broken. It's true that methane is natural: it exists in Nature. But it's easy to see that the industrialisation and pollution created by gas mining are man-made. When people thought about the hidden carriages in the train of thought it was obvious that the positive images and words did not reflect reality or justify the implication that operating gas fields in populated areas is safe and good. Counter-slogans came readily to mind: 'CSG: it's natural, like arsenic, cancer and death', and so on.

Words in Therapy

Clinical psychologists also combine simple words to take advantage of juxtaposed images, emotions and associations. If I ask you to 'Remember a happy time when you felt safe and in control', you readily understand each word from its dictionary definition. My words have little specific content, but when 'happy time' is paired with 'felt safe' and 'in control', they invite you to explore your personal history to find unique experiences that bring to mind feelings of pleasure, security and competence.

In a word spell known as the 'yes set', a therapist pairs a true statement with a beneficial idea, image or action that they hope a client will take up. The art is well developed in the field of clinical hypnotherapy.

Hypnotic inductions, the words that guide a person into trance, typically consist of pairs of simple statements. In the suggestion 'As you listen to my voice, you can relax more deeply', the first phrase is known as the 'pace' because it matches, or paces, the client's experience; it's undeniably true that the client is hearing the hypnotist's voice. Stock pacing phrases such as 'while I count backwards', 'as each second passes', 'with each breath you take', will be true regardless of the circumstances of the session. And it's a good bet that if you've been staring at a spinning watch, when the hypnotist says 'your eyelids feel heavy' it's going to be true. The second phrase 'you can relax more deeply' is known as the 'lead' because it directs the client where the therapist wants them to go: in this case, more deeply into relaxation.

Rapport is deepened when a pacing statement matches a listener's experience because it gives the impression that the speaker understands what the other person is going through. An injured child will better respond to soothing words if you first acknowledge their pain by saying 'That must really hurt' than if you dismiss their suffering with 'That's nothing'. The child gets the impression that the adult is sympathetic and is, in a sense, with them in their world.

To enhance the rapport building effect of the pacing phrase, hypnotists adjust the timing of their suggestions to accord with bodily signs in the client. They deliver their 'You are getting sleepy' line when they see a client's eyelids flutter. They initiate 'arm levitation', the hypnotic phenomena in which the arm floats up automatically, with a suggestion to 'Notice the lightness in your hands' timed to coincide with the in-breath. Try it for yourself. Sitting down, rest your hands on your thighs. Do your hands feel slightly lighter as you breathe in, and heavier as you breathe out?

The persuasiveness of the pairing of a true pacing statement with a beneficial suggestion stems, in part, from its similarity to a One Thought Solution. Both forms of communication take the listener from a simple true statement to an implied conclusion via a concealed train of thought. There is no rational connection between 'As you listen to my voice' and the suggestion 'you can relax more deeply'. But they seem linked when they're put together in hypnotic language.

In therapy, words in a One Thought Solution pattern can legitimately communicate complex ideas when the hidden carriages in the train of thought are themselves beneficial and likely to be true. For instance, hiding behind the suggestion that 'You can relax more deeply' are the implications that you've already begun to relax and are capable of even deeper comfort.

Of course, during hypnotherapy, you will never get a chance to explore the hidden carriages of thought or wonder about what's being said. The patter keeps coming, suggestion after suggestion. It's hypnosis after all, and it's expected that the conscious mind will be a bit confused while the deep mind responds to helpful ideas.

The 'yes set' is not always used to help and heal. It's also employed by those who seek to manipulate for power and profit.

Using Truth to Deceive

Thanks to Sir Antony Jay and Jonathan Lynn's creation Sir Humphrey Appleby, we know how to manipulate the 'yes set' to influence surveys of political opinion. For instance, a hypothetical series of 'yes set' questions designed to elicit support for military intervention in the Middle East might go: 'Are you concerned about the threat of terrorist attacks?', 'Do you agree with strong action to protect our citizens?', 'Do you believe that a nation has the right to defend itself?', culminating with 'Should we send troops to the Middle East?'

An alternate series of 'yes set' questions designed to elicit opposition to military intervention might go: 'Are you concerned about innocent people being killed in war?', 'Do you agree that the only thing we have to fear is fear itself?', 'Do you believe that the sovereignty of nations must be respected?', and ending with 'Should we refuse to send troops to the Middle East?'

My friend "Jack" didn't know what to say when a politician used a One Thought Solution to justify gas mining: 'You need gas for your barbecue, don't you?' It's true that you need gas to run a gas barbecue, but there are many concealed carriages in the train of thought that connects that statement to the implied conclusion that we need gas fields in populated areas. As with all One Thought Solutions used to mislead, you can see the weakness of the argument when the hidden carriages are brought into the open and questioned. 'Who told you that you can't have a barbeque unless people are forced to live in gas fields?' 'We're only short of gas because it's all exported; Australia's the only country that won't reserve gas for its own citizens.' 'We don't need to sacrifice good farming country to have gas.'

One Thought Solutions can legitimately counter harmful word spells provided that the simple statements help and protect, and the implicit arguments have integrity. Used well, simple language can stimulate a conversation about the hidden train of thought and trigger a deeper appreciation of the complexity and true nature of a challenge.

When used to deceive, One Thought Solutions and the 'yes set' tactic only work when they're delivered too quickly for the listener to think about and challenge what's being said. So when you meet such word spells, slow things down. Don't let the conversation quickly move on. Bring the hidden train of thought out into the open and direct the conversation to the real issues.

The Analogy/Metaphor Strategy

Novel solutions can emerge when we recast problems with analogies and metaphors. The thought that a dieback-affected forest is like a troubled family helped Susan and me to find a solution. The analogy led to a systems theory model of how trees, birds, insects, animals, plants, soils and humans interact to create the problem. In a different context, it's easier to get a handle on a rural politician's allegiance if we ask the metaphorical question 'Which hat is he wearing: a hard hat, top hat, or Akubra?'

Up until 2012, gas industry advertising used a One Thought Solution that ran: 'Gas industry operations occupy only 2% of the land area. CSG and farming can coexist'. There was truth in the statement. From the air, the CSG wellheads and connecting roads do occupy about 2% of the land area. The claim that farming and gas mining are compatible relied on the assumption that 2% of anything isn't much, and the implication that, therefore, the impacts of CSG mining aren't worth worrying about.

I countered the 'CSG operations only occupy 2% of the land' argument with the riposte 'It's like saying to someone, don't worry about the bullet hole in your chest, it only occupies .002% of your skin area. It would take 1,000 bullet holes to occupy 2% of your skin area'. This statement revealed a concealed truth: gas field impacts go beyond the visible well pads to the damage hidden underground.

Reverse Psychology Words

Milton Erickson told a story how as a child he got a reluctant calf to go into the barn on his family's farm. When young Milton tugged on the rope, the calf resisted, but when Erickson pulled it away from the door, the calf backed itself into the barn.

What happens when you read 'Don't think of a black horse'?

Of course, you think of a black horse. Is it possible to do otherwise? Why did you do the thing that I asked you not to do? When I see the sentence, it's as if I have to mentally process the words 'black horse' first, and then take care of the 'do not' instruction.

Negative Thinking

Imagine that you've come to see me for hypnotherapy. You feel nervous and when it comes time for the hypnotic induction, I tell you that 'There's no need to relax quickly'. If we were working together in person, you wouldn't have time to think about what I said. Here you can. How do you think you would react to the statement that you don't need to relax quickly?

I can't hear your answer, but I can share my thoughts on why a therapist might use such a suggestion. The instruction takes the pressure off and the word 'relax' is processed automatically. Just as you had to imagine a black horse to understand the earlier sentence, here you have to imagine what relaxation feels like, which is not much different from actually relaxing.

When we make sense of a 'do not' statement, we have to think about whatever it is that's prohibited. When we use a negation to communicate with others, they have to think about what it is we don't want them to do or think about.

This thought experiment explores the effects of negative language.

Imagine that you're about to give a speech when someone comes up to you and says 'Don't be nervous'.

Notice the emotions that this advice brings. Rate your feelings on an Emot-o-Meter where '-10' is 'very nervous' and '+10' is 'very confident'. Record your rating. Clear your mind before continuing.

Again imagine that you're about to give a speech, but this time somebody says 'You'll be great'.

Notice the feelings that come with these words. Rate them on our Emot-o-Meter. Record your rating. Clear your mind.

Compare your two ratings.

Could you feel the effect of the negation? Did it induce you to think about feeling nervous even though that's the last thing you'd want to do at such a time?

When I was a teenager learning to ride a motorbike, a friend told me to fix my eyes where I wanted the front wheel to go while I was riding down rutted mountain tracks. 'If you look at the ruts, you'll be in them,' he said.

Saying such things as 'Don't be nervous' or 'Don't look at the ruts' encourages the thing you want to avoid. My friend's advice was sound. Keep your eyes and mind focussed on where you want to go. Avoid negations and express what you say to yourself in positive terms.

"Terry" sought my advice about difficulties he was having with self-hypnosis. He'd read a book on the subject and had inadvertently scripted his self-hypnotic suggestions in the negative, along the lines: 'I don't feel hungry', 'I will not eat fatty foods', 'I won't smoke tobacco'. Terry couldn't work out why he felt hungrier than ever and was putting on weight and smoking more. He knew consciously what he wanted to achieve, but his deep mind kept getting messages about feeling hungry, eating fatty foods and smoking tobacco. Terry was back on track when he began to talk to himself about what he wanted.

But sometimes negative language is just what's needed.

In 2012, I worked on 'the pledge' which appeared on the Gasfield Free website. It laid out why our community rejected the plan to turn the Northern Rivers into gas fields and called for a commitment to take action. I needed an ending to follow 'We will not shirk our responsibility to protect the country we love'. Susan came up with a pair of statements, both negative, which have been called the slogan of the campaign.

The Gasfield Free movement insisted throughout that only non-violent actions were acceptable, and it was essential that any call to action be worded just right.

I had the phrase 'Our opposition is non-violent'. This was true, but too emotionally deflating to finish with. The negation 'non-violent' could not be altered because of its association with the established doctrine of non-violent civil disobedience. Like all negations, 'non-violent' brings to mind 'violence', which then is mentally countered to get the meaning. We needed energising words to balance the dampening effect of 'non-violent'. Susan came up with 'non-negotiable' – another negation – and it worked a treat.

'Our opposition is nonviolent, but non-negotiable' appeared in our February 2012 open letter to the NSW Premier, and then I had the pleasure of delivering it to 700 people. As I said 'Our opposition is non-violent' I could feel the energy flatten as the audience processed the negation. Then, with the words 'but non-negotiable', they smiled and energy surged. An unlikely sentence in which one negation perfectly counterbalanced another; 'non-violent, non-negotiable' continues to work.

This double negation was effective, but it's an exception. As a rule, when setting goals for yourself, it's best to use words that express where you want to go and what you want to achieve.

Words to Set Goals

> In the long run you hit only what you aim at.
> Therefore, though you should fail immediately,
> you had better aim at something high.
> Henry David Thoreau (1817–1862)

I smoked tobacco when I was young. At the time, anti-smoking advertisements were showing tar being wrung from lung-shaped sponges accompanied by dire predictions of ill health and death. As intended, these warnings made me anxious. So, like many other smokers who falsely believe that the habit relaxes them, I responded by having another cigarette. I managed the fear of cancer and death with the One Thought Solution 'If I've done that much damage, having another fag won't make much difference'.

Thankfully, at a party, a medico friend undid that nonsense in an instant. I became a non-smoker again when he told me to forget all that stuff about lung cancer; the best reason for quitting tobacco is that you'll get your wind back, your lungs will heal and in a few years you'll be as fit as ever.

Bad Habits

We can motivate ourselves by either thinking about the negative consequences we want to avoid, or by focussing on the positive reasons for making a change. You can frighten yourself out of doing something pleasurable that might harm you in the future, but it's easier to stick with a new routine when the goal is to become fit and healthy.

Head towards what you want, not away from what you don't want. It was easier to maintain energy during the Gasfield Free campaign by thinking about what would make the Northern Rivers safe, instead of focussing on the horrors of living in a gas field. When a client prepares for surgery, I encourage them to think about the things they'll be able to enjoy as a result of their decision to go for good health. With their conscious minds occupied by such positive thoughts, their deep mind can get on with taking care of all they have to do to realise that outcome.

Words that Bind

"Fred", a man I knew years ago, bought the plainest, poorest pony I'd ever seen. Myrtle was her name. I couldn't believe Fred bought the horse, but he seemed happy. The dealer had given him four choices and he'd picked the horse for himself. Fred had done business with a used horse dealer who knew how to direct a buyer to a particular animal while giving the buyer the impression that it was their choice. By the time Fred had rejected the horse with kick and no kindness, the too-small pony and the unbroken gelding, old Myrtle looked good enough to buy, so he did.

Philosophers know the tactic as the 'false alternative'. It works by setting things up so it seems that there is a fixed choice between certain alternatives when, in reality, other options are possible. Fred couldn't see beyond the horses in front of him. He didn't realise that the dealer probably had other horses for sale or that he could go to other dealers.

Psychotherapists use a similar word spell, which they know as the 'double bind', to steer clients towards beneficial ideas and actions. Milton Erickson described his childhood experience of such a bind. When he was a boy on the farm, Erickson's father would give him choices about which chores he could do first: 'Do you want to feed the chickens first or the hogs?' All the chores had to be done, but young Milton's father was allowing him 'the primary privilege' of deciding which task he would do first.

Effective double binds are based on things you are willing to do. If used for personal advantage, binds such as 'Will you give me $5 or $10' are easily resisted.

The following double binds direct your attention to what choice you're going to make, and away from any doubt that you're capable of performing the requested action: 'Would you like to go into a trance now or later?', 'Which hand will feel lighter first?'

Could you feel the effect? It's as if you have to begin to enter hypnosis to answer the question.

Troublesome Words

No one succeeds all the time or is forever immune to stress. Bolstering confidence with words that exaggerate how good and strong we are (e.g., 'Nothing bothers me', 'I always come out on top') leaves us vulnerable to a single setback. The downside is more serious when we use words that exaggerate the power of people and forces that threaten us. For problem solvers, words such as 'always', 'every', 'never', 'nothing', 'all', 'none', 'everybody' and 'nobody', have their place, but not when they compromise confidence and personal power or magnify the scale and seriousness of difficulties and the potency of opponents.

Beyond troublesome words that exaggerate, some words predictably feed fear and strangle hope because they suggest danger, imply failure and create pressure and guilt.

What Ifs

Asking 'what if' distracts attention from what's happening now. It leads us to either think about the past and how things could've been different, or how things might turn out in the future. Used in moderation, such thinking helps us to learn and anticipate. But little good comes from just going over unpleasant things that have already occurred or that might yet take place.

Catastrophic thinking begins with a 'what if' question: 'What if I'd been in the car accident?', 'What if I get cancer?' There's no end to such questions. How many bullets, metaphoric and real, miss us in a lifetime? What if I'd gone to the Vietnam War? What if I'd hit the stump I narrowly missed when thrown from my horse forty years ago? A good friend died that way at 20 years of age.

When we're entranced by the 'fallacy of hindsight', our thinking gets stuck as we look back and question why we did things that now seem clearly ill-considered. But at the time, we didn't know what we know now. And when our attention fixes on what could yet go wrong, we're vulnerable to the One Thought Solution that the future will be safer if we worry enough.

To break 'what if' trances that trap you in the past or the future, ask whether the answer to the question can teach you something of value. If so, explore and learn from what you have done or might yet do. But if there's nothing much of value left to learn, drop the 'what ifs' and switch to more productive thinking.

Failure Words

This thought experiment examines the implication that lies behind the word 'try'.

Say a few times, 'I will try to do better'.

Now rate how confident you feel that you'll actually do better on an Emot-o-Meter where '-10' is 'very doubtful' and '+10' is 'very confident'. Record your rating. Clear your mind.

Now say to yourself, 'I will do better'.

Rate on the Emot-o-Meter how confident you feel that you will do better. Record your rating. Compare it with your previous confidence rating.

Did your level of confidence change with the different statements?

The verb 'try' implies that failure is possible, even likely. If you were feeling anxious, would you prefer someone to say 'Try to relax', or would a simple 'Relax' be better?

I probably should – but won't – resist quoting Yoda, who told Luke in *Star Wars*: 'Do. Or do not. There is no try'.

'Try' is not the only word that generates feelings of doubt.

Hope is a wonderful emotion in dire times. As Desmond Tutu said, 'Hope is being able to see that there is light despite all of the darkness'. But 'hope' used as a verb is different from the word used as a noun. Would you feel confident that a job would be completed on time if a tradesperson said, 'I hope to get the work done'?

Pressure Words

Psychologist Dr Albert Ellis coined the term 'musterbation' for the too frequent use of the word 'must'. He described 'must' and 'should' as two of the most energy-depleting words in the English language. These words cast spells that can deliver a punch, especially if we're under pressure.

Let's explore this effect.

Run the following sentences and rate the feelings that they bring. You'll have to pay close attention because the sentences are trivial and likely to have only a slight emotional effect.

Repeat a few times, 'I must buy some milk'.

Notice the feelings that come with these words. Rate the emotion on an Emot-o-Meter where '-10' is 'very pressured' and '+10' is 'very relaxed'. Record your rating. Then clear your mind.

Now repeat the sentence, 'I want to buy some milk'.

Notice the feeling and rate it on the Emot-o-Meter. Record your rating. Clear your mind. Compare your two ratings before you read on.

Did it feel different when you switched from saying 'must' to 'want'? If you noticed a change, can you name the feeling associated with the word 'must'? Can you point to where in your body you felt this?

Some people feel pressured by the word 'must'. It's as if they're being pushed to do something. And they sense the impact in their stomach or chest.

If such a trivial statement about milk can induce a negative feeling, it's no wonder that self-talk peppered with statements such as 'I must get better' and 'I must get back to work' can create problems when people feel very down.

"Rhonda's" depression lifted when she changed her habitual use of the word 'must'. How could Rhonda not feel pressured? She didn't limit herself to saying 'I must clean the house' and 'I must do the shopping'. Rhonda even made demands on the weather: 'We must get some rain', 'It must fine up soon'. She felt better when she used alternative sentences such as 'It would be good if we get some rain' and 'I would like to do the shopping'.

Let's look at another pressure word that induces a different unpleasant emotion.

Say the sentence, 'I should do more to help'.

Notice the feelings that this engenders. Rate the emotion on an Emot-o-Meter where '-10' is 'very unpleasant' and '+10' is 'very pleasant'. Record your rating.

Can you describe the feeling and give it a name? Clear your mind. Now say the alternate sentence, 'I would like to do more to help'.

Notice the feeling that comes with these words. Rate the feeling on the Emot-o-Meter. Record your rating. Can you describe the emotion? Compare your two ratings.

The effect of using the word 'should' is usually subtle, but it tends to foster a sense of obligation. For someone who is depressed, using the word 'should' can be immobilising. In the above example, 'should' implies that we do wrong if we don't do more to help. This sets us up to feel guilty. When we apply 'should' to other people (e.g., 'He should do this', 'She should do that') it encourages a critical, judgmental attitude.

To counter harmful spells created by words such as 'what if', 'try', 'must' and 'should', notice when you use them and think about how you can better express what you want to say. Interrogate your thinking with what's known as 'Socratic questioning'. Like the ancient Greek philosopher, query the emotions and challenge the hidden assumptions and beliefs that come with these problematic words. Ask yourself, 'What can I learn from this?', 'How do I know that?', 'Where's the evidence?' and so on.

Warm-up Words

Sports people warm up to get blood flowing, stretch muscles and focus their minds before going out to play. Physical exercise can also warm up our mental muscles, but for problems more cerebral than physical, you can get ready without leaving your chair.

Before we saw a family for therapy, my psychology supervisor got me to warm up by generating seven ideas about what could be causing their problems. It didn't matter that these might all be wrong; the exercise stimulated flexible thinking and an open, searching attitude. Get your mind ready for creative problem-solving by asking questions such as 'What do I really know?', 'What's the big picture here?' and 'What alternatives are possible?'

You can also wake up your creative mind by thinking 'yes and …' instead of 'yes but …' when you come upon a new idea. A popular warm-up exercise is to generate random sentences from arbitrarily chosen words. Sometimes, the best preparation for creative thinking is to recite the alphabet, or to just resolve that you're ready to think the unthinkable.

The Alphabet Technique

When you next struggle to remember someone's name, tap into the mental filing system that stores such information. Recite the alphabet slowly letter by letter and let your mind flash on gender-appropriate names (e.g., 'A, Alison, Anne, Audrey, B, Betty …') and the name you're looking for will likely pop out when you come to the right letter. But you can use the alphabet for more interesting challenges.

When clients are considering a career change, I sometimes give them an alphabet-based task to do at home. They're to consider, and not reject out of hand, every possible job from A to Z, and I lend them a book that alphabetically lists all professions in Australia. No one has yet taken up aeronautical engineering or zoology, but most find that the exercise frees up their thinking. Even if they decide to stay in their job, thinking things through and rejecting other options confers a satisfying sense that leaving things as they are is an active choice.

Think the Unthinkable

A lifetime of using One Thought Solutions can predispose us to censor ideas before we even have them. Resist the urge to criticise and reject new thoughts the instant they come to mind, even when they're obviously absurd and unworkable. Allow yourself to think the unthinkable. What harm would it do to spend a few minutes contemplating what life would be like as an aardvark trainer or a zither tuner? The unexpected ideas that spin off those thoughts might surprise you. Wonder and let your mind wander. Stay open to new possibilities however unlikely they seem. It might be scary at first, but creative thinking becomes possible as you free up your deep mind.

Deconstructing Complex Information

When we take on those who seek to mislead and harm, we have to understand what they're saying and how they're using language. Such writers use all the tricks and tactics we talked about earlier, and they like to repeat themselves. It's as if they think a 'weighty argument' has to have lots of words. To understand complex written information, you have to first take it apart.

Keep a reference version of the original on your computer, and make a working copy that you can edit. Begin with the first sentence. Ask yourself what it is saying. Create a heading for that kind of statement, and then cut and paste the first sentence under that heading.

To illustrate, I'll use extracts from a letter a gas company executive sent me. The letter began:

> Dear Dr Somerville,
>
> NSW and Northern Rivers residents need energy for heating, lighting and cooking in their homes and to power domestic appliances. We all need transport fuels and in the workplace our

jobs depend on reliable energy supplies to power equipment and to provide heating and cooling. Our lives depend on reliable energy supplies.

Natural gas from coal seams currently meets a third of eastern Australia's gas supply needs and our industry has a proven and safe track record over a number of decades. Exports of natural gas from Australia are helping less developed countries to reduce the extent of air pollution and associated illness.

The first three sentences suggested the heading 'Why we need energy'. So we could set up our working copy as follows, with headings underlined.

Why we need energy

Sentence 1 – 'NSW and Northern Rivers residents need energy for heating, lighting and cooking in their homes and to power domestic appliances.'

Sentence 2 – 'We all need transport fuels and in the workplace our jobs depend on reliable energy supplies to power equipment and to provide heating and cooling.'

Sentence 3 – 'Our lives depend on reliable energy supplies.'

The fourth sentence breaks fresh ground and warrants a new heading, as follows.

Why we need CSG

Sentence 4 – 'Natural gas from coal seams currently meets a third of eastern Australia's gas supply ...'

We need another heading for the rest of Sentence 4.

Why CSG is safe

Sentence 4 (continued) – '... our industry has a proven and safe track record over a number of decades.'

Then we need another heading.

Why CSG is good for the environment

Sentence 5 – 'Exports of natural gas from Australia are helping less developed countries to reduce the extent of air pollution and associated illness.'

Continue like this, breaking the material down sentence by sentence. Rearrange every statement until it's placed under its appropriate heading.

By the time you're finished, you will have broken any spell that the author hoped to weave by repeating potent words. In the first four-line paragraph of our example, 'energy' is repeated three times, 'power' twice, 'need' twice, 'reliable' twice and 'depend' twice. That's a lot of power words.

You're now ready to think about each point. Consider the sentences under the headings you've created. What do they really say? What evidence is offered? Then fire up your train of thought, add carriages and work out how you'll deal with each claim.

Use this method to analyse any study, report or article that the author of the piece you're working on cites to back their argument. You might find that the information they refer to doesn't actually support the claims they make.

Countering the word spells in complex letters, policy documents and reports takes time and effort but, with practice, you'll be able to identify weak and strong arguments and take them on.

Getting Your Words Out

What's the good of having something to say if people who can make a difference don't get to hear it?

Work out who you want to communicate with. Your audience might include those who could benefit from knowing what it is you wish to share, as well as those who by virtue of position or personality can influence public debate. Your intended audience will depend on the challenge or problem you're working on and the kind of information you wish to share. Ask where your words might have the greatest effect, where you can apply 'leverage'.

Look for allies in unexpected places. Be inclusive, not exclusive. Don't waste your work by sending it to just the responsible minister. Chances are they're the least likely to care about what you think. Cast your work widely. Go beyond your networks of like-minded people. You never know who your ideas might affect or who might pass your words on. Even if the person to whom you address your work doesn't read what you've written, someone else in their office might, and good could come from that.

Be prepared for personal attack when you communicate with politicians. Such tactics aim to deflect attention away from the issue, and the strategy succeeds if you become angry. Be civil. Remember that in this digital age the things you write could be around for a long time. It's your ideas that are important, not your reaction to an insult.

During the Gasfield Free campaign, the mailing lists for our reports, submissions, letters and articles included local protectors and concerned citizens, environmental groups, scientific and academic organisations, medical and mental health professionals, local government councillors, and members of every State and Federal Parliament.

Once you know who you want to share your ideas with, decide how you're going to get the message out.

In the Gasfield Free campaign, Susan and I mailed letters to every household in the Kyogle Shire. Some Groups Against Gas purchased multi-stack burners to produce DVDs by the thousands. Compared to the high cost and limited coverage of newspaper and television advertising, these methods were cost-effective and efficient.

New Media and email

If privacy is not important, then email has advantages over letters sent via the postal service. You can attach documents and send an email to hundreds of people at minimal cost. You increase the chance of your words being read if you address each email individually using the appropriate salutation.

Thanks to friends, everything I wrote during the Gasfield Free campaign ended up on Facebook. You will know more about Twitter than I do.

At first, press releases seemed a good way to get ideas out. But as the Gasfield Free campaign gained traction, newspaper articles adopted a format that appeared balanced but, in effect, misrepresented important issues. A half-hour interview with a journalist boiled down to a few sentences which were then paired with a similar amount of gas industry spin. This style of reporting implies that truth is relative and all arguments deserve equal column space. The hidden assumption is that if I say gas mining is bad and the industry says it's good, the truth must lie somewhere in between. But some things are true and some are false.

If I say that the capital city of Australia is Canberra and someone else claims that the capital is Perth, that doesn't mean that the real capital is midway between the two, near Maralinga on the edge of the Great Victoria Desert.

Newspapers are more than just articles and ads. For getting your words out, few options beat a letter to the editor. These are usually printed verbatim and lots of folk read them.

I'll end this chapter with some observations about how you can use silence to better communicate complex ideas when you speak.

Using Silence

Tune your ear to what speakers do with the spaces between words, the slivers of silence that writers signal with a comma, a dash – or a full stop. Good public speakers use the gaps between words, phrases and sentences for emphasis and to breathe. Less accomplished speakers try to fill all the available space with sound, so they obliterate silences with a stream of 'um' and 'er' fillers.

When there are no pauses in speech, it's harder both to deliver a message and to understand what's being said. Audiences have no time to mentally process what one sentence means before they have to attend to the next one. And if the going gets tough, the lack of gaps in the stream of sound can put pressure on a speaker.

Giving expert evidence in court taught me the value of silence and leaving gaps in speech. Witnesses are meant to direct answers to the judge or magistrate, but barristers try to keep attention fixed on them. They know how to pace their questioning to develop rapport and induce comfort, so they deliver the opening question 'Is your name Dr Wayne Somerville?' in an easy-paced manner. Right then, at the beginning, it matters how you use the space before you answer. There's only one response possible, so I confirm that I am indeed he, but the timing matters. First impressions count. If from nervousness or an attempt to sound decisive, I answer quickly and leave little gap between the question and my answer, I create the impression that I'll answer all questions promptly.

The pace increases as the barrister shifts from establishing rapport to posing more demanding questions. If I was to follow the barrister's lead and answer quickly, when the time comes that I need to stop and think before answering, the silence stands out. The pause is unexpected, so the break in speech surprises. Everyone in the court looks up and wonders why you need time to answer this question. Let's rewind the scenario and start again.

The barrister asks 'Are you Dr S?' I pause, take a breath, look at the judge, answer 'Yes', and turn back to the barrister. I don't need time to think about whether I am indeed the said Dr S or to answer easy first questions such as 'Where do you practice?' But when the questions get harder and I need to think before I speak, the pause will not seem out of place.

Control the impression you make. Use the gaps in your speech to good effect. Slow down when you speak in public. Let silence be heard. When you need to take time to think, you will appear thoughtful and considered, and you will give your audience a chance to absorb what you're saying. That is, after all, why you're taking the trouble to speak in public.

We now leave the realm of language to explore emotion, the Key Mental Process that gives reason its sense. Is anxiety a symptom or a signal? What role do anger, guilt and courage play in life? How can we use our emotions to tap into our deep minds when we take on big challenges? These are some of the questions we'll look at.

Chapter 10

Emotions: Reason's judge

When a man is prey to his emotions,
he is not his own master.
Baruch Spinoza (1632–1677)

Reason is, and ought only to be the slave of the passions.
David Hume (1711–1776)

PHILOSOPHER DAVID HUME'S NOTION that emotions should control reason still surprises and provokes.[1] Since Freud, most believe that in a healthy person, the ego, with its reason and connection to external reality, needs to contain the id's cauldron of dangerous emotions. The idea goes back to the ancient Greek philosopher Plato's description of the human soul as made of three elements, with '*nous*' (reason) ruling over '*epithumia*' (appetite or passion) and '*thumos*' (spirit or fortitude). But neither extreme – reason without emotion or emotion without reason – works in the real world.

If emotion ruled without reason, society would be at risk of a dark age of superstition and barbarity. I know of no time when reason ruled without emotion – *Star Trek*'s Mr Spock and the Vulcans don't count – but such a society wouldn't seem human.

There is no essential conflict between reason and emotion. We need both. Emotion and reason dance constantly. It's not possible to judge the relative value of things by reason alone: we need to desire one choice over another. How could we plan or make decisions if we did not prefer this over that?

Defective emotions affect the reasoning abilities of some influential people. In politics and business, the ability to lie shamelessly and act without empathy can confer a competitive advantage. The apparent irrationality of some policies that harm people is best understood as arising from an emotional rather than an intellectual deficit in the creators of the legislation.

Emotions come in two basic forms: positive and negative. As children, we learn that emotions like happiness, love and compassion are good, and emotions like anxiety, anger and guilt are bad. So we adopt a One Thought Solution of avoiding the bad and desiring the good. This can induce us to think that negative emotions are symptoms of illness, and we try to suppress or escape unpleasant feelings as soon as we can. In thinking like this, we misunderstand the true nature of our emotions.

Emotions motivate and inform. Negative emotions are often signals, not symptoms. We are well served by our ability to feel courage and fear, security and anxiety, love and hate, compassion and anger, happiness and sadness, attraction and repulsion, cooperation and competition, innocence and guilt, and much more. Even depression signals the breakdown of old ways of thinking and prepares us for change.

Emotions protect us and help us to survive. They can also bring suffering. The task is not to avoid or eliminate unpleasant feelings, but rather to work out what they're telling us so we can solve the underlying problem. We can then usually let go of the negative feelings.

We'll concentrate on emotions that you're most likely to encounter when you take on life's challenges.

Fear and Anxiety

> Just as courage imperils life; fear protects it.
> Leonardo Da Vinci (1452–1519)

Difficult challenges that make us anxious do not go away just because we figure out how to stop worrying about them. In an adult version of the child's belief that if you wish hard enough for something it will come true, some think that they can solve serious environmental problems by simply not believing in them. They would rather be comfortably ignorant and risk disaster, than be concerned and informed and take appropriate action.

Thinking that fear and anxiety are symptoms rather than signals, confuses solutions with problems. Psychologists typically work to reduce a client's anxiety, but less often address the stress-triggering threat. Fear and anxiety do not indicate weakness, illness or faulty learning. Rather, Nature designed these emotions to protect us. If a mother is anxious that her children could be injured by pollution from a nearby gas compression factory, the primary therapeutic goal is not to allay her fears, but rather to investigate the danger and to help her respond appropriately and effectively to the threat. Fear and anxiety warn us that danger's about and prepare us to take action. As with an activated warning light on a dashboard, the problem is not the flashing, but what it's telling us.

But feeling anxious or fearful does not necessarily mean that we're under threat of imminent harm. We need to stay with our feelings long enough for our deep mind to work out what's really going on and decide what we should do about it.

Using Anxiety as a Tracer

If you think of fear and anxiety as signals, the question shifts from 'How do I get rid of these horrible feelings?' to 'What are they trying to tell me?' Hang with your anxiety, think about what it's saying, and it becomes a kind of tracer or link to the root of the problem. Insights emerge when you resist the impulse to escape.

Anxiety can signal a threat that comes from within or from without. Seeing a fin break the surface at the beach indicates a danger from without which triggers a rapid exit from the surf. The shiver of fear from hearing about a shark attack on the radio signals a threat that comes from within, perhaps from our empathetic imagining of what it would be like to be attacked or from a childhood memory of a gory story or a day at the beach when the shark alarm sounded. When we work out what our anxiety signals, we can go about managing the real threat.

When anxiety and fear do their job and we remove the danger, stressful feelings can subside. But what happens if the threat doesn't go away?

Letting Go of Unnecessary Emotion

When a menace persists, sustained high levels of anxiety can cause harm. We need to tone down the signals while still heeding what they're telling us.

If you find yourself in such a situation, first assess the level of anxiety you feel on an Emot-o-Meter where '0' is 'no anxiety' and '+10' represents 'extreme anxiety'.

Now think about the actual threat. Rate your rational, considered estimation of the real danger on an Emot-o-Meter where '0' is 'no threat' and '+10' is 'very severe threat'.

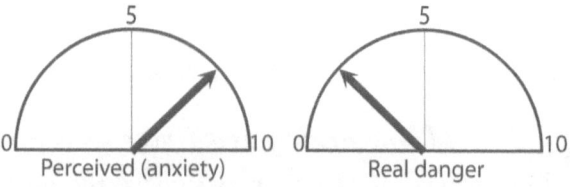

Measuring Unnecessary Anxiety

Compare the gap between your ratings. You can safely let go of the anxiety that exceeds your estimate of the current, actual level of threat. Keep only as much anxiety as you need for protection. Or perhaps promise yourself to go back to worrying on a specified day in the future, as your deep mind continues to work on the problem.

We now look at an ever-present physical activity that's often implicated when anxiety seems overwhelming.

Remember to Breathe

I used to pace my rate of breathing to that of a client for a few minutes to see what it felt like to breathe like them. I gave up the practice because it usually felt awful. Susan has a 'Remember to breathe' sticker above her desk, and lots of us could benefit from this advice. We tend to not notice our breathing when it works well, and when it's faulty, we rarely recognise the anxiety-arousing effect it has on us. For some unfortunate folk, circumstances, disrupted breathing and a One Thought Solution combine to create a mental disorder.

Attend to your breathing. When you inhale, do you breathe with just your abdomen, or do you inflate the upper part of your chest as well? How often do you breathe? A healthy rate of breathing is about once every four seconds. Anxiety creates muscular tension which restricts breathing, and sitting at a desk for a long time magnifies the effect. Put your arms in front of you as if you're working on a keyboard and take a few breaths. Now pull your arms back, open your chest and breathe. Can you feel the difference that posture makes to the rate and depth of your breathing?

If you've done much skin diving, you know that to get fresh air into the snorkel the in-breath is deeper and the out-breath stronger than normal breathing. If you breathe shallowly while you're snorkelling, you'll soon feel light-headed and unwell because rebreathing the exhaled air in the snorkel disrupts the balance of oxygen and carbon dioxide in your blood.

The windpipe from mouth to lungs is like a snorkel, and habitual shallow breathing when you're on dry land can also create unpleasant physical effects. Add an inflammatory One

Thought Solution along the lines 'I'm losing my mind' or 'I'm dying' and you're on your way to a 'panic attack'.

My client "Robert" believed he was going insane. Robert had always enjoyed car travel in his work, but now he dreaded driving, he'd quit his job and his life was unravelling. Robert's breathing was chaotic; I wasn't game to mirror it. I asked Robert to take me for a drive down some back streets so I could see what was happening with him.

It's common to hold your breath for a bit when you concentrate, and as we set off Robert held his breath. He then kept holding it as we went down the road, turned left, then left again – a psychologist and a client who looked as if he might never breathe again, together on a drive of discovery.

The first panic attack often coincides with a stressful event or some illness such as influenza that affects breathing. In Robert's case, his first panic occurred when he was on the way to a funeral. At this point, all Robert suffered was the effect of disturbed breathing. But when he thought he was having a heart attack, his anxiety shot off the scale and a full-blown panic attack had arrived.

During therapy, Robert's anxiety eased after he changed the way he thought about his problem and retrained his breathing to a healthier pattern.

As a trainee psychologist, I visited 46-year-old "Jill" at her home. Jill was housebound. Her first panic attack ambushed her at the shops and she had adopted a One Thought Solution to avoid embarrassment: 'I almost passed out at the supermarket, so I won't go there again'. Jill's protective strategy produced the fear and avoidance of panic attacks that define 'agoraphobia'. Jill quit her job and cut off contact with her friends. When I saw her, Jill avoided every room in her house where she'd had a panic attack. She only felt safe sitting in one particular chair. Jill benefited from improving her breathing.

Agoraphobia is debilitating, but it makes sense as a misinformed attempt to solve the problem of panic. When sufferers learn about the connection between breath and anxiety and retrain their disrupted breathing, they have the new information they need to craft a successful response.

Anger

Anger is a natural response that prepares us to fight off danger. The emotion worked well in the simpler world in which our kind evolved. The adrenaline spike with its supercharged strength and devil-may-care disregard for personal well-being are just what's needed to repel a wild animal that wanders into your cave. Using anger is trickier in modern times. The ability to throttle a dangerous animal was once a valuable skill but is not so useful now that predators can wear suits and attack from afar.

Cranky Cow

If anger doesn't fulfil its purpose and remove a threat, the emotional energy tends to be redirected. Turned outward, anger can lead to abuse of family, friends and other blameless people. If turned inward, anger can result in depression.

An anger-induced trance fixes attention, limits awareness of what's going on around us, and restricts our ability to think rationally. People entranced by anger tend to say and do uncharacteristic things that they later regret. If you melt down, as soon as you come out of the angry spell, take responsibility for your actions. If you've hurt others, apologise promptly and sincerely. Don't let embarrassment stop you from making things right. It's important for both you and the person who bore the brunt of your anger to finish with an apology so you can put the experience behind you.

Just as it's best to repair a leaky roof when the sun's shining, work on your anger when you feel calm. To break anger's hold, think things through and draw on all your Key Mental Processes. Ask questions such as 'What triggers my anger?' and 'Why do I lose control?' Explore the beliefs, memories and thoughts that feed your anger. Imagine how you might respond differently in the future. Think about how you can channel such strong emotion to help, rather than block, your creative problem-solving.

As Mahatma Gandhi explained, we need to control our anger to transmute it 'into a power which can move the world'.

Finding Courage

Courage harnesses fear, anxiety and anger in the most difficult times. It gives us strength to take on a dangerous challenge and stay with the struggle. Courage is not mere bravado. Acts of courage define our personal and social histories. But for so important an emotion, there's little information about what courage is and how to foster it. I don't recall hearing much about courage during my professional training, and yet it's the outstanding quality I see in my clients as they overcome trauma and tribulation. Then, I found practical ideas about courage in two literary genres: wartime speeches and the novels of J.R.R. Tolkien.

For insights into the nature and nurture of courage, read the speeches of historical leaders such as Queen Elizabeth I and Sir Winston Churchill.[2] Their words steeled soldiers and citizens to stand against deadly foes. The oratory of German and British wartime leaders embodies the infamy and the glory of World War II. Neither Hitler nor Churchill went to university, both were soldiers who loved art and the theatre, and their words shape our culture still. Hitler's writings foment racist hatred, while Churchill's oratory continues to inspire and instruct.

Winston Churchill's use of language to foster bravery was similar to the way a clinician paces a client's experience and then leads them to change. He first told the truth about what lay ahead. In Churchill's maiden speech as British Prime Minister, he did this with the words, 'We have before us an ordeal of the most grievous kind. We have before us many, many long months of struggle and of suffering ...' There's no false comfort offered in those words. Like a pacing statement in psychotherapy, this truthful assessment built rapport between Churchill and his audience. The British people knew straight away that their leader understood and respected their fear and would not understate the danger they faced.

Churchill then let his audience know that they were a part of something worthy and greater than themselves. He said, 'You ask, what is our policy? ... It is to wage war ... against a monstrous tyranny, never surpassed in the dark, lamentable catalogue of human crime'. Churchill then gave a realistic assurance that victory was possible by saying, 'I feel sure that our cause will not be suffered to fail among men. At this time I feel entitled to claim the aid of all ...'

J.R.R. Tolkien served as a soldier in World War I and saw the impacts of coal mining and the Industrial Revolution on the English countryside: experiences which informed his epic fantasy novels. Professor Tolkien's words, delivered by fictional characters, also demonstrate pacing and leading language patterns.

In Tolkien's *Lord of the Rings*, Aragorn prepares his troops for battle and likely death. Aragorn tells the men that he can see in their eyes the fear that he feels. He says that the day may come when 'we forsake our friends and break all bonds of fellowship' but it's not going to be this day. He then calls on his men to fight.

For five months, citizens at the Bentley blockade coped with anxiety and fear under a constant threat of intervention by the NSW riot police. In a letter to the editor of a local newspaper, I wanted to bolster the resolve of protectors and reduce the likelihood of violence. There was no place for the fighting words that inspire courage in war. The letter had to evoke emotions other than anger and aggression. It was essential that protectors maintain non-violent resistance, regardless of how harshly the police treated them. I had to acknowledge the threat and distress; the risk of serious injury or death was real. I wrote:

> The Bentley Protectors could soon confront a massive police operation. The NSW Government appears locked into a high risk 'shock and awe' strategy. They hope that riot police can end our community's resistance to gas field industrialisation. But Minister Roberts' courageous policy of 'mining by martial law' can only succeed if we allow it to – and why would we do that?
>
> 'Shock and awe' only works if we are indeed shocked and awed. But what happens if we are just prepared and bored, and respond with humour and compassion rather than fear and anger?
>
> When you see columns of police looking mean and nasty, remember the big picture, draw on the fellowship and support of the good people around you, find your humour and compassion, and savour the moment. You will be privileged to witness an event of historical importance. The riot police might win this skirmish, but our determined citizens will win the war.

Thankfully, I have only once needed to draw on Tolkien's words during therapy. "Tom", a husband and father of two young sons, faced a cruel task. I was helping Tom's wife, "Alicia", cope with terminal cancer. I felt so sad for Tom – a good man who had to lose both the wife he loved and the life they shared. Tom was afraid and troubled by visions of Alicia's funeral. All I could think to say were words along the lines, 'The day will come when you will go to Alicia's funeral, but this is not that day. The time will come when you will have to care for your sons by yourself, but that time is not now. On this day, tomorrow, and on the days that follow, you do what you have to do. Your job is to enjoy being with Alicia and the boys. Draw on your strength as a man to do what you have to do'.

To find courage when you're fearful, respect your emotions and look honestly at the danger. Remember the friends, family and neighbours who support you. Commit yourself to do what you need to do, regardless of how afraid you are.

But when courage deserts us and we do something we shouldn't have done, or we don't do what we should have, guilt reminds us of our failing.

The Voice of Conscience

Guilt is the emotion that lets us know we've done something wrong. If guilt motivates us to own up to our failing and put things right, we can usually let go of the feeling. When the emotion is strong, shame dissuades us from talking to others, and our desire to avoid unpleasant feelings can prevent us from thinking deeply about what happened. If left unresolved, guilt can blight an entire life.

Children learn that they're rewarded for doing right and punished for doing wrong. This makes them vulnerable to the false belief that if something goes wrong in their lives they must have done something to cause it. Children can believe that they are responsible for an accident because they argued with their mother that morning, or didn't tell her that they loved her, or for some other reason that seems irrational to an adult. But children are not the only ones susceptible to simple, misleading thinking about punishment and reward.

For some adults, childlike notions about why good and bad things happen to people spawn One Thought Solutions such as 'Good things happen to me, so I must be good', 'Bad things happen to other people, so they must be bad', and so on. In reality, bad things can happen to good people and good things to bad people.

Guilt is an especially difficult emotion for war veterans. War provides many opportunities for guilt-generating acts such as killing innocent people, failing to keep promises made to dying mates, or even just surviving when others didn't. And politics and social attitudes can exacerbate the shame veterans feel.

Some who lack empathy can do terrible things and feel no remorse. "Charlie" should never have been in the army. Referred to me by his psychiatrist, Charlie arrived heavily medicated and with diagnoses of posttraumatic stress disorder and 'psychopathic personality'. I agreed with his psychiatrist that, for all the atrocities Charlie had committed in Vietnam and during his postwar career as an assassin for hire, there was a likeable part of Charlie that struggled to form a conscience. I thought I should address his guilt, but Charlie straightened me out on that. He explained that for some crimes there can be no redemption or forgiveness.

There are also people who suffer terrible guilt when they've done no real wrong. Guilt had worn "Carol" out. She had a dilemma. Her two young daughters were keen to visit their grandfather, Carol's father, and he was also pressuring to see the kids. Carol's father sexually abused her when she was a child, and she could not reconcile her wish that her daughters have a relationship with their grandfather and her need to protect them.

Pointing out the mismatch between Carol's 'offence' of wanting to protect her children and her father's crimes didn't lessen her guilt. Work with Carol's disturbing memories went well but didn't ease her guilty feelings. I'm not sure what triggered the idea – perhaps it was using the word 'offence' – but I decided to put Carol on trial for her crimes.

Long-term guilt is a severe punishment. It's like a self-imposed prison sentence for a crime that never went to trial. The law specifies penalties for every offence and when the offender pays their debt to society they are set free. The punishment meted out by guilt can be a life sentence with no parole. Under Australian law, only the most heinous crimes attract such a penalty.

When preparing a pre-sentence report, my job as a clinical psychologist is to help the judge determine the appropriate penalty for an offender who has pleaded guilty to criminal charges. The judge wants an opinion about the offender's insight into their actions, the contrition or sorrow they feel for what they've done, their attitude to making changes that might reduce the risk of further offending, and any other mitigating circumstance.

Carol's day in the quasi-court held in my office went something like the following.

'Carol, you feel guilty because you believe you've done something wrong.' Carol nodded.

'Under Australian law, every offence has a specified penalty. When the offender pays the fine, works off the community service order, or serves the sentence, the debt is paid in full.' Carol nodded.

'But before a judge imposes a sentence, the defendant needs to answer some questions. Are you ready?' Carol was ready.

'Carol, by your own admission you've done something wrong. Please describe your offence in detail, as it might appear on a police charge sheet.'

This wasn't easy for Carol. She'd never before spelt out what she'd done wrong. I sensed her attitude already shifting from meekness to something spikier.

'I guess it's my fault that my daughters can't visit their grandfather … but … but…' Carol was ready for the next stage, so I continued.

'Are there any mitigating circumstances that we need to know about? Anything else you would like to say about your offence?' With that, Carol began a long overdue conversation with herself.

'But I can't leave my daughters with him. He sexually abused me as a child. I couldn't live with myself if he abused them. I have to protect my girls.'

I asked, 'Did the police ever charge your father for his crimes?' 'No.'

'Has your father apologised for what he did? Has he ever talked to you about it?' 'No.'

When I asked, 'How do you feel about your offence? What do you think you should do differently?' Carol burred up.

'What offence? I've done nothing to hurt him. I never did anything wrong. He's the one who committed the crimes, not me. It's his fault I can't trust him with his granddaughters. I'm not going to do anything different. I won't ever let the girls be alone with him. Maybe one day when they're older I'll explain it to them.'

I didn't expect my next question to get far, and it didn't. 'Perhaps your guilt is not enough. Do you deserve more punishment for your crime?'

Carol's defence of herself was over. She had, in effect, withdrawn her earlier plea of guilty. Her dilemma had lost its horns. She now believed that she was right, not wrong. Carol was ready for release from her self-imposed sentence.

Asking guilt-suffering clients to specify their crime and how they should be punished can work well. The conversation rarely gets through the quasi-court routine before their attitude changes, even when, unlike Carol, they truly have done something wrong.

For "James", his offence was clear. When fighting in Vietnam he promised a dying mate that he would take care of his friend's wife and family when he got back to Australia. James felt ashamed because he'd never fulfilled his promise. The mitigating circumstances were that he was young at the time and was in shock from battle and seeing his friend die. There's a time for every crime. James had already had more than 20 years of beating himself up with guilt, but he felt he needed to do more. James decided that after so many years he couldn't seek out his friend's family. Instead, he repaid the debt he felt through welfare work with other veterans.

Nature gives us guilt for a reason. The emotion tells us how our actions measure up against the moral principles that matter to us and our community. But unexamined guilt that runs on automatic generates stress and depletes energy. If you get stuck with guilt, think about why you feel that way. Consider what it is that you've done or not done that's causing you grief. Perhaps, like Rob, the war veteran who created a new ending for his memory about leaving a young soldier in the jungle, you will free yourself of guilt by seeing what happened from a new perspective. Perhaps you need your day in 'court' to work out what you can do to set things right.

Balancing

Burning out is an inelegant solution to the problem of caring. If we had unlimited mental and emotional resources, we could care about all the suffering in the world, take on the biggest challenges and still be optimistic and thrive. But our energy is finite and we need to ration our emotions. If we can't take care of ourselves, how will we help others?

You are important to all the people you care for and who care about you. As someone looking to tackle challenges and solve problems, you are a most precious asset. Anything that you do to nourish and protect yourself is an investment in the future well-being of your family, friends and community. What happened to the goose that was forced to lay too many golden eggs? Or to use a bush metaphor, what happens if you cut wood but never stop to sharpen your saw? Long-term success depends on our taking care of ourselves and balancing our concerns with our capabilities.

We need to reserve our deepest compassion for those who we're most responsible for and have the greatest ability to help. If we give too much of our heart to those we'll never meet or be able to assist, we'll use up the energy we need to care for those closest to us. And we should extend our compassion to ourselves.

Our emotions protect, motivate and soothe us. Respect and heed the emotions that protect you from threat and danger. Work with those feelings that motivate and give you the energy to tackle challenges. Nurture compassion, warmth and kindness to care for others and for yourself.

To complete our journey together, we're now off to the parts of our mind that seem most foreign to our conscious, waking selves – the Key Mental Processes that operate at unconscious, intuitive levels and while we sleep and dream.

Chapter 11

Intuition, Sleep and Dreams

> Even a soul submerged in sleep is hard at work and helps make something of the world.
>
> Heraclitus (540–c.480 BC)

OUR INTUITIVE, DEEPER MENTAL processes are not unconscious in the sense that they lack awareness, are incapable of being rational, or operate in a realm that's cut off from the rest of our mind. Rather, our intuition is subtle – more like the light of the moon than the glare of the sun – and is easily overlooked.

When our daughters were young, we rode horses in the moonlight. Once our eyes adjusted we could see well and we'd ride for miles. It seemed a different world when daytime colours gave way to grey and the night creatures came out to play. Like riding at night, when we adjust ourselves to the subtle insights of the intuitive mind, we discover a world that's always been there.

But what are we dealing with here? What kind of beast of nature is this? How should we understand a process that's a part of us, but seems so apart?

Is the Unconscious Ally or Foe?

We base our notions about the deep mind on Sigmund Freud's division of the human psyche into three parts: the 'superego' with its conscience, the rational ego in contact with external reality, and the id dominated by unconscious aggressive and sexual instincts. The common idea is that the superego and ego operate at conscious levels and are good, while the id is unconscious and is bad. But that's not what Freud really said.

Freud believed that large portions of the ego operate outside of conscious awareness. He understood that our deep mind can act rationally even when we have no inkling of what it is doing.

Most of us have heard of Freud's 'ego defence mechanisms': those mental strategies that protect us from knowing stressful things. If someone says that we're 'projecting', we understand that they think we're unconsciously attributing our own undesirable feelings or traits onto someone else: as when an angry person falsely accuses others of being angry. Like all One Thought Solutions, the 'projection' defence mechanism is quick and easier than having to think things through.

The ego defence of 'repression' simply blocks us from remembering or thinking about something that's upsetting. With 'reaction formation', an individual adopts an opposite persona to manage unpleasant emotions and personality traits: a bitter person might profess great love for others and pursue a life of service. With the familiar defence of 'rationalisation', our conscious mind generates all kinds of poppycock as cover stories to put our dubious feelings and dodgy thinking in the best light. And according to Freud, our unconscious mind even protects us while we sleep and dream.

In his *Interpretation of Dreams*, Freud described a 'dream censor' which operates beyond conscious awareness while we're asleep.[1] The censor makes sophisticated decisions about what we are capable of handling in our dreams. Freud realised that dreams deal with emotional stuff, but if the level of feeling becomes too intense, we wake up. So, to protect sleep, the censor determines what we'll dream about before we dream about it. If it judges some material as likely to cause trouble, it's symbolically transformed in the dream – hence 'Freudian dream interpretation'. And no, I don't buy the idea that dream images of towers and snakes always represent phalluses and images of caves and flowers are visual code for wombs and vaginas. As the saying goes, sometimes a cigar is just a cigar.

Have you ever set your clock for an early morning getup only to wake a few minutes before the alarm goes off? To do this, our sleeping minds have to remember what we want, accurately judge the passage of time, and be able to wake us when needed. Such experiences, and Freud's notions of ego defences and the dream censor, show that even while we're asleep, cooperative, rational, unconscious mental processes routinely access, evaluate and manipulate parts of the mind to achieve our goals and to protect us.

And that's how Milton Erickson described the unconscious mind.

Tides and Waves of Consciousness

Superimposed on our lives, ancient biological rhythms determine whether we're awake or asleep and how our conscious and deep minds interact at any time. A daily tide of consciousness washes over us as we pass from wakefulness to sleep and back again. Not fully synchronised to the cycle of day and night, we spend about a third of our lives asleep: in a life of 75 years, we sleep for 25 years.

Culture and climate shape local variations such as the siesta, but human societies universally structure their daily waking routines around a biological rhythm known as the 'basic rest activity cycle': waves of consciousness that pulse through our bodies and minds every 90 to 120 minutes or so.[2]

In a working day that begins at 9 am, our energy levels are up and concentration comes easy for about 90 minutes. By mid-morning, our mental activity shifts as we enter the 20 minute period that Milton Erickson dubbed the 'natural everyday trance'. As the morning break approaches, time distorts and the clock's minute hand seems to slow down. Our reflexes dull. Staring into space seems a good thing to do and our minds wander off after vague thoughts. We yawn and stretch, notice that we're hungry and want to get up and walk around. Then the morning break arrives.

About 20 minutes later, we attribute our feeling refreshed to partaking of stimulants and socialising, rather than the passing of the trough in the wave of consciousness. Work comes easy for the next 90 minutes or so until the next cycle runs its course, the trough arrives again, and it's time for lunch. If you've ever tried to interest an audience after the lunch break, you know what glazed eyes and drooping heads look like. During this phase of the cycle, you'd do better to declare nap time and get back to teaching about 20 minutes later when drowsiness lifts.

So our daily life goes. The ebb and flow of alertness and drowsiness continues on through the afternoon and into the night. And the cycle rolls on as we fall asleep.

When we're awake, our eyes dart around and the electrical activity that pulses across our brain is fast, complex and chaotic: a mix of alpha frequencies (8 to 12 cycles per second) and beta activity (13 to 40 cycles per second). During this time we mostly think, but sometimes we have dreamlike experiences.

As we relax in bed at night, our minds drift, our eyes can roll slowly in their sockets, the brain's electrical activity begins to synchronise, and alpha wave frequencies increase. When asked, we usually say that we're thinking, but sometimes we're watching fleeting images.

Then, at the point of falling asleep where you can't keep your eyes open and your head drops forward onto your chest, our brains return to an electrical pattern similar to when we're awake and our mental experience changes dramatically. Reports of thinking become rarer as we enter the 'hypnagogic' period with its vivid, uncontrollable, hallucinatory visions.

After a few minutes of hypnagogia, the imagery disappears as abruptly as it arrived. For the next 30 minutes or so, our mind returns to prosaic thinking as we drift deeper into sleep. The brain's electrical activity becomes more rhythmical and slower as we pass through sleep Stages 2 and 3 until, in our deepest Stage 4 sleep, delta wave pulsations of 3 to 4 cycles per second dominate. We remain in deep sleep for about 20 to 30 minutes as our bodies produce human growth hormone which assists physical healing. Then off we go again.

During the next 20 minutes or so we cycle back up through sleep Stages 3 and 2 as our brain's electrical activity quickens. Then, during what's known as 'rapid eye movement' or 'REM' sleep, we have our first fully fledged dream of the night. The electrical activity is similar to when we're awake, but our brain consumes more energy dreaming than it does during the daytime. Everyone dreams. People who claim that they don't dream just don't remember their nightly adventures.

Have you noticed the eyes of a sleeping partner dart around under their closed eyelids? These are the eye movements that give REM sleep its name. If there wasn't a switch that disconnects our bodies from our dreaming minds, we'd be forever falling out of bed as we acted out dreams. The switch is not perfect. When a sleeping dog or cat growls or meows and flexes its paws, it's probably dreaming of chasing a ball or a mouse. Like our pets, as we dream, the minute jerky movements in our muscles and the movements of our eyes track the action in the dream.

The first REM dream of the night ends after about 10 minutes, and then off we go again down to deep sleep before we cycle back up to the second dream of the night.

The sleep cycle repeats five to seven times every night, and as the evening goes on our dreams become progressively longer, more vivid, sexier and more aggressive. Then as we wake up, we spend a few minutes absorbed in vivid 'hypnopompic' imagery that's similar to the hypnagogia of sleep onset.

We now look at how you can work with deeper, intuitive mental processes as your mind shifts through the basic rest activity cycle and the daily tides of wakefulness and sleep.

The Day Shift

While we're awake, slight bodily echoes of thought allow us to converse with our otherwise mute, deep mind.

I won't discuss the Ouija board or the automatic writing and drawing that can occur during hypnotic trance. I prefer a simple head nod or finger movement or the ideosensory signals that we use in this book. But we will look at one other method for communicating with the intuitive mind.

You might have heard of people trying to predict the sex of an unborn child by swinging a ring on a piece of string above the belly of the mother-to-be. They were using 'Chevreul's pendulum', named after Anton Chevreul who in the eighteenth century discovered that you could convert minuscule ideomotor finger movements into the more obvious sweep of a pendulum.

The first step is to establish the meaning of signals. These are usually 'yes', 'no', 'don't know' and 'don't want to answer', for the four possible movements of the pendulum: a clockwise circle, a counterclockwise circle, a straight line from right to left, or a line towards and away from you.

Hold the string of the pendulum with your fingertips and think 'yes ... yes ... yes' until the pendulum settles into a movement which you can take to represent 'yes'. Continue in this way to set up your signals for 'no', 'don't know' and 'don't want to answer'.

Now that you have ideosensory, ideomotor or pendulum signals set up, work out what you want the deep mind to do for you.

Begin by asking if your intuitive mind is willing to cooperate. That might sound strange – though probably not so much given that you're still reading this book – but your deep mind knows more about you than you do. It might have good reasons for not agreeing to your request.

A guiding principle for inner work is that there is no failure, only information. A 'no' signal when you want and expect a 'yes' does not mean that anything has gone wrong. Rather, such unexpected responses indicate that you need to do more. Thank your deep mind and take things from there. Ask for more information and think about why your intuition might have a contrary take on what you need. When your deep mind agrees to cooperate, you can go to work.

Simply ask your deep mind to carry out whatever it is that you want. If you're after a 'yes' or 'no' answer, proceed as if you're playing a game of 20 questions. If you want your deep mind to carry out a more complex task, ask it to do what you want it to do. It's as simple as that.

It's trickier to work out what it is you want your deep mind to do. Take this where you will. To get started, here are examples of some things you might request. At each step along the way, check with your intuition that it's all right to proceed.

To induce self-hypnosis ask, 'Deep mind, please take me into a hypnotic trance and give me a "yes" signal when this is done'. That's often all it takes to induce hypnosis.

To locate specific memories ask, 'Would it be alright for me to remember all that happened during my fifth birthday party?' (Insert here whatever memory you're looking for.) When 'yes' is signalled ask, 'Please allow the memory to come fully to the conscious level so I can hear, see and feel everything that happened back then'.

To find the source of a personal problem ask, 'Deep mind, please locate the first memory that has anything to do with my shyness (Insert here whatever issue you're working on) and give me a "yes" signal when that's been done'. When 'yes' is signalled ask, 'Would it be alright for me to know what happened back then?' When 'yes' is signalled, ask the deep mind to bring the memory to a conscious level.

To find good memories ask, 'Deep mind, please locate a particularly good memory, a time of confidence, strength and pleasure that I haven't thought about for a long time'.

To initiate new learning ask, 'Deep mind, please help me learn to become more confident'. (Insert here whatever skill, knowledge, strength you want to develop.)

Ernest Rossi's Problem-Solving Procedure

We end this section on working with the deep mind while you are awake with Ernest Rossi's three-step problem-solving procedure.[3] I was fortunate to see Dr Rossi demonstrate the technique in person.

> Sit comfortably where you can freely move your hands. Place your hands up in front of your face with the palms facing each other about six to eight inches apart.
>
> Ask your intuition to indicate that it's all right for you to work on the problem or issue that concerns you by moving your hands towards each other slowly, as if a magnetic force draws them together. If your hands don't move, engage with your deep mind to explore what you need to do.
>
> As your hands touch, ask your deep mind to allow one hand to move down, but only as quickly as you explore all aspects of the problem.
>
> Your hand might drift down slowly and steadily. It might pause and hold its position for a while. As your hand moves you might feel your mental gears turning, insights or imagery could come, or perhaps the work will go on while you think about something else.
>
> Next, access your creative resources. As your hand touches and settles on your leg, ask your intuition to let your other hand drift down all by itself, but only as quickly as you explore all possibilities for solving the problem or achieving your goal.
>
> As your hand makes its downward journey, you might enjoy the sense of accomplishment that comes with working on a challenge.
>
> When your hand comes to rest on your leg, ask your deep mind to continue this problem-solving into the future and while you sleep and dream.
>
> Then drift back to your surrounds, remembering what you need to remember and forgetting what you need to forget. Bring the good feelings with you as you stretch and open your eyes.

Could you sense your creative mind working during Rossi's procedure? Do you feel that you know more about your challenge and how you might tackle it than you did before?

We now turn to a deep mind technique that you can use during the day while you're awake but feeling drowsy.

The Natural Everyday Trance

Milton Erickson made good use of the waves of consciousness with their regular troughs of daytime drowsiness.[4] He'd tell clients boring stories until their eyelids fluttered and they were ready to drift into natural hypnosis, which is an ideal time for creative problem-solving, relaxation, self-hypnosis and working with imagery.

At One with the Universe

The signs of approaching natural hypnosis are subtle and easily disguised by external demands and coffee. When working with yourself, look for the telltale clues: wanting to stretch, yawn, sigh or take deep breaths; feeling tired, hungry or thirsty; needing to use the toilet; poor concentration, wandering thoughts, slower reflexes, clumsiness, doodling and staring vacantly into space.

It matters what you call the breaks you take during these episodes of natural hypnosis. Some call them 'nanna naps', and in our hyperkinetic, never-think-deeply age, taking time off from attending to the world around us can seem indulgent. In the business world, these breaks are known as 'power naps' and corporations like Google encourage employees to take them. No one has a problem with lunch and morning and afternoon tea breaks, so what could be wrong with taking 20 minutes off to enhance your health, recharge energy and boost creativity?

Timing is important. Inner work is easiest when you pick the right time to catch the consciousness wave. It doesn't matter what technique you prefer. You might intone a mantra or think about something pleasant like sitting beside a creek, walking through a garden or being on the beach at sunset. Or perhaps you'll simply notice the comfort. When your mind and body are ready, these and many other methods will take you where you need to go. But when you feel the press of time, it's good to have a backup plan.

To use the natural hypnotic break when you're under time pressure, give up altogether the idea of relaxing or meditating. Just pay attention to your breathing for a while. Notice how it feels to breathe in and to breathe out. Close your eyes and count each breath: '1' for the first in-breath, '2' for the out-breath, and so on to '100'. This will only take minutes and there's no pressure on you to relax because all you're doing is counting your breaths. You might be surprised by what happens when you're not paying attention.

You don't lose control or 'go under' during the natural everyday trance. It feels like a daydream and you can open your eyes and deal with things as you need to. If you're a bit sleep deprived, when you first begin to practice natural hypnosis you might fall asleep and wake feeling groggy. Keep practising and your sessions will become lighter and after about 10 to 20 minutes you'll stretch, open your eyes and enjoy the day with renewed energy and insights.

In my early university days, I found that I could better understand what I was studying if I just closed my eyes for a while during the drowsy phase of the basic rest activity cycle. Most of the time, insights came without effort on my part. The method works as well for me now as it did 45 years ago.

We can work on challenges at conscious and unconscious levels while we're awake, but it's when we're asleep that perhaps our most productive and creative Key Mental Processes come into play.

The Night Shift

> We sleep, but the loom of life never stops, and the pattern which was weaving when the sun went down is weaving when it comes up in the morning.
>
> Henry Ward Beecher (1813–1887)

A barrier of amnesia separates our waking and sleeping selves. There are important exceptions, but when we're awake we usually don't remember what we think and dream about while we're asleep, and when we're asleep we usually don't remember being awake. This leads to the mistaken belief that when we fall asleep we stop thinking and our minds go blank. For some, sleep even seems like a form of death.

Shakespeare wrote, 'We are such stuff as dreams are made on, and our little life is rounded with a sleep'. Lord Byron rhymed, 'Death, so called, is a thing which makes men weep, and yet a third of life is passed in sleep'. Mahatma Gandhi felt that 'Each night, when I go to sleep, I die. And the next morning, when I wake up, I am reborn'. Byron and Gandhi were wrong. Thinking goes on all the time. Our minds play whether we're awake or asleep.

If you gently rouse a sleeper and ask them what's going through their minds, they'll either be thinking or they will be dreaming, immersed in a hallucinated drama.

Before we get into interesting dream stuff and how you can use your deep mind creatively while you sleep, we first need to get the basics right. Good dreaming is built on sound sleep.

Sleeping Well

Good sleep is precious and many things can disrupt it.

Pile on too many blankets and you'll sleep hot and disrupt your healing deep sleep. Excessive noise has a similar effect. Coffee reduces sleep time. Alcohol relaxes the body, but it leaches out the colour and reduces the vividness of dreams until our bodies metabolise the alcohol. But speaking from personal experience, there's nothing more important during sleep than breathing.

Sleep Apnoea

Apnoea means 'without breath' and in 'obstructive sleep apnoea' breathing repeatedly stops when relaxing throat muscles cut off the airway. Sleep apnoea is a shared joy. Bleary-eyed partners spend hours on alert waiting for their afflicted others to prove that they're still alive by gasping for breath.

When the disorder is severe, breathing can stop hundreds of times each night. This plays havoc with sleep cycles and health as oxygen levels fall and the blood becomes acidic. Sleep apnoea is underdiagnosed, even in older men who are most at risk, but this is a potential problem for both sexes of any age.

Children nowadays rarely undergo tonsillectomies and adenoid-ectomies. An unfortunate consequence of this has been an increase in children suffering undiagnosed apnoea symptoms related to respiratory tract infections. It's unknown to what extent this breathing disorder contributes to behavioural and emotional problems in children.

A sufferer is unlikely to know that they have sleep apnoea. It was inconceivable to me that I was waking hundreds of times every night. I was sure I was asleep when, in truth, I was repeatedly waking up, although never for long enough to lay down a memory of being awake.

It's worth medical follow-up if you feel tired during the day and have great difficulty staying awake while watching movies or when you're a passenger in a car. Perhaps the most telling diagnostic question is, 'Does your partner say that you stop breathing and gasp for breath while you're asleep?'

Managing my sleep apnoea with 'positive airway pressure' gear has been a revelation. I've rediscovered the joys of breathing. I can recommend a good night's sleep as the foundation for creative problem-solving, and just about everything else for that matter.

Make Good Use of Your Time

Apnoea screws up your sleep cycles, but insomnia can eliminate them altogether.

Bovine Insomnia

When I first set up my 1976 study of falling asleep, none of my subjects would fall asleep. It didn't matter how tired they were or how long I left them lying in the dark, they just wouldn't nod off. The problem was that they were trying to fall asleep, which you can't do. When I stopped talking about sleep and simply asked them to lie in the dark, everyone fell asleep within minutes.

Relaxing and falling asleep are things you can't force. The more you try, the more unlikely they become. If getting to sleep is a problem for you, take the pressure off. Remind yourself that missing some sleep is no big deal. Staying awake is only an issue if you think it is. Insomnia becomes a problem when you give it a name. Before then, it's just a change of routine.

If you've been awake for a while, don't lie there worrying or imagining that you're pushing sheep up a hill. Sheep are skittish creatures, prone to ricocheting, and even if you get them to cooperate, sleep is not guaranteed. Rather, get up and do something useful with your time. Sit somewhere that's not very comfortable: a chair designed for work is best. In an hour or so the next wave of consciousness will have you wanting to yawn and stretch. That's the signal to go back to bed, slip under the covers and imagine something repetitive and pleasant. If you're still awake after 10 minutes or so, get up and get back to work.

First and Second Sleeps

Ours is an illuminated age. By that, I don't mean that we're enlightened or free from confusion, but rather that we live with lots of artificial light. Due to light pollution, 60% of Europeans and nearly 80% of North Americans can no longer see the Milky Way.[5] It wasn't always so.

Back a few generations, our sleep cycles were more in sync with the natural cycle of day and night. There's only so much you could or would want to do by candle or firelight. From medieval times back, humans retired to bed not long after sunset for what they knew as the 'first sleep'.[6] Go to bed this early and you'll wake around midnight, which was when medieval Europeans would get out of bed, dress and get up to mischief for an hour or two. When they felt sleepy again, they went back to bed for their 'second sleep'. Such was the routine in less well-lit times.

If you find yourself wide awake in the middle of the night, hopefully with a head full of good ideas, don't despair. You're not suffering from insomnia. Do like your ancestors, get out of bed and get on with it until it's time for your second sleep.

Use Your Bed Wisely

Beds are for sleeping, musing and making love. Never use them for worry or work; don't check emails in bed. Do you recall our earlier conversation about conditioning? Ring a bell as you feed a dog and pretty soon it will salivate when it hears the bell. You're a human, so all you have to do to salivate is imagine eating something delicious. If you work or worry in bed it'll become a 'conditioned stimulus' and, like the bell with a dog, your bed, or even just the thought of your bed, will bring on a 'conditioned response' of being awake and on the job.

Bucolic Sleep

That's why you need to get out of bed if you don't feel like sleeping. There's a proper place for every activity. It's okay to worry and work in your office because you're conditioned to do such things there. Match task to setting and what you're doing will come easy. Get it wrong and the mismatch creates tension.

Hypnotherapists sometimes have a special chair for trance work. Once you've associated the comfort of hypnosis with that chair, all you have to do to induce trance is sit in it. Meditators practice where the physical cues of a comfortable seat, mandala, candle or soft music act as conditioned stimuli to encourage the desired mental state. Hence the advice: keep your bed for sleeping, musing and making love.

Creative Sleep and Dreams

> Before you sleep, read something that is exquisite,
> and worth remembering.
>
> Desiderius Erasmus (1466–1536)

Creative thinking can go on all through the night. Sigmund Freud proclaimed night dreams to be the 'royal road to the unconscious'. When you know how to work with them, there are various forms of mental activity during sleep that can take you to the deep mind.

What goes on when we're awake affects what we think and dream about when we're asleep, and we take the legacy of the night into the next day. The concerns might be the same, but the mind handles them differently when we're awake and when we sleep and dream.

When we're asleep, our mind lays down new memories from the previous day and works on whatever information, experiences or emotional issues seem relevant to it at that time. Freud called it the 'day residue': the unfinished things that we didn't or couldn't pay attention to during the day. Our dreams incorporate the day residue as our minds work on personally important issues. And if we pay attention to emotional things before we go to bed, we can inadvertently set the agenda for the night.

Respect your sleeping and dreaming mind. Prime it properly and it will work creatively through the night, rewarding you with ideas and solutions in the morning. But go to bed after watching a violent movie and you'll likely spend the night running from zombies and playing out scenarios from the drama. Read a vexing email before you retire, and you could mull it over all night long. Hence the advice: check your emails long before bedtime, and never retire soon after watching the evening news or a violent movie. Make it a routine to finish your day with thoughts and experiences that leave you feeling good.

As Albert Einstein described the creative process, there's an intuitive leap and 'the solution comes to you and you don't know how or why'. I guess it sounds strange, but my affectionate nickname of 'the weasel' for my sleeping creative mind has stuck. It has its own moniker because I bear witness but do not will its good work. I'm its benefactor, not its boss. The name 'weasel' came one night and suited the spirited flood of ideas that woke me up. It's definitely more 'weasel' than 'wombat' or 'possum'.

But sometimes the payoff for our mind's work during the night comes not as ideas, but as dreams that, under certain circumstances, we remember when we're awake.

The Magic Theatre of Hypnagogia

Accounts of altered states of consciousness at sleep onset have appeared in Western literature for 2,500 years and even longer in Eastern writings. In the mid-1800s, these vivid, hallucinatory visions were named 'hypnagogic imagery'. Hypnagogic dreams have inspired scientific breakthroughs such as August Kekule's discovery of the structure of the benzene atom, and literary creations including Enid Blyton's *Noddy* and other books.

As research for my honours degree, I studied what goes through our minds as we fall asleep. After I attached electrodes to their scalps to record brainwaves and to their faces to monitor eye movements, my subjects lay on a bed in a dark university laboratory. In an adjacent room, I watched their brain wave patterns on a printout. When subjects drifted off, I interviewed them over an intercom and then left them alone until they fell asleep again. Over two nights, each subject gave eight reports of sleep onset experiences.

It begins with a bizarre slideshow. The following were typical early sleep onset answers to the question, 'What's going through your mind?'

> Buccaneer ships ... and a child listening to a tape recorder ... all superimposed ... it looked sort of like a photograph.

> There were several things in quick succession ... I think the last thing was a newspaper ... sort of held open ... before that was sort of an animal's head that was sort of like a cross between a lizard and a crocodile ... that looked like it had a bonnet on it of some sort ... and then before that there was ... something else.

> People sitting on a very large pineapple doughnut ... (laughs) ... I moved my head and I started to ... almost dream. I started to get visual pictures and I just saw this ridiculous picture of all these people sitting on this enormous pineapple doughnut and they all fell over backwards.

After a minute or so, the slideshow settles into a brief dream, like the following:

> I was in a ... I was observing a Mexican police station ... and the captain was asking a policeman to read a chart ... something like an eye chart ... and the word he had to read was 'si', you know 'si', the Mexican 'yes'.

> There were two men in a room ... and one guy was saying how he reckoned he could control people's thoughts ... and the other guy was sort of ... more or less disagreeing with him. He was somewhat wary of him because ... the one who was disagreeing was sitting down ... in a dark suit ... they were both black guys ... and the room was sort of a library type room. And the one talking was standing up sort of stomping around and the other guy was listening and seemed to be rather worried because the speaker was getting very ... emotionally excited.

The following dream was based on a memory:

> I was travelling around looking at different places ... and trees ... I was in a caravan park that I've been to ... about seven years

ago in England ... and I was looking at the lupins flowering ... was the summertime.

And some dreams, like the next two, seem randomly bizarre:

> There was a rabbit in a field ... just about to jump onto this disk that was spinning around ... there was a dog there and there was a rabbit and there were three people there ... and the rabbit was jumping across the yard. The rabbit was trying to get to the person ... in order to do this it had to jump over this disk ... it was just about to jump on it and get spun off.

> About being on a road actually ... lying in the gutter of a road ... first of all there was just this little trickle of water going down the gutter ... and I could see in slow motion like parts from a movie this great torrent of water coming down the road and dashing about the sides of the buildings and things and the road but ... when it reached me it was really soft and cushiony ... it was really quite pleasant but it never ... as soon as it reached me it cut off.

The following hypnagogic dream worked with a concern common to university students in those days:

> (Laughs) ... there was a big wide street ... motorcycles sort of ... police motorcycles. And they were ... there was this big demonstration a lot of people walking down this big main street and there were ... they were stopped by the police ... but the police ended up driving away on their motorcycles all in formation down the road ... the police talked to some of the people in the crowd ... and they said ... that's right, they agreed that there shouldn't be any bloodshed ... so they ... the police drove off.

For my client "Michael", his hypnagogic experiences took on a sinister significance. The closest most of us come to catching a sleep onset experience is thinking that we've heard our name called out as we fall asleep. But for some, our natural ignorance of hypnagogia can have serious consequences. Michael felt stressed and couldn't sleep. He had started to notice his bizarre hypnagogic images and, not understanding what they were, feared that he was going insane.

Michael's was not the only case of normal phenomena being mistaken for symptoms of psychosis.

A 1970s psychiatric textbook gave the following experiences as examples of psychotic hallucinations. Can you see why these could have been normal hypnagogic phenomena?

> I had a strange vision. As soon as I had laid down in my bed, a light came over the room.

> The first I saw of them was the brown man. He was leaning over my bed at arm's length; I could easily have touched him ... I was wide awake ... though it was night and the room was dark.

> I did not read in bed, but blew out the candle immediately. My head had scarcely touched the pillow when a man's voice ... proceeding apparently from the large armchair by the fireplace, asked clearly and aloud, 'Are you awake?'

You can catch your own hypnagogic visions and you don't need fancy equipment. Let your partner know what you're up to, and when they see your head nodding as you drift off, get them to gently ask, 'What's going through your mind?' A good time is when you're sitting quietly at night while reading or watching television. As with all dreams that you want to remember, as soon as you can, write them down or say them out loud.

Night Dreams

Dreams are never concerned with trivia.
Sigmund Freud (1856–1939)

The classic tale of horror, *Frankenstein: or the modern Prometheus* came to Mary Shelley in a dream. Over dinner, Mary, Lord Byron and her future husband Percy Shelley decided to compete to see who could write the best horror story. During the conversation, Mary heard accounts of electrical current making frogs' legs twitch. That night she dreamt about a scientist who created life and unleashed a horror.

Dreams can do more than inspire creativity. They sometimes solve big problems.

My dreaming self must have known what I needed, so it gave me my first 'lucid dream'. I became aware that I was in a dream and did not wake up. I can tell you about it now because I wrote the dream down as soon as I woke.

About 25 years ago, my father died of pneumonia and emphysema. I was alone with Dad throughout his final night and he died in my arms. Dad's death wasn't easy, but it freed him from suffering.

I felt shocked and couldn't sleep much for weeks after Dad's death. I tried to distract myself, but memories kept taking me back to that night until I had an extraordinary dream. From then on, whenever I think of my father, only good times come to mind.

In the dream, I was sitting in an auditorium. My brother was on my left, my sister on my right, and next to her my father and my mother. When I saw my father I instantly became lucid. I knew Dad was dead, so this had to be a dream! I turned to my brother and said, 'Listen carefully. This is a dream. We're in a dream together. Dad is over there but he's dead. You're probably asleep at home. I want you to remember this when you wake up'.

When I touched my father's arm, it felt real. I was elated, lucid and sound asleep. Here was my dead father, as alive and as real as could be, in a dream that I knew was a dream. I told my sister and mother that Dad was dead and we were all in my dream together. When I told Dad that he'd died, he looked at me and the scene changed.

Still lucid in the dream, I pushed Dad in a wheelchair across an open field where we came across seemingly bottomless pits in the ground: round, about 20 feet across with sloping sides, they disappeared into the depths. I was calm but knew these holes were dangerous. We got around them easily. We came to a concrete building and entered a tunnel. As I wheeled my father along, water lapped at my feet and began to rise. Dad panicked. He was afraid of drowning, but I reassured him that this was just a dream and we would be all right. I felt the rising water against my skin but knew that we'd be able to breathe underwater. When the water covered my mouth, the scene changed again.

Up ahead I could see a brightly lit hospital room – I think I was looking at my father's death from a distance. I turned to Dad and said words to the effect, 'We both know what that's about. We don't need to go there again'. I think I said some other things, and then I woke.

The lucid dream ended my grieving. Of course, I knew it was just a dream and that my father was really dead. Nonetheless, I felt deeply reassured that I could dream about my father without getting lost in his death scene. I put up a photo of Dad and knew that he'd always be a part of my life.

We have about six dreams every night, so with a mean life expectancy of 82 years, the average Australian will have close to 180,000 dreams in their lifetime. You've got to think that humans have this ability for a reason. Nonetheless, we spontaneously recall so few dreams. It's likely that if there was an evolutionary advantage to remembering dreams, we would do so. It seems that our waking minds do not need to know the details for effective learning and problem-solving to take place in our sleep and dreams. But there are times when it's useful to ask for a specific dream that we can remember.

Sweet Dreams

The process is much the same if you're requesting a night dream, hypnagogic imagery or a daydream to help you with a specific goal. As you prepare for sleep or a daytime break, think about what it is you want to achieve. Some recommend that you write what you want on a piece of paper and hold it in your hand, but I haven't done that.

The dreams that my clients have after they make a request to their 'dreaming self' are always useful and to the point, and often profoundly so. When clients unlock the code to understand their unconscious creations, they discover a deep intelligence within.

To request a specific type of dream, as you retire to bed, respectfully ask your dreaming self to give you an experience that helps with what you want to achieve. For example, you might ask for a dream that tells more about a problem, gives a solution, or advises about what you should do next.

Keep a notepad and pen by your bed. If you wake during the night, go over the dream and write it down so you'll remember it. Record all dreams, no matter how brief or bizarre. Anything you remember will be relevant. When you have your dream reports, it's time to decode them.

For working with dreams, I prefer a method based on Carl Jung's dream analysis.

> Begin by reflecting on the dream. Retell the dream story from a 3rd person perspective, as in 'the dreamer did this, then that happened …' Ask yourself how the dreamer was feeling and think about the general mood. Contemplate how this dream story might relate to your waking life.
>
> Then objectively define each dream element. Give everything in your dream a dictionary definition. For example, if there was a car, you might define 'car' as 'a vehicle, a means of transport that moves people from place to place'. The question to ask is, 'What's a car?' rather than 'What's a car mean to me?' Continue until you have an objective definition for every dream element.

The next step is to uncover your subjective associations. For each element, read your definition and then ask yourself what this could represent in your life. What does it remind you of? What else is like this? What's it mean to you? With our example of dreaming of a car, which you might objectively define as 'a vehicle that moves people around', your subjective association could be 'my body'. Look for the first impression that comes to mind. When you have associations for every element, retell the dream story to incorporate the new information.

Go back through the dream from the beginning, but this time add your subjective associations for each element. For example, you might say 'The dreamer drove in a car, which she associated with her body,' and so on. As you do this the meaning of the dream will emerge. Refine your retelling of the dream. Put the message into words.

The final step is to put the dream message to work. What do you think the dream is telling you? You can now either apply the insights and ideas you've gained to the task that motivated you to request the dream in the first place, or you might use what you've learned as 'grist for the mill' and the next night put a follow-up question to your dreaming self.

And that, Dear Reader, brings to an end what I want to tell you about the Key Mental Processes and how you can use them to go beyond shallow thought to harness the creative power of your deep mind.

But we're not finished until we bring the Key Mental Processes back together again.

Chapter 12

What It Will Take

> You chose the best among us – a strong man:
> For where he fixt his heart he set his hand
> to do the thing he willed, and bore it through.
>
> Alfred Lord Tennyson (1809–1892)

WE'RE CUSTODIANS OF A flame that's burned since life began. The human spirit is strong, but in times like these, the ancient, simple ways of thinking and behaving that got us here threaten to take us out. The way we use our minds is both the problem and the promise. Our thoughts and actions will determine what follows for us and for the generations to come.

As individuals, the way ahead is clear. Your life is unique – you steer your own course. Your success in tackling life's challenges will depend in large part on the skills and knowledge you put to work. We had to artificially separate the Key Mental Processes to see how each operates. In reality, there is no separation; perception, memory, imagination, beliefs, language, emotions, intuition and dreaming interact seamlessly in a unified mind. The task for you now is to bring together what you've learned.

Build complex skills from the ground up, bit by bit. To learn to play tennis, you have to master grip and how to move your feet and swing your arm before you practice the serve, volley and ground shots. And after you add knowledge of the rules, strategy and gamesmanship, you're ready to bring it all together. Then you just go out and play tennis, enjoying the flow as you tailor each shot to the circumstances of the game. It will be a similar process as you practice using your deep mind.

Breaking the trances of simple thinking and One Thought Solutions is difficult at first. Habits resist change until you update them, and this usually takes a few weeks of practice. As with any new skill, master your Key Mental Processes by breaking the job down into smaller tasks that you deal with one at a time. Early on, you'll think about something, sleep on it and revisit the issue the next day. This will become easier and more natural over time.

Remember that your conscious attention is limited and much goes on that you are not aware of. Reflect on the way that your mind creates the reality you perceive. Take control of your imagination and memory to learn from the past and plan the future. Free yourself from limiting beliefs and take on attitudes that foster success. Break word spells that harm, mislead and restrict. Choose words that power your thinking and use language respectfully to influence others. Appreciate your emotions and listen to what they tell you. Stay with tension so anxiety can guide you to a problem's source and solution. Practice the art of thinking things through and get used to driving a train of thought with lots of carriages. Cultivate your intuition. Respect and listen to the ancient but subtle wisdom that doesn't speak in words. Do all these things and you'll be richly rewarded and enjoy yourself along the way.

But beyond the personal, what's the likely future for the challenges I told you about in Part 1 of this book?

The Three Case Studies

Human societies will never be free of shock and trauma. But there's much we could do to more compassionately relieve suffering and better protect ourselves and others.

My career as a clinician is nearly done. In professional workshops, I've passed on what I know about treating traumatic stress to about two hundred fellow practitioners. Some colleagues will continue to develop gentle ways to ease stress, but my profession of clinical psychology still indulges some out-of-date ideas and unnecessarily harsh ways. Beyond directly helping clients, what becomes of my work largely depends on you, Dear Reader. This book is my best chance of passing on what I've learned.

Thanks to generous support, the bush regeneration work on our Creek's Bend property continues and more of our forests are becoming healthy again. As news spreads that you can free landscapes from lantana's suffocating grip, people are taking up the challenge to save their eucalypt forests.

Nonetheless, the threat of forest dieback is immense and growing. The impacts on native plants and animals and the collapse of ecosystems are not yet generally recognised. A persistent, pessimistic mindset that assumes all environmental problems are too difficult to solve stymies efforts to make things better. The future for Australia's east coast eucalypt forests will depend on whether enough people come to understand the problem and take effective action in time.

There's been much to celebrate and some things to lament since our community drove the unconventional gas industry out of the Northern Rivers. As years go by, the hardships fade to memory. Our community is now strong, unified and proud in ways that only the successful defeat of a great threat can confer. A renewed appreciation of our natural gifts and a belief in the collective power of people now protects the region and steels it for the challenges ahead.

As books and films record lessons learned, the message is spreading – social movements can change history. Elsewhere, the campaign goes on to put people before profits and to protect communities from invasive industrial development. All the while, the image of a gas field free Australia sharpens and looks more likely to become reality.

We know how to treat trauma victims humanely, address native forest dieback and protect communities from coal mining and gas fields. But knowing how to tackle such challenges doesn't mean that these problems are solved or ever will be. The necessary extra ingredient is a critical mass of well-informed, motivated people who take effective action.

Big Challenges Ahead

Disparate forces are in play. The thoughts and actions of like-minded people working together are going to propel us towards either nightmare scenarios or genuine prosperity and solutions that promote the interests of all. It's up to us how this turns out.

If we are to realise a brilliant future, enough of our kind will have to give up the comforts of shallow thinking to practise a deeper wisdom. It won't be easy – nor should it be too hard. Sometimes, complex problems yield to straightforward solutions once we find the key.

Knowledge, numbers and cooperation are essential. Dark forces can brush aside a few hundred citizens, but if enough people of goodwill take a stand, they will prevail. When Northern Rivers folk learned the truth about invasive gas fields, 10,000 turned up to march, thousands stood in the mud at dawn to defy riot police, and hundreds were prepared to put their bodies on the line.

Imagine what would be possible if the passion that 100,000 fans bring to a football grand final was redirected to the even more compelling drama that will determine the fate of their team Earth. To take effective action, the hundred thousand don't need to be in the same place. They just need to share a common goal.

Unfortunately, some corporate interests assault rationality and good policy and make the task harder. Feeding on a natural human proclivity for shallow thought, they mock and devalue science and reason while promoting emotive, superstitious and mean-spirited sentiments. They could trigger a new 'dark age' in which nuclear-armed forces play out with dire consequences for all.

We need a bright light to counter the growing dark – intense enough to illuminate a new age of enlightenment. Knowledge and truth have to counter ignorance and lies. We've done it before. We need to do it again.

In the 18th century, the Enlightenment transformed the world with the idea that reason, not wealth, class or religion, is the primary source of authority and legitimate power. Leaders taught ideals of freedom, tolerance and equality, and defended the rights and dignity of people. They promoted the scientific method and the rational search for truth. Meetings, books and pamphlets inspired political and social revolutions in an increasingly literate population. Poetry, art and literature celebrated science. The 'scientific revolution' created our modern world as philosophers denounced slavery and promoted democracy. Coffee houses became 'penny universities' where citizens from all walks of life met to discuss ideas. But that Enlightenment has stalled.

We need a 'new enlightenment' to revitalise commitment to reason and human dignity. As popular as coffee is, this revolution will not begin in Starbucks or the Coffee Club. Nor can we count on our universities to lead the way; they now teach vocational skills, rather than philosophy and revolution. Vested interests control funding and research and compromise institutional science. As for politics, we'll find some allies there, but the party-based system and our public service are unlikely to generate the light that needs to shine. So, it's going to come down to the people.

We're impressive. So are untrained horses. Our thinking is similarly flighty, fast and shallow. We're capable of marvellous things even in our untrained, natural state. But like the horse, we're capable of much more if we get the right training.

Good horse handlers don't take it personally if an uneducated horse wants to bite and kick. They understand that these behaviours have protected the horse through evolutionary time, but that doesn't mean that they tolerate such acts. Rather, they take account of these natural impulses as they teach the horse sophisticated new skills.

Like horses, untrained people are liable to strike out if they're frightened or don't get their way. As with horses, it's a mistake to overreact when people bite and kick and act with prejudice, ignorance or violence. It's better to understand the evolutionary function of such behaviour and go beyond it to teach more effective ways of being.

What I have in mind is people taking control of their own education and destiny. We no longer need universities to obtain knowledge; the World Wide Web can give us that. We don't need coffee shops or halls to get together and share ideas; we can do that with new media. We can't rely on politicians, professionals or professors to save us; the people and only the people can do that.

We have to understand who we really are, what we're up against, and what we have to do to meet the challenge. We need to study how practitioners of the dark arts of persuasion go about their trade. Not to emulate them, but to work out how we can effectively counter their destructive messages.

Imagine an army of skilled, creative protectors prepared to respond with integrity to whatever misinformation, insult or obstacle comes their way. For them, philosophy is a contact sport. They look always to get on the front foot and take the argument forward. They promote their ideas and ideals with style and relentless reason.

Can you envision a critical mass of educated, activated people committed to the ideals of a new enlightenment? I can.

Dark forces got the jump on us, but when we get ourselves together, we'll run them down for sure.

References

Chapter 1 – Nature's Basic Problem-Solving Strategy

1. Phelps, P. 2013. Debate in NSW Legislative Council on the environmental movement. *Hansard of the Legislative Council*, NSW Parliament.
2. Calaprice, A. 2005. *The new quotable Einstein.* Princeton University Press.
3. Ohman, A., & Mineka, S. 2001. Fears, phobias, and preparedness: Toward an evolved module of fear and fear learning. *Psychological Review, 108(3)*, 483–522.
4. Cook, M., & Mineka, S. 1990. Selective associations in the observational conditioning of fear in Rhesus monkeys. *Journal of Experimental Psychology: Animal Behavior Processes, 16(4)*, 372–389.
5. Silove, D. 1998. Is posttraumatic stress disorder an overlearned survival response? An evolutionary–learning hypothesis. *Psychiatry, 61*, 181–90.
6. Hirata, S., Watanabe, K., & Kawai, M. 2001. 'Sweet-potato washing' revisited. In T. Matsuzawa (ed.) *Primate origins of human cognition and behaviour.* Japan: Springer.
7. Watanabe, K. 2007. Long-tailed macaques use human hair as dental floss. *American Journal of Primatology, 69(8)*, 940 – 944.

Chapter 2 – War Trauma and a New Psychology

1. Kay, J. 2015. 'Napalm girl' Kim Phuc receiving laser treatment for Vietnam war scars. *The Sydney Morning Herald,* 26 October 2015.
2. Masson, J.M. 1984. *The assault on truth: Freud's suppression of the seduction theory.* USA: Farrar, Straus & Giroux.
3. Holt, R. 1964. Imagery: The return of the ostracized. *American Psychologist, 19(4)*, 254–264.
4. Erickson, M. 1975. Preface. In R. Bandler & J. Grinder. *Patterns of the hypnotic techniques of Milton H. Erickson, M.D., Volume 1.* Meta Publications: Cupertino, California.

5. Gordon, D. & Meyers, M. (1981). *Phoenix: Therapeutic patterns of Milton H. Erickson.* Cupertino, California: Meta Publications.
6. Erickson, M. (1948). Hypnotic psychotherapy. *The Medical Clinics of North America*, 571–583.
7. Somerville, W. R., & Jupp, J. J. 1992. Experimental evaluation of a brief 'ideodynamic' hypnotherapy applied to phobias. *Contemporary Hypnosis, 9*, 85–96.
8. Yuste, R., & Church, G.M. 2014. The new century of the brain. *Scientific American, 310*, 38 – 45.
9. Breuer, J., & Freud, S. 1893. On the psychical mechanism of hysterical phenomena: Preliminary communication. In A. Richards (ed.). 1974. *Studies on hysteria: The Pelican Freud Library, Vol. 3.* Great Britain: Penguin Books.
10. Schubert, S., & Lee, C. 2009. Adult PTSD and its treatment with EMDR: A review of controversies, evidence, and theoretical knowledge. *Journal of EMDR Practice and Research, 3(3)*, 117.
11. Cochrane, A. 1972. *Effectiveness and efficiency. Random reflections on health services.* London: Nuffield Provincial Hospitals Trust.
12. Bandler, R. 1985. *Using your brain – for a change.* Moab, Utah: Real People Press.
13. Somerville, W. 2004. Cognitive Control Therapy for PTSD. *Doctor of Psychology dissertation*, Department of Psychology, Bond University, Gold Coast, Queensland.
14. Foa, E. B., & Kozak, M. J. 1986. Emotional processing of fear: Exposure to corrective information. *Psychological Bulletin, 99*, 20–35.
15. Reynolds, M., & Tarrier, N. 1996. Monitoring of intrusions in posttraumatic stress disorder: A report of single case studies. *British Journal of Medical Psychology, 69*, 371-379.

Chapter 3 – Native Forest Dieback

1. Somerville, S., Somerville, W., & Coyle, R. 2011. Regenerating native forest using splatter gun techniques to remove Lantana. *Ecological Management & Restoration, 2(3)*, 164.

2. Wardell-Johnson, G., Stone, C., Recher, H., & Lynch, A. 2006. Bell Miner Associated Dieback (BMAD) independent scientific literature review: A review of eucalypt dieback associated with Bell miner habitat in north-eastern New South Wales. *Australia Occasional Paper DEC 2006/116*. Department of Environment and Conservation (NSW).
3. Silver, M. & Carnegie, A. 2017. An independent review of Bell Miner Associated Dieback. *Final report prepared for the Project Steering Committee: Systematic review of Bell Miner Associated Dieback*. Office of Environment and Heritage (NSW).

Chapter 4 – Unconventional Gas

1. Somerville, W. 2015. *How could CSG air pollution in the Darling Downs be an acceptable risk to health?: The elephant that can't get into the room*. Independent report, available for download at www.drwaynesomerville.com.
2. Groundwater (Deep Aquifer Modelling) for Santos GLNG project. *Environmental Impact Statement*, 31/3/2009.
3. Maher, D.T., Santos, I.R., & Tait, D.R. 2014. Mapping methane and carbon dioxide concentrations and $d^{13}C$ values in the atmosphere of two Australian coal seam gas fields. *Water, Air, & Soil Pollution, 225*, 2216. doi:10.1007/s11270-014-2216-2.
4. Turner, A., Jacob, D., Benmergui, J., Wofsy, S., Maasakkers, J., Butz, A., Hasekamp, O., & Biraud, S. 2016. A large increase in U.S. methane emissions over the past decade inferred from satellite data and surface observations. *Geophys. Res. Lett., 43*, 2218–2224.
5. The Brisbane Times. 2017. Condamine River on fire in CSG mining area. *The Brisbane Times*, 23 April 2017. http://www.brisbanetimes.com.au/Queensland/Condamine-River-on-fire-in-CSG-mining-area-20160422-godaoo.html.
6. Somerville, W. 2013. *CSG and your health: Understand the risks, protect your family. Independent report on the health impacts of CSG and shale gas mining with self-help risk management tools*. www.drwaynesomerville.com.
7. Albrecht, G.A. 2005. Solastalgia: A new concept in human health and identity. *PAN (Philosophy, Activism, Nature), 3*, 41–55.

8. McCarron, G. 2013. *Symptomology of a gas field: An independent health survey in the Tara rural residential estates and environs.* Independent report, download from: https://sites.google.com/site/frackingireland/symptomatology-of-a-gas-field
9. O'Kane, M. 2014. Final report of the independent review of coal seam gas activities in NSW. *NSW Chief Scientist and Engineer.*
10. Somerville, W. 2014. *Is CSG safe? A failed public debate in the interests of community health.* Independent report from www.drwaynesomerville.com.
11. Hannam, P. & Cubby, B. 2012. Minister slams 'unscientific' report on gas leak. *The Sydney Morning Herald*, 20 Nov 2012.
12. Phelps, P. 2015. Debate on Petroleum (Onshore) Amendment (Prohibit Coal Seam Gas) Bill 2015, second reading. *Hansard of the Legislative Council*, NSW Parliament, May 2015.
13. Phelps, P. 2014. Speech in Legislative Council, NSW Parliament, *Hansard of the Legislative Council*, NSW Parliament, May 30.
14. Colless, R. 2013. Speech on carbon emissions reduction, NSW Legislative Council debate, *Hansard of the Legislative Council*, NSW Parliament, June.
15. Phelps, P. 2014. Speech on ecologically sustainable development. *Hansard of the Legislative Council*, NSW Parliament, 8 May 2014.
16. McKenzie, L., Guo, R., Witter, R., Savitz, D., Newman, L., & Adgate, J. 2014. Birth outcomes and maternal residential proximity to natural gas development in rural Colorado. *Environmental Health Perspectives.* http://dx.doi.org/10.1289/ehp.1306722.
17. Kassotis, C., Tillitt, D., Davis, J., Hormann, A., & Nagel, S. 2013. Estrogen and androgen receptor activities of hydraulic fracturing chemicals and surface and ground water in a drilling-dense region, *Endocrinology*, endo. endojournals.org, doi: 10.1210/en.2013-1697.
18. Phelps, P. 2015. Debate on Petroleum (Onshore) Amendment (Prohibit Coal Seam Gas) Bill 2015, second reading. *Hansard of the Legislative Council*, NSW Parliament, May 2015.
19. Metgasco. *Metgasco drilling notes.* NSW Department of Trade and Energy Digital Imaging of Geological Systems (DIGS) website. http://www.resourcesandenergy.nsw.gov.au/miners-and-explorers/geoscience-information/online-services/digs

20. McNally, L. 2015. Gloucester CSG suspension: NSW vows investigation after chemical found at site. *ABC News Online.* 28 January 2015.
21. Goodell, G. 2012. The big fracking bubble: The scam behind Aubrey Mc Clendon's gas boom. *Rolling Stone*, 1 March 2012.
22. Chessell, J. 2014. Queensland LNG doesn't add up, says ex-Woodside boss Don Volte. *The Australian Financial Review,* 11 Sep 2014.
23. Deem, R. 2016. *Gasfield free NSW Northern Rivers: Non-violent, non-negotiable.* Australian eBook Publisher.
24. Shoebridge, B. 2016. *The Bentley Effect.* Smiling Dragonfly.
25. Permanent Peoples' Tribunal. 2019. Session on human rights, fracking and climate change, 14–18 May, 2018: Advisory opinion. *General Secretariat.* www.permanentpeoplestribunal.org.
26. Schraufnagel, D., Balmes, J., Cowl, C., De Matteis, S., Jung, S-H., Mortimer, K., Perez-Padilla, R., Rice, M., Riojas-Rodriguez, H., Sood, A., Thurston, G., To, T., Vanker, A. & Wuebbles, D. 2019. Air pollution and non-communicable diseases: A review by the Forum of International Respiratory Societies' Environmental Committee, Part 1: The damaging effects of air pollution. *Chest, 155(2),* 409 – 416. Part 2: Air pollution and organ systems. *Chest, 155(2)*, 417 – 426.
27. Hansen, C., Barnett, A. & Pritchard, G. 2008. The effect of ambient air pollution during early pregnancy on fetal ultrasonic measurements during mid-pregnancy. *Environ Health Perspect. 116(3),* 362–369.
28. McCarron, G. 2018. Air Pollution and human health hazards: a compilation of air toxins acknowledged by the gas industry in Queensland's Darling Downs. *International Journal of Environmental Studies,* DOI: 10.1080/00207233.2017.1413221

Chapter 5 – The Key Mental Processes

1. Miller, G. A. 1956. The magical number seven, plus or minus two: Some limits on our capacity for processing information. *Psychological Review, 63*, 81–97.

Chapter 7 – Memory and Imagination

1. Bartlett, F. C. 1932. *Remembering.* Cambridge, Eng.: Cambridge Univ. Press.
2. Loftus, E. F., & Palmer, J. C. 1974. Reconstruction of auto-mobile destruction: An example of the interaction between language and memory. *Journal of Verbal Learning and Verbal Behavior, 13*, 585–589.
3. Loftus, E.F. 1993. Make-believe memories. *Am. Psychol. 58*, 864–873; and Loftus, E.F. & Pickrell, J.E. 1995. The formation of false memories. *Psychiatr. Ann. 25*, 720–725.
4. Braun, K.A., Ellis, R., & Loftus, E.F. 2002. Make my memory: How advertising can change our memories of the past. *Psychol. Marketing, 19*, 1–23.
5. Braun-LaTour, K.A., LaTour, M.S., Pickrell, J., & Loftus, E.F. 2004. How (and when) advertising can influence memory for consumer experience. *J. Advertising, 33*, 7–25.
6. Paling, E. 2016. Fox will remove violent X-Men billboards after outcry. *The Huffington Post Canada,* 6 April 2016.
7. Eisenberg, N. and Cohen Silver, R. 2011. Growing up in the shadow of terrorism: Youth in America after 9/11. *Amer. Psychologist, 66(6)*, 468–481.
8. Holmes, E. A., Creswell, C., & O'Connor, T. G. 2007. Posttraumatic stress symptoms in London school children following September 11, 2001: An exploratory investigation of peri-traumatic reactions and intrusive imagery. *Journal of Behavior Therapy and Experimental Psychiatry, 38*, 474–490.
9. Seery, M., Silver, R., Holman, E., Ence, W., & Chu, T. 2008. Expressing thoughts and feelings following a collective trauma: Immediate responses to 9/11 predict negative outcomes in a national sample. *Journal of Consulting and Clinical Psychology, 76(4)*, 657–667.
10. Somerville, W. 2004. Cognitive Control Therapy for PTSD. *Doctor of Psychology Dissertation*, Department of Psychology, Bond University, Gold Coast, Queensland.
11. Nigro, G., & Neisser, U. 1983. Point of view in personal memories. *Cognitive Psychology, 15*, 467–482.
12. Covey, S. 1989. *The 7 habits of highly effective people.* N.Y.: Simon & Schuster.

Chapter 8 – Beliefs

1. Watts, A. 1975. *Tao: The watercourse way.* New York: Pantheon Books.

Chapter 9 – Language

1. Spencer, S., Steele, C. and Quinn, D. 1999. Stereotype threat and women's math performance. *Journal of Experimental Social Psychology, 35*, 4–28.
2. Bargh, J.A., Chen, M., & Burrows, L. 1996. Automaticity of social behavior: Direct effects of trait construction and stereotype activation on action. *Journal of Personality and Social Psychology, 71*, 230–244.
3. Doyen, S., Klein, O., Pichon, C-L., & Cleeremans, A. 2012. Behavioral priming: It's all in the mind, but whose mind? *PLoS ONE, 7(1)*, e29081.
4. Rosenthal, R., & Fode, K. L. 1963. The effect of experimenter bias on the performance of the albino rat. *Behavioral Science, 8*, 183–189.
5. Rosenthal, R. and Jacobson, L. 1966. Teachers' expectancies: Determinants of pupils' IQ gains. *Psychological Reports, 19*, 115–118.

Chapter 10 – Emotions

1. Hume, David. 1748. 'Of the Passions' in *An enquiry concerning human understanding*.
2. Rose, J. 2014. *The literary Churchill: Author, reader, actor*. New Haven & London: Yale University Press.

Chapter 11 – Intuition, Sleep, and Dreams

1. Freud, S. 1913. *The interpretation of dreams*. Third edition, translated by A. A. Brill. New York: The Macmillan Company.
2. Kleitman, N. 1982. Basic rest-activity cycle – 22 years later. *Journal of Sleep Research and Sleep Medicine, 5(4)*, 311–317.
3. Rossi, E. L. Cheek. D. B. 1988. *Mind-Body therapy: Methods of ideomotor healing in hypnosis*. New York: Norton and Co.
4. Rossi, E. & Nimmons, D. 1991. *The 20-minute break: Using the new science of ultradian rhythms*. Los Angeles, CA: Jeremy P. Tarcher, Inc.
5. Falchi, F., Cinzano, P., Duriscoe, D., Kyba, C., Elvidge, C., Baugh, K., Portnov, B., Rybnikova, N. & Furgoni, R. 2016. The new world atlas of artificial night sky brightness. *Sci Adv, 2(6)*, e1600377.
6. Ekirch, A.R. 2005. *At day's close: Night in times past*. New York: W.W. Norton & Co.

Index

Names in double quotation marks indicate stories about people. Page numbers for all cartoons, photographs, and other graphics are in the Illustrations.

9/11 (World Trade Centre), 174–76

A

Abetz, Eric, 119
Adams, John, 39
Adelson, Edward, 164
affect bridge, 57
AGL, 131–33, 136, 137
agoraphobia, 28–29, 250–51
agricultural revolution, 32
air pollution, 111–12, 124
alcohol, 272
alphabet technique, 238–39
American Psychological Society, 6
analogy and metaphor, 227–28
"Andrew" (supervisor), 97–98
anger, 66–67, 251–52
"Anne" (piano), 26
Anthropocene, 220
anxiety and fear, 247–51
apnoea, 272–73
aquifer contamination, 129, 133–36
aquifer depressurisation, 112
arm levitation, 225
arrow of time, 161–62
asbestos, 119, 129
atomistic thinking, 15–16
automatic thoughts, 54
Aurelius, Marcus, 88
Australian Psychological Society, 6
avoidant strategy, 203
awareness, 158–159

B

balancing emotions, 259
Bandler, Richard, 80
Barrett, Damian, 113
barrier of amnesia, 271
"Barry" (dentist's chair), 83–84
baseline testing, 127–28
basic rest activity cycle, 263–65, 269–71
Beecher, Henry Ward, 271
behaviourist psychology, 45–47, 69–70
    classical conditioning (Pavlov), 32
    demise of, 46–47
    habituation, 70, 76
    operant conditioning (Skinner), 32
beliefs
    big picture, 207
    learning new things, 206–7
    optimism and pessimism, 203–5
    predicting the future, 210–11
    self-esteem and efficacy, 205–6
    suffering and evil, 17, 213–14
    time, 209–10
    truth and lies, 208–9
    world's end, 211–12
Bell Miners (bellbirds), 94, 98–100
Bender, George, 115
Bentley blockade, 149–50, 253–54
Bible, The, 17
Big Pharma, 64–68
"Bill" (changing memories), 80–83
binds and false alternatives, 233
Blake, William, 161
blind sight, 49
Blyton, Enid, 277

BMAD (Bell Miner Associated Dieback)
   Bell Miners, 94, 98–100
   family therapy for forests, 97–100
   forest function, 105
   forum, 95–97
   glyphosate herbicide, 95–96, 103–5
   Hunter, John, 94–96, 101
   lantana, 94–100, 103
   Lantana Associated Dieback, 102
   lerps, 99
   logging of native forests, 94, 99
   model of, 99–100
   names and labels, 101–3
   psyllid insects, 99–100
   splatter gun, 95–96, 101
   Toonumbar Valley, 93–94
bob creadur, 156–57
body language, 56
brain
   electrical activity in, 264–65
   frontal lobes, 23, 49, 73
brain injuries, 49–50
   blind sight, 49
   Capgras delusion, 49
breaking the law, 147–48
breathing
   anxiety and, 249–51
   counting breaths, 270
BTEX (benzene…), 111–12
Buckingham, Jeremy, 113, 139
Buddhist attitude to evil, 213–14
   Yin-Yang symbol, 17
burden of proof, 126–27
burning out, 70, 259
Byron, Lord, 271, 280

C

Camden, 125–26, 131–33
Capgras delusion, 49
carbon cycle, 122–23
carbon footprint, 104
cargo cult, 138–39
"Carl" (Exposure Therapy), 70
"Carol" (quasi-court), 256–58
cartoon voices, 82, 188
castration complex, 44
catharsis, 43–44, 70
"Charles" (9/11), 174–75
"Charlie" (contract killer), 256
chequer board illusion, 164, 166
Chevreul, Anton, 266
Chevreul's pendulum, 266
ch'i energy, 76
Chinchilla, 137
Churchill, Winston, 221–22, 252–53
cinematic metaphor (memory), 79
circus monkey, 24, 189–90
classical conditioning, 32
climate change, 122, 219–20
clinical psychology, 44, 64–66, 68, 73, 76–77
Coal Seam Gas (CSG). *See* Unconventional Gas
Cochrane, Archie, 74–75
Cognitive Control Training, 80–83, 85–86, 90
cognitive revolution, 47
Cognitive Therapy
   automatic thoughts, 54
   unconscious mind in, 54
Colless, Rick, 122–23, 140
colour/black and white (imagery), 184
computer
   mind-body problem, 48–51
   programs, 50
   relevance for psychology, 47–51
Condamine River, 113
Confucius, 93
conscription, 39
control group problem, 75
conversion disorder, 44
cooperation, 23
courage, 252–55
curse of memory, 61–63

D

Dalai Lama, 213
Darling Downs, 108–9, 111–13

"David" (phobia), 59–61
da Vinci, Leonardo, 247
day residue, 276
deconstructing language, 239–41
Deem, Richard, 151
deep mind
    nature of, 53–54, 156, 261–63
    working with, 4–6
demand characteristics, 217
denial and intrusion in PTSD, 86
depression, 246, 251
dieback. *See* BMAD
diesel emissions, 111, 116
Disneyland and Bugs Bunny, 172
dissociative disorder, 44
distance in imagery, 82, 181–82
Doctor of Psychology, 85, 182–92, 197–98
domino theory, 40–41
double binds, 233
double blind, 75
double standards for proof, 125–27
Doubtful Creek, 148
"Dr Allen" (lobotomy), 73–74
dreams and dreaming
    amnesia for, 176, 282
    basic rest activity cycle, 263–65, 269–71
    day residue, 276
    dream censor, 262–63
    hypnagogia, 264, 277–80
    hypnopompic imagery, 265
    lucid dream (father's death), 281–82
    "Michael" (hypnagogia), 279
    naps, 270
    natural everyday trance, 263, 269-71
    nightmares, 78–79, 83–84, 192
    REM (rapid eye movement), 265
    working with, 283–84
    See also sleep
drilling notes (Metgasco), 134–35
DSM (diagnostic manual), 62
duck illusion, 168
duty of care, 117–18

E

ego, 53, 245, 261–63
ego defence mechanisms, 262–63
Einstein, Albert, 4, 14, 16, 161, 277
electra complex, 44
"Elizabeth" (memories), 85–86
Elizabeth I (queen), 252
Ellis, Albert, 236
EMDR (Eye Movement…)
    "Gillian" (EMDR), 73
    rating scales in, 90
    as treatment for PTSD, 68, 72–73
Emotional Freedom Technique (EFT), 76, 90
Emotions
    anger, 64–67, 251–52
    anxiety and fear, 247–51
    anxiety as a tracer, 247–48
    balancing, 259
    breathing and anxiety, 249–51
    "Carol" (quasi-court), 256–58
    "Charlie" (contract killer), 256
    courage, 252–55
    depression, 246, 251
    fear and learning ("Miss Dowdy"), 25–27
    Freud's model of, 43–44, 53,
    function of, 66–67, 78, 156, 246, 258
    guilt, 78–79, 237, 255–59
    hope, 235
    humour, 189–90
    "James" (guilt), 258
    "Jill" (agoraphobia), 250–51
    phobia, 27–30
    reason and, 245–46
    reductionism and, 64–67
    "Robert" (driving), 250
    talking about, 175–76
    "Tom and Alicia" (cancer), 254
Emot-o-Meter, 4
emperor has no clothes effect, 208–9
Enlightenment, 289
environment, what is the, 15

envision the future, 198–200
epidemiological research, 128–29
Erasmus, 276
Erickson, Milton, 51–55
  calf story, 228
  double binds, 233
  Ericksonian Hypnotherapy, 6, 51-55
  natural everyday trance, 263, 269-71
  role of therapist, 53
  unconscious mind, 53–55
evidence-based treatment, 73–77
  alternative to, 86
  Cochrane, Archie, 74–75
  control group problem, 75
  double blind, 75
  limitations of, 76–77
  lobotomy as, 76
  placebo, 75
  randomised controlled trials, 75
Exposure Therapy, 68–71, 76
  "Carl" (Exposure Therapy), 70
  caveats and risks, 71
  imaginal, 68
  in vivo, 68
  symptom scales in, 89–90

F

fallacy of hindsight, 234
falling asleep, 264, 273–74
false memories, 171–73
family therapy
  "Andrew" (supervisor), 97–98
  for forests, 97–100
  Systemic Family Therapy, 53
Fell, Chris, 111
Ferguson, Martin, 120–21, 137
fight-or-flight response, 18–19, 30, 84, 114
first and second sleeps, 274–75
Foa and Kozak's PTSD model, 87–88
forest dieback. *See* BMAD
forest function, 105
fracking (hydraulic fracturing), 108, 110, 119, 136

Frankenstein, 280
"Fred" (plain pony), 233
Freud, Sigmund
  castration complex, 44
  catharsis, 43–44, 70
  day residue, 276
  dream censor, 262
  dreams as 'royal road', 276
  ego, 53, 245, 261–63
  ego defence mechanisms, 262–63
  electra complex, 44
  hysteria, 44, 69
  id, 53, 245, 261–62
  libido, 43–44
  Oedipus complex, 44
  penis envy, 44
  projection, 262
  psychoanalytic theory, 43–45
  rationalisation, 262
  reaction formation, 262
  repression, 262
  superego, 261
  trauma resolution, 173, 175
  unconscious mind, 53, 262
friends of coal, 122
fugitive emissions and methane, 107, 112–14

G

"Gail" (restore eyesight), 213
Gandalf's conundrum, 37
Gandhi, Mahatma, 145, 252, 271
Gasfield Free campaign actions
  Bentley blockade, 149–50, 253–54
  breaking the law, 147–48, 150
  CSG as 2% land area, 227–28
  Doubtful Creek, 148
  Glenugie blockade, 146
  health professionals, 141–43
  letter to NSW premier, 140
  locking on, 147, 150
  non-violent direct action, 147–48
  'non-violent, non-negotiable', 140, 231

INDEX

Gasfield Free campaign actions (*cont.*)
   protectors, 144–50, 253–54, 290
   Shannonbrook, 146
   Simmo (lock on), 148
Gasfield Free campaign events
   CSG the Musical, 145
   Don's party, 145
   Lismore Town Hall meeting, 146
   NSW parliamentary inquiry, 139–40
   polls, Fairfax media/Nielsen, 146
   Victorian Government ban, 150–51
Gasfield Free campaign groups
   Gasfield Free Ballina group, 144
   Gasfield Free Communities, 145–46
   Girls Against Gas, 145
   Groups Against Gas (GAG), 144, 242
   Keerrong Gas Squad, 144
   Knitting Nannas Against Gas, 145
   Kyogle GAG, 144
   Lismore GAG, 144
   Lock the Gate, 144
   Neighbourhood Environment Centres, 144
   Northern Rivers Guardians, 144
   Northern Rivers Regional Alliance, 144–45
   Richmond Valley GAG, 144
   Rock Valley Gas Rangers, 144
gas wells, 109–11, 134, 149
Genesis spark, 22
ghost train of thought, 11
"Gillian" (EMDR), 73
Girls Against Gas, 145
Githabul Rangers, 96
Gladstone LNG export hub, 108, 139
Glenugie blockade, 146
global warming. *See* climate change
Gloucester, 136
glyphosate herbicide, 95–96, 103–5
goal setting and motivation, 231–32
Goodnow, Jacqueline, 13–14
ground water levels, 112
Groups Against Gas, 144, 242
guided imagery, 201
guilt, 78–79, 237, 255–59

H

habits, 24–27, 231–32, 286
habituation, 70, 76
Happy and Honey (horses), 20–21
head injuries. *See* brain injuries
Heffernan, Bill, 135–36
Henderson, Peter, 119, 130–33
Heraclitus, 261
Hitler, Adolf, 208, 211, 252–53
Hobbes, Thomas, 222
holistic thinking, 15–16
homo sapiens. See human
homo sapiens halliburtinus, 108
'hope', 235
horse
   evolution of, 18–21
   Happy and Honey, 20–21
   long face, 19–20
   memory, 21
   Myrtle (plain pony), 233
   Ra (Arab gelding), 21, 35
   sleep, 21
   training, 21, 34–36, 52
   vision, 19, 166
horse sense, 34–35
human
   cooperation, 23
   evolution, 22–23
   face recognition, 23
   love of sport, 23
   potential to learn, 36–37, 289
   resilience, 22
   stereotyping and prejudice, 22
Hume, David, 245
humour, 189–90
Hunter, John, 94–96, 101
Hutton, Drew, 139
hypnagogia, 264, 277–80
hypnopompic imagery, 265

hypnosis and hypnotherapy
  affect bridge, 57
  arm levitation, 225
  Chevreul's pendulum, 266
  Ericksonian Hypnotherapy, 6, 51-55
  induction of, 229, 267
  natural everyday trance, 263, 269–71
  new hypnosis, 51–55
  pace and lead, 224–25, 253
  "Peter" (former client), 90–91
  phobia treatment, 59–61
  quit smoking, 24–25
  Rossi procedure, 268–69
  "Sylvia" (hypnotherapy), 55–57
  "Terry" (self-hypnosis), 230
hysteria, 44, 69

I
id, 53, 245, 261–62
ideomotor signals, 5, 56, 266
ideosensory signals, 5–6
illusions. *See* perceptual illusions
imagery and imagination
  9/11 effects on children, 175
  "Charles" (9/11), 174–75
  dangers of, 70–71
  Lara Croft game, 174
  media, 173–75, 177
  working with, 178–79
  See also memory
imagery transformations
  characters, 190–91
  circus monkey, 82, 189–90
  colour vs black and white, 184
  distance, 82, 181–82
  envision the future, 198–200
  guided imagery, 201
  new endings, 77–78, 191–92
  perspective, 81, 87, 88, 185–86
  size, 82, 182–83
  sound and volume, 187–88
inner coach, 194–96
inner mind. *See* deep mind
insomnia, 273–76

intelligence, 13–14
intuition. *See* deep mind
IQ (intelligence quotient), 13, 217

J
"Jack" (gas barbecue), 226–27
"James" (guilt), 258
"Jan" (soup kitchen), 213
Janet, Pierre, 80
"Jill" (agoraphobia), 250–51
"Jim and Claire" (PTSD), 30–32
"Joan" (water phobia), 29–30
Jung, Carl, 27, 283

K
Kahneman, Daniel, 13
Keerrong Gas Squad, 144
Kekule, August, 277
Kendall, Henry, 101
Key Mental Processes, 155–60, 285–86
  awareness, 158–59
  bob creadur, 156–57
  learning to use, 285–86
Kingfisher well (accident), 124–25
King, Martin Luther, 145, 148
Knitting Nannas Against Gas, 145
Kyogle GAG, 144

L
labels. *See* names and labels
language
  alphabet technique, 238–39
  analogy and metaphor, 227–28
  binds and false alternatives, 233
  'climate change', 219–20
  communication of ideas, 241–44
  courage, 252–55
  deconstruction of, 239–41
  demand characteristics, 217
  goal setting and motivation, 231–32
  'hope', 235
  hypnotic, 224–26
  "Jack" (gas barbecue), 226–27
  'must', 236–37

language *(cont.)*
  names and labels, 101–3, 218–21
  'natural' as a word spell, 223–24
  'non-violent, non-negotiable', 140, 231
  pacing and leading, 224–25, 253
  priming, 215–17
  'radical' vs 'conservative', 220
  reverse psychology words (negations), 228–31
  Romeo and Juliet (a rose…), 218
  rule of three (triplets), 221–22
  'should', 237
  silence in speaking, 243–44
  "Terry" (self-hypnosis), 230
  think the unthinkable, 239
  'try', 235
  warm-up words, 238
  'what ifs', 234–35
  word pairs, 221
  'yes' set, 224–27
lantana, 94–100, 103
Lantana Associated Dieback, 102
Lao Tzu, 155, 206
Lara Croft game, 174
learning
  cultural transmission of, 32–34
  fear in, 25–27
  new things, 206–7
lerps (sugary coatings), 99
libido, 43–44
Lincoln, Abraham, 107, 203, 222
Lismore GAG, 144
Liverpool Plains, 108
lobotomy, 73–74, 76
locking on, 147–50
Lock the Gate, 144
logging of native forests, 94, 99
logs on road illusion, 163
London, Jack, 215
lost-in-the-mall, 172
lottery of death, 39
love of sport, 23
Loy, Jeff, 149–50

LSD-25, 49
lucid dream (father's death), 281–82
Luther, Martin, 117, 211

M

Macbeth, 62
MacDonald, Scot, 121, 125–26, 135, 139
Maher, Damien, 112–13, 120
many lines illusion, 162–63
Marcuse, Herbert, 143
"Mary" (writing mistakes), 26
Master of Clinical Psychology degree, 59–61
maths problem (bat and ball), 13
meaning information in memories, 87–88
media hypnotists, 173–75, 177
media prescription, 177
medications for emotional problems, 66–67
Melbourne Cricket Ground, 111
memes, 32–33
memory
  adding new information to, 87–89
  "Barry" (dentist's chair), 83–84
  "Bill" (changing memories), 80–83
  Cognitive Control Training, 80–83, 85–86, 90
  complexes, 27
  curse of memory, 61–63
  Disneyland and Bugs Bunny, 172
  Doctor of Psychology, 85, 182–92, 197–98
  "Elizabeth" (memories), 85–86
  emotional effects of, 71, 173
  fallacy of hindsight, 234
  false memories, 171–73
  lost-in-the-mall technique, 172
  meaning information in, 87–88
  networks (Foa and Kozak), 87–89
  as reconstruction, 171–73
  response information in, 87

memory (cont.)
  "Rob and Cathy" (changing trauma memory), 77–79
  stimulus information in, 87
  talking about trauma, 175–76
  training memories, 179–80
  working with imagery, 178–79
  See also imagery and imagination
memory transformations
  cartoon voices, 82, 188
  characters, 190–91
  circus monkey, 82, 189–90
  colour vs black and white, 184
  distance, 82, 181–82
  inner coach, 194–96
  multistage techniques, 194–200
  new endings, 77–78, 191–92
  perspective, 81, 87, 88, 185–86
  size, 82, 182–83
  sound and volume, 187–88
  supporting younger self, 59–60, 83, 196–98
Metgasco, 119, 124–25, 134–35, 148–50
methane and fugitive emissions, 107, 112–14
"Michael" (hypnagogia), 279
Milligan, Spike, 139
mind-body problem, 48–51
  psychology students, 64–65
  reductionism, 64–68
Mine Safety Investigation, 124–25
"Miss Dowdy" (singing teacher), 26
model for BMAD, 99–100
monkeys
  learned fear response, 29
  potato washing, 33
  teeth flossing, 33
Monty Python, 203
Moratorium marches, 40
Muller-Lyer illusion, 163–64
multistage imagery techniques, 194–200
'must', 236–37

Myrtle (plain pony), 233

N

names and labels, 101–3, 218–21
napalm girl, 40
naps, 270
National Pollution Inventory (NPI), 111–12
native forest dieback. See BMAD
'natural' as a word spell, 223–24
natural everyday trance, 263, 269–71
natural trauma resolution, 86–87
Neurolinguistic Programming (NLP), 6, 53
new age of enlightenment, 288–90
new endings for memories, 77–78, 191–92
new hypnosis, 51–55
Newman, Campbell, 140
new media and e-mail, 242–43
nightmares, 78–79, 83–84, 192
Nile, Fred, 136
Nixon, Richard, 42
nocebo effect, 142
non-violent direct action, 147–48
'non-violent, non-negotiable', 140, 231
Northern Rivers, 108, 112, 139–40, 143–46, 148–51
Northern Rivers Guardians, 144
Northern Rivers Regional Alliance, 144–45
NSW Chief Scientist (Mary O'Kane), 117, 124
NSW Dept of Trade and Energy (DIGS), 134
NSW Parliamentary Inquiry into CSG, 139–40

O

Oedipus complex, 44
O'Farrell, Barry, 140, 148
O'Kane, Mary (NSW Chief Scientist), 117, 124

INDEX   307

One Thought Solution, 9–12, 15,
    36–37
  ghost train of thought, 11
  one carriage train of thought, 2
  role in personality, 27
operant conditioning, 32
optimism and pessimism, 203–5
Origin Energy, 113–14

P

pacing and leading, 224–25, 253
particulates, 112, 116, 128
Pavlov, Ivan, 32
penis envy, 44
perception, 19, 49, 161–69
  arrow of time, 161–62
  colour, 19, 166
  sensory systems, 165–66
perceptual illusions
  chequer board (Adelson), 164, 166
  duck, 168
  logs on road, 163
  many lines, 162–63
  Muller-Lyer, 163–64
  rainbows, 167
  US Air Force radar operators, 47
  young woman, 168–69
perspective in imagery, 81, 87, 88,
    185–86
"Peta" (young activist), 213
"Peter" (former client), 90–91
Petroleum Health Watch program,
    130–31
pharmaceutical industry. *See* Big
    Pharma
Phelps, Peter, 15, 121-22, 126-27, 134,
    140
phobia, 27–30
  agoraphobia, 28–29, 250–51
  "David" (phobia), 59–61
  "Joan" (water phobia), 29–30
  preparedness for, 29
  social phobia, 29
  specific phobia, 28–29, 59–61

  therapy for, 29–30, 59–61, 68, 199
Pilliga State Forest, 108, 135–36
placebo, 75
planning, 200
Pocock, David, 147
polls (CSG), 146
pollution debt, 104
Positive Psychology, 58
posttraumatic stress disorder (PTSD)
  changing trauma memories, 80–84
  Cognitive Control Training, 80–83,
    85–86, 90
  conversion disorder, 44
  dangers of imagery, 70–71
  denial and intrusion, 86
  dissociative disorder, 44
  Doctor of Psychology, 85, 182–92,
    197–98
  "Elizabeth" (memories), 85–86
  EMDR (Eye Movement…), 68,
    72–73, 90
  Exposure Therapy, 68–71, 76
  Foa and Kozak's model, 87–88
  "Gillian" (EMDR), 73
  guilt in, 78–79
  hysteria, 44, 69
  "Jim and Claire" (PTSD), 30–32
  meaning information in memories,
    87–88
  medications and, 63–68
  memory in, 61–62, 70–71, 87–88
  name for, 39, 62
  natural trauma resolution, 86–87
  new endings for memories, 77–78,
    191–92
  nightmares, 78–79, 83–84, 192
  "Peter" (former client), 90–91
  reliving trauma, 68–69
  response information in memories,
    87
  "Rob and Cathy" (changing trauma
    memory), 77–79
  stimulus information in memories,
    87

posttraumatic stress disorder (*cont.*)
   symptom ratings (SUDS), 89–90
   symptoms as protective, 31–32
   talking about trauma, 175–76
   third form of learning, 32
   treatment of, 32, 69, 77–79, 89–90
   two-step treatment process, 88–89
   vicarious traumatisation, 70–71
post-truth, 1, 208
power naps, 270
pressure words, 236–37
priming, 215–17
"Prof X" (traumatic amnesia), 58–59
programs (computer), 48
projection (Freud), 262
proof. *See* scientific evidence
protectors, 144–50, 253–54, 290
Proust, Marcel, 171
psychoanalytic theory, 43–45
psychological therapies. *See* Cognitive Control Training, Cognitive Therapy, Emotional Freedom Technique, Exposure Therapy, Eye Movement Desensitisation & Reprocessing, hypnosis and hypnotherapy, Narrative Therapy, Neurolinguistic Programming, Psychoanalysis, Solution Focused Therapy, Systemic Family Therapy
psychology, 43–51
   assessment (rating scales), 89–90
   Freud and psychoanalysis, 43–45
   medications as therapy, 63–68
psyllid insects (BMAD), 99–100

Q
quasi-court for guilt, 256–58
Queensland floods, 175
Queensland Government health report, 132
quit smoking, 24–25, 231–32
QWERTY keyboard, 77

R
'radical' vs 'conservative', 220
rainbows, 167
randomised controlled trials, 75
rationalisation, 262
rat psychology, 45–47
reaction formation, 262
reductionism, 64–68
REM (rapid eye movement), 265
renewable energy, 104
repression, 262
repressive tolerance, 143
resilience, 22
response information in memories, 87
reverse osmosis filtration, 111
reverse psychology words (negations), 228–31
"Rhonda" ('must'), 236–37
Richmond Valley GAG, 144
Riflebird E4 and E5 (gas wells), 134–35
risk management (gas industry), 117–36
"Rob and Cathy" (changing trauma memory), 77–79
"Robert" (panic driving), 250
Roberts, Anthony, 125, 254
Roberts, Tom, 52
Rock Valley Gas Rangers, 144
Romeo and Juliet (a rose…), 218
Rossi, Ernest, 268–69
Rousseau, Jean-Jacques, 171
rule of three (triplets). *See* language

S
salt, 111
Santos, 112, 135–36
Santos, Isaac (scientist), 112–13, 120
scientific evidence, 125–29
self-esteem and efficacy, 207–8
set and setting, 178–79
Shakespeare, William, 62, 218, 271
shale gas, 109
Shannonbrook, 146
Shapiro, Francine, 72

Shelley, Mary, 280
Shelley, Percy, 280
Shoebridge, Brendan, 151
'should', 237
Siberian gas field, 113
silence in speaking, 243–44
Simmo (lock on), 148
size in imagery, 82, 182–83
Skinner, B.F., 32
sleep
  alcohol effects on, 272
  apnoea, 272–73
  barrier of amnesia, 271
  basic rest activity cycle, 263–65,. 269–71
  creativity during, 276–77
  falling asleep, 264, 273–74
  first and second sleeps, 274–75
  as a form of death, 271
  horse, 21
  hygiene, 272–74
  insomnia, 273–76
  light pollution, 274
  naps, 270
  sleep stages, 264–65
  See also dreams and dreaming
smoking and tobacco, quitting, 24–25, 231–32
social phobia, 29
Socratic questioning, 237
solar panels, 104
solastalgia, 115
Solution Focused Therapy, 53
Somerville, Susan, 20
  activism, 140, 149, 209, 230–31, 242
  forest dieback work, 94–96
Southern Cross University, 95, 113
specific phobia, 28–29, 59–61
Spinoza, Baruch, 245
splatter gun (BMAD), 95–96, 101
stereotyping and prejudice, 22
stimulus and response. *See* behaviourist psychology

stimulus information in memories, 87
subconscious mind. *See* deep mind
superego, 261
supporting younger self, 59–60, 83, 196–98
Sydney Harbour Bridge, 110
"Sylvia" (hypnotherapy), 55–57
symptom rating scales (SUDS), 89–90
symptoms as solutions, 24–25
Systemic Family Therapy, 53
systems theory, 15–17, 51, 98-100, 207

T

talking about trauma, 175–76
Tara health survey (McCarron), 116
Tara, Queensland, 113, 116
television news, 173–75
Tennyson, Alfred, 285
"Terry" (self-hypnosis), 230
therapy for phobia, 29–30, 68, 199
The Who, 42
think the unthinkable, 239
Thoreau, Henry David, 231
thought experiments, 4
tight sands, 109, 124–25, 149
"Tim" (quit smoking), 24–25
time
  arrow of, 161–62
  country attitude to, 210
  deep time, 107
  past and future, 209–10
  taking time to think, 14
tinnitus, 84
Tolkien, J.R.R., 37, 252–53
"Tom and Alicia" (cancer), 254
Toonumbar National Park, 94
Toonumbar Valley, 93–94
training memories criteria, 179–80
triplets (rule of three), 221–22
truth and lies, 208–9
'try', 235
Tversky, Amos, 13
two-step PTSD treatment process, 88–89

U

unconscious mind. *See* deep mind
Unconventional Gas companies
  Australian Gaslight (AGL), 131–33, 136, 137
  Metgasco, 119, 124–25, 134–35, 148–50
  Origin Energy, 113–14
  Santos, 112, 135–36
Unconventional Gas economics
  cargo cult, 138–39
  land values, 136
  Ponzi scheme, 138
Unconventional Gas environmental impacts
  air pollution, 111–12, 124
  aquifer contamination, 129, 133–36
  aquifer depressurisation, 112
  Buckingham, Jeremy, 113, 139
  Condamine River, 113
  diesel emissions, 111, 116
  ground water levels, 112
  methane and fugitive emissions, 107, 112–14
  National Pollution Inventory, 111–12
  salt, 111
  Santos, Isaac (scientist), 112-13, 120
  Siberian gas field, 113
  volatile organic compounds (VOCs), 111–12
  waste water, 111, 132–33, 135
Unconventional Gas health impacts
  Bender, George, 115
  BTEX (benzene, toluene…), 111-12
  children, 116
  dangerous chemicals, 115
  particulates, 112, 116, 128
  Queensland Government health report, 132
  sleep disturbance, 114
  solastalgia, 115
  Tara health survey (McCarron), 116

Unconventional Gas industry
  Camden, 125–26, 131–33
  Chinchilla, 137
  Darling Downs, 108–9, 111–13
  Gladstone export hub, 108, 139
  Gloucester, 136
  Liverpool Plains, 108
  Northern Rivers, 108, 112, 139–40, 143–46, 148–51
  Pilliga State Forest, 108, 135–36
  Tara, 113, 116
Unconventional Gas mining
  chemicals used in drilling, 110
  drilling notes, 134–35
  fracking (hydraulic fracturing), 108, 110, 119, 136
  gas wells, 109–11, 134, 149
  Kingfisher well (accident), 124–25
  reverse osmosis filtration, 111
  Riflebird E4 and E5 (gas wells), 134–35
  shale gas, 109
  tight sands, 109, 124–25, 149
Unconventional Gas risk management
  attitudes to scientists, 120–22
  baseline testing, 127–28
  burden of proof, 126–27
  carbon cycle, 122–23
  costs and benefits, 117, 136–37
  double standards for proof, 125–27
  duty of care, 117–18
  epidemiological research, 128–29
  ignorance defence, 119–20
  industry approach, 118
  Mine Safety Investigation, 124–25
  misrepresent information, 129–33
  personal attack, 120–22
  Petroleum Health Watch program, 130–31
  regulations, 123–25
  risk management principles, 117–18
  rocks and gases as friends, 122–23
  scientific proof, 128–291
  time, 119

INDEX

US Air force radar operators, 47

V

vicarious traumatisation, 70–71
Victorian Government gas ban, 150-51
Vietnam War, 39–43, 61
   domino theory, 40–41
   lottery of death, 39
   Moratorium marches, 40
   napalm girl, 40
   welcome home march, 41
Virgil, 205
Voelte, Don, 138
volatile organic compounds, 111–12
Voltaire, 9

W

wallabies, 17–18
   apple eating wallaby, 33
warm-up words, 238
waste water (gas industry), 111, 132–33, 135
Watts, Alan, 213–14
'what ifs', 234–35
Whitlam, Gough, 39
wisdom, 12–15
word pairs, 221
World Health Organisation, 103
World War I, 41–42
   grandfather's service, 41–42
World War II, 82
world's end, 211–12

Y

Y2K, 212
Yes Minister, 120, 226
'yes' set, 224–27
Yin-Yang symbol, 17
young woman illusion, 168–69

About Dr Wayne Somerville

As a clinical psychologist and trauma specialist, Wayne has helped many find relief from the aftermath of violence and catastrophe. During 40 years of living on their property, 'Creek's Bend', Wayne and his wife Susan have farmed, worked horses and developed a treatment for forest dieback. Wayne is a prominent voice in the campaign against gas field industrialisation of rural Australia.

Wayne holds the degrees of Bachelor of Arts with 1st Class Honours in Psychology, Master of Clinical Psychology, and Doctor of Psychology. He has researched gentle therapies for phobia and posttraumatic stress disorder, published a journal paper on hypnotherapy for phobia, and presented workshops, seminars and training programs on trauma, stress management and hypnotherapy.

With his wife Susan, Wayne co-authored a journal paper on the treatment of forest dieback and has presented workshops and seminars on bush regeneration. In a parallel career as an environmental activist, Wayne has made himself a nuisance to the gas mining industry.

Wayne lives with Susan, his wife of 45 years. They have two grown-up daughters and four grandchildren.

You can contact Wayne by email at: drwaynesomerville@gmail.com

At www.DrWayneSomerville.com you'll find editions of *Shallow Thought, Deep Mind* for sale, downloads and other resources.

And don't forget to sign up for Wayne's email letter to keep up to date with developments.